FIGURE IT OUT

mascotbooks.com

FIGURE IT OUT:

My Thirty-Two-Year Journey While
Revolutionizing Pro Football's Special Teams

For more information, please contact:
Mascot Books
620 Herndon Parkway #320
Herndon, VA 20170
info@mascotbooks.com

CPSIA Code: PRV0222A
Library of Congress Control Number: 2021923891
ISBN-13: 978-1-63755-271-1

Printed in the United States

To my son, John, and my three grandsons—
Tom, Sam, and Nathan—for their great
support and always being foremost
in my thoughts.

FIGURE IT OUT

My Thirty-Two-Year Journey While Revolutionizing Pro Football's Special Teams

---

Mike Westhoff

with *BARRY WILNER*

Contents

PROLOGUE

I always thought that I would like to start a book by describing standing on the sidelines during the national anthem at the Super Bowl. It didn't happen for me, but I came close, coaching in four conference championship games and one heartbreaking playoff loss when I was with the New Orleans Saints in 2017. We were beaten by "The Minneapolis Miracle" or whatever they call it up in Minnesota—we lost on a final crazy play, a pass down the right sideline that somehow Stefon Diggs not only caught but took to the end zone to steal the win. We would have had a chance to advance to another conference championship.

No, I never got that opportunity to get to the Super Bowl. I coached in 657 total games, including playoffs, Pro Bowls, and the preseason. That's a lot of NFL games.

That I was not able to go to the Super Bowl was very disappointing for me because of a promise I made to myself on July 3, 1988.

On that date, I was finishing my last chemotherapy treatment at Jackson Memorial Hospital, which today is Sylvester Cancer Center. I had already received two chemotherapy drugs, Adriamycin and cisplatin—both very strong drugs. I had gotten sick, and I didn't have a hair on my entire body. I had surgery on my left leg to remove a malignant tumor, and I'd gone through some therapy and five months of chemotherapy. I was feeling better by then and hoped to move forward.

But that night as I sat there in that bed, I looked out the window across to the other side of the highway at the site of the Orange Bowl stadium. They were having a Fourth of July fireworks celebration, with the accompaniment of a band. I could see the fireworks in the distance and hear the music.

I asked a nurse if she would raise the window so I could see the fireworks and hear the music better. It was a nice night, and she raised the window for me. I can still picture it through the windows on my left as I looked up from my bed.

During the grand finale, they played the national anthem. It occurred to me how very fortunate I was at that point in time. Primary bone cancer—osteogenic sarcoma—at that time had only a 20 percent survival rate, and here I was going to get up out of that bed, go home the next day, and begin a normal life. I was proud to be an American and to live in a country where we had so many resources available to us.

I promised myself that every time I heard that song, I would repeat a pledge that I would show my thankfulness to this wonderful country and how much I appreciated what so many people had done for all of us—myself very much included. On that day, I would make sure that I tried to do my job better than anyone had ever done it. That was my goal.

Did I achieve it? I don't know, but I know I came close. It was always my goal as I stood there every Sunday listening to the national anthem and returned in my mind to that hospital room. I could picture myself sitting up in that bed and looking out the window. I'd remember how appreciative I was, and how I'd promised to show that appreciation. And 657 times, I tried to do that very thing.

I love that moment, but I always wanted one more chance to do it at the Super Bowl. Nonetheless, it guided me and inspired me throughout my career to say thank you to so many people who gave so much for us in this country. I was a direct recipient. I was able to fight through a very, very serious illness and a set of major surgeries to be in a position to live a wonderful life with a great family and hold the greatest job in the world as a coach in the National Football League.

CHAPTER 1

A Spunky Kid

I was born in Pittsburgh in a row house in a mostly Irish neighborhood. Many of the city's sections were divided somewhat racially and ethnically.

My mother didn't work when I was young; she had a full-time job taking care of six little ones. She was the brains of the family, however, with an exceptional IQ and advanced reading ability. When I was in college, she became a teacher's aide for learning-disabled children and excelled at it. She was respected and loved by the entire school.

I was the eldest of our six, with two brothers—Greg and Tom—and three beautiful sisters: Karen, Kristen, and Kelly. I am so proud to be part of such a successful, supportive, and highly competent family.

The traits that led me to a level of success as a player, and especially as a coach, were developed in my youth. We played ball in the street, made our clubhouse on the garage roof, and fought with neighbor kids. One such encounter stands out.

Behind our apartments was a series of very small garages. We claimed the roofs of those garages as our territory. I was about eleven years old—just old enough to get into some trouble. Between the garages and a factory next door was a very small walkway that anyone traveling in our neighborhood to the main street had to pass through. As a group of boys from another neighborhood was passing through the walkway, we threw bags of dirt into the wall to rain down on them. Of course, it was a direct hit. You really couldn't miss.

We ran away across the roof, thinking it was hilarious. Those other kids didn't share the humor. One day, they cornered me in an alley. They beat the hell out of me—and I mean they beat the HELL out of me. To cap it off, they used me to send a message.

At that time, there had been a very popular movie about corruption in New York and New Jersey: *On the Waterfront*. Marlon Brando earned an Academy Award for his performance in the film as an ex-fighter in conflict with the corrupt syndicate running the dockworkers' union. In one of Hollywood's iconic scenes, Brando's brother—who worked for the Mafia and was played by Rod Steiger—was given instructions to make his brother stay away from the investigators. When the outcome of that meeting between brothers was in doubt, the Mafia executed Steiger's character. He was shot in the chest several times and hung in an alley on a hook commonly used by dockworkers—left there for Brando to find.

After beating me, the guys from the other neighborhood must have had the same thought. They hung me up on a hook by my shirt in a garage. They told my brother to get my mother to let me down.

I had to learn to fight back after that. It took a while, but I got even with every single one of them. I learned how to fight.

Fighting is not always about winning, especially if you are a skinny little shit. But it's always about figuring things out and never quitting. I learned how to box; believe it or not, I can hit a speed bag better than Rocky Balboa—with a little practice, even to this day.

I always wanted to be a football player, but when I was young, Little League football was not an option. So we played in the yard or at neighborhood parks. Little League baseball was the sport of choice.

My brothers were both good ballplayers. Greg, who is about two years younger than I am, was our excellent athlete. He was an outstanding pitcher who could really throw. His fastball was, well, fast, and if you got too close to the plate, you might find one coming at your head. A shoulder injury pulled the plug on his career. It would have been interesting to see how far he could have gone.

My father was an amateur coach and a very good player. He had all the natural talent. At 6-4 and 245 pounds, "Big Jim" was a well-known amateur athlete in Pittsburgh. As a quarterback at Central Catholic High School, he set many of the city of Pittsburgh records—only to see them beaten by some guy named Dan Marino.

Early in my years with the Miami Dolphins, my father and I played golf with Dan. My father and Dan rode in a golf cart together and talked for hours about growing up in the same Pittsburgh neighborhood and playing football at the same high school. My father laughed at how easy it must have been for Dan to break his records.

My dad could throw a football 80 yards and easily hit a golf ball 300 yards. In high school, he also ran in the city's 100-yard dash finals.

Me? I took after my mother, the cute little Irish gal. My father never exercised; I never stopped.

I grew up in the city, but we moved to the suburb of Bethel Park when I was in junior high school. My parents had started me in school a year early, not knowing what a disadvantage being younger than my classmates was going to be. It was hard for me.

I was slow to grow and mature. I was a skinny little kid who was a year behind while still having to compete at a level for which I was not physically prepared. Trying to play sports in school when you are twelve and your classmates are thirteen—a year bigger, stronger, and more mature—is a very discouraging experience.

As a sophomore in high school, I was fourteen years old. I didn't turn seventeen until January of my senior year. Always trying to catch up is not the best path through high school. Schoolwork was hard for me, and I was not a very good student. I loved to read, and English and history were my favorite subjects. Unfortunately, I was very poor at math and science and fell very far behind. I never really did catch up.

I constantly worked out, trying to get bigger. I was intimidated and very self-conscious about being undersized and a poor student. I tried to overcome my fears by reading everything I could find and fighting anyone who questioned my size or courage.

I did gain a level of academic confidence by reading. I always was working my way through a book. I could escape from my fears of not being a top-level student by being immersed in a book.

From the shelter of the books I read, I didn't feel like the student who was afraid to raise his hand in class. Reading made me feel as though one day I might really become the student I dreamed to be.

So, yeah, I lacked confidence in myself both physically and academically. It made me very sensitive to any type of teasing or derogatory remarks. I developed a quick trigger and a bad temper. I had zero tolerance and would quickly fight anyone who said the wrong thing or even looked the wrong way at me. I certainly didn't always win; I was always the physical underdog. But I learned to fight and would do so at the drop of a hat.

Because I was constantly told I was not big enough, I tried to eat everything and always lifted weights. I wouldn't walk up the steps in our house without stopping in the middle of the stairs to do twenty push-ups. While watching TV, I sat on the floor and did sit-ups.

I used to keep track, and from the time of my youth through my years in high school, I had been in more than thirty street fights. That probably didn't happen to everyone. It gave me a mental outlook and set a standard of how I would live my life. Later in life, I would learn to fight with my brain against NFL opponents—or against cancer and the effects of the accompanying surgeries.

Football was going to be my answer to success. I would be the first person in my family to go to college, and a scholarship would be necessary for me. I was the oldest of six children; we got by fine, but there was never much extra.

My sophomore football season approached in August 1962, and every bit of my energy had gone into preparing. I was a skinny kid, but my body was all muscle and in good shape. I could run all day, and I was tough.

Our head coach was a great gentleman and an excellent coach. He was a veteran and a big, powerful man: Dan Galbraith, who was affectionately known as "The Bear." His son, Danny, at the time was in the fifth grade. Danny has become a good friend and was himself a very good football player, a high school track star, and a longtime weightlifter. He currently lives in Anderson, Indiana, where he and his brother Rick own a fencing company.

Later, we would discuss our high school days and my 1964 undefeated team. He told me that, as a youngster, he would accompany his father to practice and work as a field manager.

"In 1962, I was eleven years old and in the fifth grade," Danny said. "My father, known as 'The Bear,' was the head coach at Bethel Park High School in a community just south of Pittsburgh. High school football in western Pennsylvania was considered the very best in the United States. Joe Namath, Johnny Unitas, and Mike Ditka were just three of the many stars with their roots firmly entrenched in western Pennsylvania high school football.

"I used to go with my father to practice and help in any way possible. One thing I learned early on was that whatever I heard stayed with me and was never to be shared.

"My dad's practices were tough and always set up the same way. They started with running and calisthenics, followed by individual drills such as blocking and tackling on sleds and dummies. Those were followed by individual work, in which Joe Nicoletti, one of my father's assistants, would take the quarterbacks and running backs and work on plays while my father would have the linemen and would conduct the somewhat famous (or infamous!) 'line scrimmage.'

"Dad did everything full speed, and the line scrimmage was very aggressive. He always went to a specific area of the field right below a grassy hill. During the line scrimmage, there was always a large crowd sitting and watching this highly aggressive and, for them, highly entertaining part of the practice.

"As we were driving [one day], Joe asked my dad, 'Bear, is there anything new with your part (line scrimmage)? Is anyone raising eyebrows?'

"My dad answered, 'Joe, I don't know what to think. I brought up Mikey Westhoff today (from junior varsity to practice with the varsity), and he knocked Biff Baker right on his butt. Not once, but several times.'

"Biff Baker was a senior offensive tackle at 6-3, 255 pounds, and the team captain who accepted a full scholarship to the University of Miami. Biff was at least three years older than Mike and probably seventy-five pounds heavier. Biff was a good football player, and for him to have gotten beaten in a full-speed drill in front of everyone—that was special. Well, to Mike. Maybe not so much to Biff.

"The Bear never swore. But my dad then said, 'You know, Joe, that damn Mikey is tough. I am going to keep him up for a while and see what happens. We might have found ourselves an out-side linebacker.'

"Mike never did go back down to the junior varsity. He stayed up and went on to be the first sophomore to start every game in the history of the high school. I didn't know Mike back then, but for him to do that at such a young age was really something special. It must have given him a lot of confidence."

Even back then, Danny seemed to know I could handle any challenge.

"He was a good player and an exceptional leader," Danny said. "Over the next several years, he was the leader of his class and other classes.

"And I have never heard of anyone else doing this during the summers: Mike organized what he called 'captain's practice.' He ran the practice and pretty much made everyone who was playing football participate in the conditioning workouts. He was always in great condition and led everyone through the workouts.

"I remember reading about Walter Payton of the Chicago Bears and his famous running up and down hills. Mike Westhoff was running the very difficult hills around our school before I ever heard of anyone training that way. What was once a steep, grassy hill seemingly straight up and down was covered with worn-out trails when Mike finished his 'captain's practices.'

"My dad gave Mike a chance and Mike *figured it out.* He was not going to go back down to the junior varsity, no matter what. That skinny little kid was going to take advantage of that opportunity and make it work. That day in the line scrimmage he became a leader.

"They had an excellent season the next year, losing only two games. But it was in 1964, Mike's senior year, that he led them to an undefeated season and arguably the No. 1 ranking in the state of Pennsylvania."

Yes, we were a good high school program. I wasn't a star but was always one of the team's best players. I was a smart player who understood the game and was tough enough to always be willing to play a physical brand of football. In 1964, our team went unbeaten—and I was a captain. Danny's brother Rick was our quarterback and an excellent athlete and football player.

I had learned to love being the underdog, probably because I was the classic example. Being a year younger, always trying to gain weight and deal with feeling inadequate as a student made me never stop working. As a coach in the NFL, I never shied away from an undersized player. I saw the end result, not the ongoing process. Poor students never scared me if there was a good work ethic. Each year I looked out at the room full of faces and only saw NFL players. I knew I could teach them what they had to know. I only had to figure out how to do it.

My special teams units were going to be the smartest, toughest, and most diverse. They would become physically dominant and unquestioned experts at their various positions.

My propensity for reading helped me overcome my classroom inabilities and poor test results. As time progressed, I improved as a student and figured out how to deal with college both at Wichita State and in my one year at Wyoming.

I was redshirted as a player and received an extra year in college. I graduated in five-and-a-half years with a Bachelor of Arts in history. I chose history for several reasons. First, I was terrible in math and only average in science. But I loved to read and was fascinated by how we humans have developed through our history.

I went to graduate school at Indiana University and received a master's degree in education, with an emphasis in psychology on the educational level, not clinical. I was intrigued by how we learn. I always felt inadequate as a student, and I was obsessed with how we learn and how we teach.

I got my degree in one calendar year and received all A's. I guess I figured out the "classroom thing."

In dealing with my players, I adopted the educational philosophy of an Israeli psychologist, Haim Ginott. He dealt with children and believed that if you have a particular goal for a child and you see him and treat him in that manner, his chances of achieving that goal will dramatically increase. If you call him a dummy, he might become one.

No matter what educational background my players possessed, I saw them as "magna cum laude." I just had to find a way. I never gave up, and I never stopped trying.

Danny Galbraith understands exactly what I mean.

"As I look back on it, and having already followed his NFL career, I realize that, in 1962, that skinny kid in Bethel Park was Larry Izzo, Bernie Parmalee, Taysom Hill, and so many others to whom Mike gave a chance," Danny said. "I am sure that he made it clear to them that this chance could change their lives.

"It gives me great pride to picture my father in front of that crowd at practice, on the hill coaching the line scrimmage, and him giving Mike Westhoff—a kid from nowhere—an opportunity. And where that opportunity would someday lead.

"It formed a foundation as to how he would conduct his NFL career. Pick a tough guy—don't care about his size or speed—and give him a chance and see if you can change his life. In my opinion, a hell of a lot of NFL players got their start in front of that hill in 1962."

CHAPTER 2

Wyoming and Wichita

Wyoming is a long way from Pittsburgh—almost another world.

Following my graduation from high school in 1965, I accepted a full football scholarship to the University of Wyoming. They were playing very good football at the time, and some part of me had always wanted to be a cowboy.

I had been recruited but not heavily. Several colleges had offered me scholarships—Louisville, Arizona—but I was only an average student. Being a year younger than a lot of my peers, I wasn't as big as most colleges would have preferred.

I knew that I would catch up and become big enough to play college football. I just needed some time.

While I was in high school, I was very interested in the University of Pittsburgh, but my number one pick at the time was Virginia Tech. They had recruited me but at the last minute turned me down, telling me that they didn't believe I was going to be big enough. Where had I heard that before?

During the summer, I ran into one of Virginia Tech's coaches who had been recruiting me at an all-star game in Hershey, Pennsylvania. By that time, I had caught up size-wise, gained fifteen pounds, and was in excellent shape. The coach had always liked me and now, seeing my new size, was impressed and tried to talk me into going to Virginia Tech. I was honored that he felt that way; it was a confidence boost. But I told him I had signed with the University of Wyoming and was very excited to get started there.

I also was accepting the challenge of going to a completely different environment. I knew they were a good football team. Jim Kiick was a big star, and they had a number of guys who were very good. I was eager to see how I would fit in.

Like most students, I worked the summers in Pittsburgh to get some spending money. I was very fortunate that I was able to work in the steel mills. A friend of mine's father worked in the mill. He had a good "in" for us there, and we got very good-paying jobs. It was hard, challenging work, but it paid well and was very much a growing experience. Working in a steel mill as a young man helps you grow up in a hurry. The responsibility and discipline that those jobs helped develop stayed with me my entire life.

As I was preparing to leave for college, my father said to me, "You know, Mike, we never have gotten to travel, much and this trip to Wyoming will be a good chance for you to see much of the country."

He then handed me a Continental Trailways bus ticket for Laramie, Wyoming.

My chance to see the country? Well, OK.

I left for Laramie from Pittsburgh at eleven o'clock on a Friday night. My girlfriend gave me a small box of brownies, and I had one suitcase. Yep, traveling light.

The trip seemed to take forever. I ate fast food and slept on the bus. Along the way as we drove across the country, we stopped in various cities and towns where we picked up one or two additional players who were also on their way to Laramie. I talked with them but never really did get to know them very well. It was kind of a lonely ride.

We arrived in Laramie around ten o'clock on Sunday morning. It was cold, and I remember getting off the bus thinking that maybe I had just landed on the moon. I could see miles of empty prairie and the mountains in the distance.

A manager from the football team pulled up in a pickup truck and told me to throw my bag in the back and climb in for the ride to the university. We stopped in front of the dormitory that was to be my new home. I can still remember it: Crane Hall. I got out of the truck, picked up my suitcase, and started to walk in. The manager stopped me and said, "Where the hell do you think you're going? Put that bag down right there, get over to the field house to get some equipment before it's all gone."

All gone? Where the hell am I?

When I got to the field house, I never saw a doctor and didn't have a physical. I never even talked to a trainer.

So just after sitting on a bus for thirty-some hours, I was getting equipment. I just hoped the equipment was going to fit properly. But the helmet felt like I could spin it around my head with my head still in it. The shoes were too tight. Nothing seemed to fit.

Yet there I was in the locker room with about fifty other players, getting dressed—and wondering what in the world I was doing there.

The freshman team coach, Bill Baker, came walking through, meeting everyone. In 1965, freshmen were not eligible for the varsity in college football. He said, "You know, we've got a nice crowd here. Let's just get outside and get a practice in."

What? Have a practice?

Here it is, Sunday morning, I've been on a bus for nearly thirty-six hours, and now I'm going to practice? There must be some sort of rule against that.

The practice consisted of exercises, running, and contact drills. We blocked and tackled and generally just ran into one another. We tackled and blocked sleds. Every crazy and violent drill that I knew in football, we ran that Sunday morning.

One was "bull in the ring." That's a famous drill in which six or so guys get in the circle with one man in the middle. A coach would then call out a number, and the guy with that number would attack and block the man in the middle. The idea was to be aware of everything on the field. That way, you could turn in time to take on that attacker.

It's definitely a barbaric drill, and it hasn't been done in football for quite a long time now. It was used back then.

I was cut and bruised all over. I got into two fights, and my nose was bleeding.

Welcome to college football.

Finally, after about an hour and a half of this torture, the practice came to an end. I took a shower thinking, "What in the hell have I gotten into?"

I learned how to *figure it out* and never quit. Very few college students experience anything like that, but it's these very experiences that helped me grow into the man and coach that I would become.

I walked back to the dorm where my bag was still sitting on the sidewalk. So—thirty-six hours on a bus, my bag on the sidewalk, no physical, equipment that didn't fit. A brutal practice and a nosebleed.

Figure it out, Mike!

Over the years, I look back on that day thinking of the times and how many friends or relatives that I've seen take their children to college. You know: a carload of luggage, a stereo, a television, a refrigerator. And, of course, a well-decorated room. Home away from home.

Me? I picked up that suitcase and, bloodied and battered, checked into the dormitory to start my college career.

Something about Wyoming

My time at the University of Wyoming didn't work out in any shape or form. I liked the school and really wanted to attend classes and play football there. At seventeen years old and now in college, I was a young kid and had a long way to go to becoming a college football player. I needed the extra (redshirt) year to help catch up physically and prepare me to become the type of college player I very so much desired.

But what they were doing as coaches was total bullshit. They started to build a good football team but helped ruin a lot of young men's lives. They would bring in a lot more freshmen players than they intended to keep. That was not what college football was supposed to be about.

But there was something about Wyoming that I always loved. Maybe since I was a "city kid" from Pittsburgh, I dreamed of being a cowboy. Minutes after I arrived in Wyoming, I fell in love with the state. The mountains, plains, forests, and wildlife captured me and stayed with me my entire life.

To this day, I visit Jackson, Wyoming, several times a year. In the summer, I go hiking in the mountains and rafting and kayaking in the Snake River. The winters there are a paradise of snow. I own two snowmobiles, and each year can't wait to go with my good friend Tim Peters—a real cowboy and Jackson resident—and snowmobile throughout the Teton Valley, Yellowstone, and the Togwotee Mountain area. Wyoming has played a major role in my life, and I am so grateful to have made such a wonderful place my part-time home.

Wyoming to Wichita State

Following my freshman year at Wyoming, I was planning on leaving the school and transferring back home to the University of Pittsburgh. In high school, I was recruited by Pitt but turned down due to my size.

I was barely seventeen years old when I graduated high school, but now, a year later, I had caught up and certainly was big enough.

One of the Pitt coaches liked me and told me that if I was big enough, I might be in line for a scholarship. We were a large family without much extra money, and I needed the scholarship to be able go to college.

Wyoming was a very good football team. It has produced a number of very good players from all over the country, including Jim Kiick, who went on to help the Dolphins win two Super Bowls. Believe it or not, the school would bring in about one hundred freshmen players and, through the process of grades, discouragement, and just being released, would end up with twenty to twenty-five scholarship players to move from freshman to sophomore class.

In 1966, with freshmen not eligible for the varsity, we converted that nearly one hundred-man roster into a very good freshman team. We only played three games but won them easily. The University of Colorado, Colorado State, and the Air Force Academy—we pounded all of them. I was playing both as outside linebacker and tight end. I was doing a good job and getting to play a lot.

We had our share of stars. Our two freshmen running backs were Vic Washington and Dave Hampton; both went on to very long and successful NFL careers.

We were a damn good team.

We pretty much practiced all winter in the indoor arena, and this continued into spring ball. We were basically playing football

all year long. How did this happen? Who the hell is going out to Laramie, Wyoming, in the middle of the winter to find out?

Following spring ball, all the freshmen players were to meet with head coach Lloyd Eaton to discuss our status. We stood in a long line in the field house and awaited our turn. It seemed like I stood there all day—and, like most everyone in that line, I was basically scared to death.

Do you wonder why I was scared to death? Remember, this was 1966 and the Vietnam War was raging. My family did not have the means to send me to college. Yes, I could have gotten a student loan, and I would have paid it back. I would not have needed Bernie Sanders' help.

I believed that I had done well in the spring, and I had gotten much bigger and stronger, but I was far from being a real good player. When my turn finally came, I sat with the coach, and he told me I had fought hard and showed enough toughness. I had gotten bigger, but he wanted me to work on my leg size and strength.

Gee, thanks. Talk to my mother.

He said that he was going to redshirt me to give me that extra year to grow and catch up. He told me that this year, out of nearly one hundred players, he had decided to keep twenty-three freshmen on scholarship, and, by the way, I was number twenty-three. He made it very clear, so I knew exactly where I was in the grand scheme of things: twenty-three out of one hundred. Well, I finished ahead of seventy-seven others.

I don't believe that is the way college football is supposed to work, but that is exactly how it happened.

I liked Wyoming and believed I could have made it work, but the entire process discouraged me. I was looking to transfer. What should I have done? Gotten a student loan, transferred to Alabama, and walked on to the Crimson Tide. They were playing a type of "small ball." It might have taken me a year or even two, but I would have matured and *figured it out*.

I certainly was no all-star, but I would have found a way to make that team and been able to play. There are very few things in my life that I wish I could have done differently. That is one of them.

I spent the entire summer of 1966 working in a steel mill and trying to obtain a football scholarship. I worked four summers in the Pittsburgh steel mills. The work was physical and dangerous, and the workers were strong and hard. I was constantly reminded: "Don't let me see you back here." Or: "Get your education and keep your ass out of here."

If you look closely, you might see that the Pittsburgh Steelers football team resembles that exact persona.

The football scholarship search was difficult. The Pitt coach who had promised me a scholarship had left and, with him, so did my scholarship hope. A number of schools were interested, and I went on weekends to visit. Several of them offered me full or partial scholarships, but none really appealed to me.

A friend of our family had gone to school with George Karras, the head coach at Wichita State University. They called me and said that if I was good enough to play at Wyoming, then I would be worth taking a chance on.

Wichita? In 1966, I didn't even know where it was. They played in the Missouri Valley Conference, and those schools had gained some notoriety, especially in basketball, because of the many very competent minority players who were playing for their universities. They bordered two very powerful conferences, the Southwest and the Southeastern, which at the time had very few if any African American players.

Wichita State was playing a good, competitive schedule, and its roster comprised many minority players, as well as transfers such as myself. In some ways, football-wise, it was the Second Chance University—and that was what I needed. There was constant movement of players and coaches. In my four years there, I played for four head coaches: George Karras, Boyd Converse, Ed Kriwiel, and Ben Wilson. Three got fired.

I played with some very good players. One of my roommates, Lynn Duncan, was drafted by the Bears, and another, Kenny Lee, a running back, spent some time with the Eagles.

Most of the very good players I played with were minorities who ended up at schools such as Wichita State after having not been recruited by Southeastern or Southwest Conference schools. In 1968, I was a captain for us, and we played North Texas State when Joe Greene was one of that school's captains. I am sure that under more normal circumstances a player such as Joe Greene would have been heavily recruited by every Southeastern and Southwest school. I don't know that he wasn't, but he was only the "best player in the state."

I remember as a player going to Arkansas and having to stay in a Little Rock inner-city hotel because we had a number of minority players. I am proud that I was personally involved in a small aspect of integration.

When I arrived at WSU, I met a young coach who had played at Wichita State and was coaching the linebackers. Bill Parcells was getting started on his coaching career, and it didn't take long to recognize that this guy knew what he was doing and was headed for big things. I didn't get to know Bill very well then, but we did know each other, and it started a relationship for me with someone I always admired and respected. It didn't end the way it should have, but for a long time, he was someone I could ask for advice and counsel.

Something very interesting occurred on my first day at WSU. Actually, this was a very typical Mike Westhoff hurdle. I was sitting in the office of the head coach, George Karras, talking about my brief college history. He told me I would be practicing against his varsity, and I would be expected to do anything that was asked. He handed me the scholarship papers and showed me where to sign. He then took the papers, held them, and said to me: "You know, I really don't know much about you. School starts in two weeks. You practice against us for two weeks, and we will meet again, and I will either hand you a signed scholarship or a plane ticket home."

Well, Mike, here you go again. Practice after a thirty-six-hour bus ride to Wyoming, and now this. My college career was not exactly normal.

I said, "Yes, sir," to Coach Karras, got up and immediately went to the stadium to see the equipment manager. He was an older gentleman named Phil, and over time he would become one of my friends. I told him I needed a helmet with a full face mask and hand and arm pads. I told him that I was going to hit every "son of a bitch" on the field and get into a hundred fights, and I had to be prepared.

Years later, long after I had been starting for three seasons and was both captain and Most Valuable Player, Phil told me that he often told first-year players of what I had to do to make the team, and if they were half as tough as Mike, maybe someday they would make it also.

Two days after being in Coach Karras' office, I was walking off the practice field and he came by me and told me to stop into his office and pick up my signed papers. He told me that he had signed the scholarship after my first practice.

I am not good at quitting, and I wasn't going to end up in a fucking steel mill.

Fourth Quarter Class

My college playing career was about as crazy as it gets. Five years under five different head coaches and five different coaching staffs. Some really good coaches and some really not-so-good coaches.

My first year in Kansas, I practiced every day, improved my skills, getting bigger and stronger, and actually becoming a pretty good player. George Karras and Bill Parcells were fired and replaced with Boyd Converse, a junior college coach from Kilgore, Texas. They had won the national championship and brought in the Alabama "small ball" style. Everyone had to lose weight and become quicker and faster.

Boyd Converse brought some good coaches with him, most notably Larry Lacewell as the defensive coordinator. He had been a graduate assistant at Alabama. He then hired Jimmy Johnson, who had just finished playing at Arkansas.

They made it clear they were going to bring in their own guys and get rid of us Yankees. Yes, the coach actually said that to me. Could there be anything more fucking stupid than that?

Here we go again, Mike.

During that winter, we were all required to take a phys ed class. I think we each received two hours credit for "The Fourth Quarter Class." It was running, agility drills, rope climbing, and combat drills. This class had two purposes: to get us in incredible physical condition and improve our speed and quickness. It also revealed how much pressure we could take and who was tough enough to endure.

Also, a number of players would be run off or quit, making room for the new coaching staff's guys. It seemed like half of our team quit, with many of them leaving the university.

Three days a week at 4 p.m. we would assemble in a gymnasium for a one-hour class. It was nonstop moving from one station to another while always being screamed at. I was always in very good condition, constantly lifted weights (not common in the 1960s), and could get myself into a zone and just keep going and going.

As a teenager, I had worked "grown men" jobs. I dug ditches, ran a jackhammer in the streets of Pittsburgh, and worked in front of a steel mill blast furnace. I sure as hell could survive their bullshit "Fourth Quarter Class."

On the first day of the class, as a group, we moved from station to station where each one was explained and demonstrated. One such place was a stick-fighting station. Two players were to get on their knees while facing each other, and each would grip a six-foot wooden shovel handle. On a signal, you had twenty seconds to try and take the handle from your opponent. To demonstrate, Coach Larry Lacewell picked me and told Coach Jimmy Johnson to get down with me.

I had lifted a lot of weights and, for my size of 210 pounds, was very strong. I knew that Johnson had played at Arkansas, but at this time looked like a short, chubby guy to me. He was certainly tough enough and fought hard, but I was stronger and was winning. Out of frustration, he threw an elbow and hit me in the mouth. I dropped the handle and went after him. We scuffled for a few seconds and were separated.

He couldn't have taken that handle from me to save his life.

He went on to become a Hall of Fame coach, but back then I saw nothing impressive. I am sure he felt the very same about me.

I will give you another example of this bullshit "Fourth Quarter Class." One of our stations was a rope climb. There were two ropes. One was short, with knots in which you were to try and not use your feet and pull up only with your hands and arms. The other went all the way to the ceiling with no knots and you were to use your feet to help hold on.

I could do both fairly easily, but the long rope was a real challenge. One of our players whose name I can't remember had tried all year long but could not climb the long rope. On the final day, everyone was called up and gathered around the rope. The coach let us all know that on this day, this particular player was going to "make it."

He wasn't strong enough, and I knew that he had no chance. He started up and the entire team cheered and encouraged him. He fought all the way, taking forever and draining all of his strength. As he reached the top, he struggled one last time but successfully touched the top.

As we all cheered, his strength gave out and he violently slid back down the rope. He maintained his grip to keep from falling. I can still hear the hissing sound of his hands on the rope as he slid down. All of the skin was torn from his hands, and he lay screaming on the floor. He was rushed to the hospital and left the university. I never saw him again.

Yeah, those guys in charge of such drills were really special.

"Fourth Quarter Class" I guess was a booming success. It seemed like much of the team quit and went home. The new staff brought in new players, but most of them were punks who never went to class. Not one went on to finish a degree or to graduate, and most of them weren't very good players anyway.

I was playing as an outside linebacker and doing OK, but I injured my knee and missed most of the year. I wasn't a good enough athlete to be playing that position, and the entire year for me was a waste.

Converse and his entire staff were fired after that one year and left with what I believe were the most violations in NCAA history. I told you, my college career was anything but normal.

Actually, though, when I look back, having survived that fucking mess helped turn me into a damn good coach—mainly by reminding me of what not to do.

My next two years saw some smarter coaches, especially an offensive line coach named Tony Yelovich, who went to work at Notre Dame for many years and who moved me to the O-line. I know, I am too small, but I was 6-1 and 230 pounds by then, and we were playing small ball. I was perfect. We ran the option and play-action passes. We scramble blocked, and my quickness and strength made this type of football perfect for me. I went on to start every game for the next two years and was made captain and won Most Valuable Player.

We were not a good team, but we had some good players who fought hard and competed every week. I learned a lot about what it took to be successful without having all the tools. I found a way to make it work by *figuring it out* with what skills I had to work with.

I am proud of what I accomplished as a player. I have no illusions of grandeur. I was just a guy on a not-so-good team but made the very best of it and more than held my own.

I went to school. I got my degree—something almost none of my teammates accomplished. No, none of my college career was normal, but I *figured it out* and made the most of it. It sure as hell helped prepare me for what was ahead.

Back to High School

Following my graduation from Wichita State, I returned to Pittsburgh and spent four years coaching at several high schools. High school football in Western Pennsylvania at that time was arguably the best in the United States. Great players and coaches helped build those programs.

Among my most special times were the two years I spent coaching and teaching at Peters Township, a high school south of Pittsburgh. I taught history and coached with one of my favorite coaching staffs. We lost only twice one year and went undefeated the next season. Our head coach was John Bacha, an excellent educator and coach. John is a perfect example of the type of individual who made Western Pennsylvania high school football so great.

Vaughn Brunazzi was a big, powerful man who coached defense and was quite a character. Ron Peters, the fourth member of our staff, left high school coaching and joined the Navy. Ron was a jet pilot flying off aircraft carriers all over the world.

This was one of the top coaching staffs I was a part of. Vaughn died a few years ago of complications from diabetes. John, Ron, and I remain very close friends, and my weekly phone conversations are some of my most cherished times.

CHAPTER 3

Lee Corso, Woody Hayes, Bear Bryant—and Me

I first became aware of Lee Corso when he was the head coach at Louisville, and I was playing for Wichita State. I was one of the team captains, and we played them late in the year on a very cold Saturday night.

Tom Jackson, who went on to star at linebacker for the Denver Broncos and became famous for his work at ESPN with Chris Berman after his playing career, was on the Louisville team.

It was an important game for me because it was one of the few times my parents were able to see me play. They were able to drive from Pittsburgh to Louisville and stay over before and after the game. So, we had the chance to visit, and they got to see me play.

I had played against Louisville several times, but now with Lee Corso as the coach, this was a different team. They had more talented athletes, especially in the skill positions, and they were much faster and more aggressive. It didn't take much to see that Lee was a talented young coach working his way up the ladder.

I remember that we lost a hard-fought game to a more talented Louisville team. I was disappointed in that I had lost very few games in front of my father. We nearly always won in Little League and went undefeated at Bethel Park High School during my senior year in 1964.

My parents were happy to see me play, and my father—who was never easy to please—was impressed with how physical I played.

Something very interesting happened in this game, and the results of dealing with it afterward stick with me to this day.

I was playing center, and on a particular running play, I was to pull and help lead the ball carrier around the end. We were playing a different kind of football at that time—smaller and faster in style. I was 6-1 and weighed 230 pounds; not offensive lineman size, but in 1969 it was a good position for me.

I pulled around the end, and their safety came up to defend the play. It was a cold night, and I can still remember (and feel) the collision. We hit helmet to helmet. He ducked his head, and the crown of his helmet hit me square in the face mask. It was the hardest hit I'd ever encountered on the football field. It would be completely illegal nowadays and might even have gotten him ejected from the game.

We both went down—hard. I was momentarily knocked out, and I am sure he was, too. It was actually a win for me because his job was to make the tackle, and that sure as hell didn't happen.

When I got to my feet, I noticed that my face mask was hanging loosely on my helmet. An official told me that my helmet was broken, and I would have to leave the field. On the sideline, I saw that the helmet had been cracked on both sides from the earhole straight up about three inches on each side.

That wasn't going to stop me—not in a big game, not in front of my parents. I was given another helmet and went onto the field.

Believe it or not, the next week, our equipment manager—at my request—repaired the helmet. He took flat pieces of plastic about three inches by three inches and screwed them in over the cracks to secure them. He knew I loved that helmet and was going to make sure I finished my senior season wearing "my helmet."

Football was a different game then. Something like that could never occur today. That helmet sits in my office to this day. While coaching with the Jets, I took the helmet with me to show the trainers. Believing that a concussion must have occurred on the collision, and with the fact that I continued to play and had a cracked helmet, well, they just laughed and said that "this answers a lot of questions."

Several years later, I was working at a high school outside of Pittsburgh, and Lee Corso, then at Indiana, came in recruiting several of our players. He actually signed one, a tackle named Jim O'Rourke who eventually went on to play at Indiana. Lee and I were talking about his recruiting visit, and he mentioned that he remembered me as a player and asked about my goals and plans. I told him that I would love to coach in the college ranks, and I wanted to finish my master's degree.

He then told me to apply to Indiana, and if I got accepted there to drive out to Bloomington and discuss what it would take for me to coach for him as a graduate assistant.

Indiana accepted me in its graduate school of education, where I would work toward a degree with an emphasis on the educational psychology area. One of my high school coaching friends had a brother who was an Olympic bronze medalist in the javelin, and he was competing in a spring track meet in Bloomington. IU also was having a spring football scrimmage. So three of our high school coaches and I drove out to Bloomington on a Saturday afternoon.

I left the track meet and walked over to the field house to meet with Coach Corso. We talked a while and then he offered me the job. He said he would arrange for me to get in-state tuition and that the football department had a "little bit" of money that he could pay me.

I couldn't wait. Welcome, Mike, to college football.

Well, almost.

I arranged with the university to start my classwork in January, thankfully giving me the entire fall to concentrate on football. My wife, Marilyn, a cytologist—lab work screening slides of cells for cancers—was very qualified and got a job at Bloomington Hospital. Between her salary and my "little bit" of money from football—I didn't know how much yet—we would be OK financially.

We found a small two-bedroom apartment, and—just before training camp was to start—I loaded up a U-Haul truck, attached my car to the back, and took off for Bloomington. My brother, who lived and worked in Cincinnati, brought one of his workers to help us move in.

My next step was at the registrar's office to get signed up for school. When I mentioned the promise of in-state tuition, the people in the office looked at me like I was from Mars.

"No," they said, "you have been misinformed. In no way are you eligible for in-state tuition."

We had no money; how was I going to be able to afford this? I had gone to school as an undergrad on a full athletic scholarship and never paid a penny for school. Now, like so many others, I took out a student loan, which, by the way, I fully paid back.

After that, I headed for the football office to talk with Coach Corso about my "little bit" of football money. And the good news just kept coming: Coach Corso told me that there was not any "little bit of football money" available.

But he had another option.

His good friend Bob Mitchell was an IU alumnus and a highly successful builder. Lee had arranged for me to meet with him and see what we could work out. He was building homes near the campus, and I would work as a carpenter.

I didn't know anything about being a carpenter. Naturally, though, I would *figure it out.*

My entire life I had worked every minute that I was not in school. Those four summers in the steel mill. Two years building roofs. I dug ditches and laid pipe, worked for a moving company, and ran that jackhammer on the streets of Pittsburgh when I was seventeen. That is, until the union discovered my exact age and that I didn't have a social security card.

Actually, the carpenter's job was a very generous offer. Following training camp, I would work Monday-Thursday from 7 a.m. until 11 a.m. I then would be able to go home, eat some lunch, and take a shower before heading to campus to start working on football and coach at practice. I was paid for five-and-a-half days. Yes, a very generous opportunity.

"I knew who Mike was from his playing days while I was at Louisville," Coach Corso said. "On a recruiting trip to Canon Mc-Millan High School in Canonsburg, Pennsylvania, I talked with Mike about joining my staff. The job was half football and half building houses. Mike took it and never blinked.

"Mike was outstanding in every way; his intensity and ability to absorb knowledge were second to none. His work ethic was on the level of very few.

"I read a letter to the staff one day that I had received from a professor who had Mike in his class. He described Mike as one of the most creative students he'd ever encountered."

So, my dream job had no tuition help and included construction work. But it also gave me a chance to coach football in the Big Ten under Lee Corso. I would be studying the programs at Michigan and Ohio State.

Who could have a better start to learning the game?

I will always love and respect Lee Corso. He was a good coach, much better than he is credited for, and his media career with ESPN's *College GameDay* program is truly the work of a star. His love and respect for the game is emphasized each week, but it's been his signature prediction at the end of each program, when he dons the mascot head of his pick, that has been the show's premier moment.

"Mike was one of my most dedicated coaches, and I was not the least surprised that he went on to such prominence in the NFL," he said. "Following his coaching days and while he was working with the media, Mike and I talked a number of times concerning the kicking game in college football for our *GameDay* show. Mike carried his knowledge and intensity from the football field to the TV and radio booth.

"There is one other part of Mike's time at Indiana that I feel I should add. Mike began his graduate school classwork and wrote a thesis and received all A's before football started in the fall. Graduate school in two semesters? How many people have accomplished that?

"I couldn't have been more proud of him."

Lee Corso was great to me, but what was really special was that he gave me an opportunity. He taught me how to think outside the box and how to *figure it out* and find a way to be successful when you're not holding the best cards.

I will never forget being in a staff meeting one day and a very specific debate developed over a play design. One of the coaches was arguing that a particular running play could be run both toward the tight end and away from him by moving one of our wide receivers in close and slightly behind the tackle. If the ball was run to the tight end's side, the wide receiver would block the defensive end and seal the back side.

Bob Otolski, the tight ends coach, was drawing his play and making his argument, and his case was looking solid—until he got up to debate it.

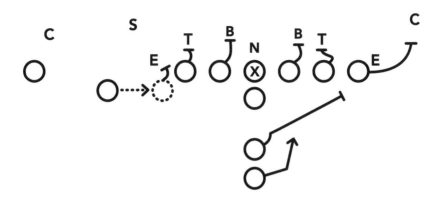

Coach Corso then walked up to the blackboard and made this point: our wide receiver is Keith Calvin, and he has to block Ohio State's All-American Bob Brudzinski (a future 1977 first-round draft pick by the Los Angeles Rams).

"Your drawing looks good," Lee said, "but this is what it's really like:"

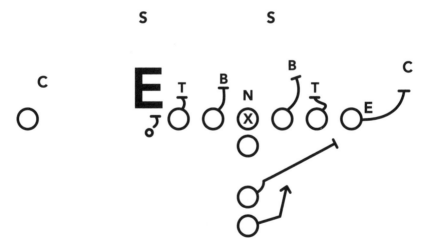

Lee then said, "I am not sure, but it doesn't look so good now."

The staff cracked up—although Bob didn't completely appreciate the humor.

It was a lesson I never forgot: we are drawing with Xs and Os, but they are real people, and we as coaches must never forget that.

Actually, for much of my career as I would draw plays, most of the time I would use numbers to draw the opponents.

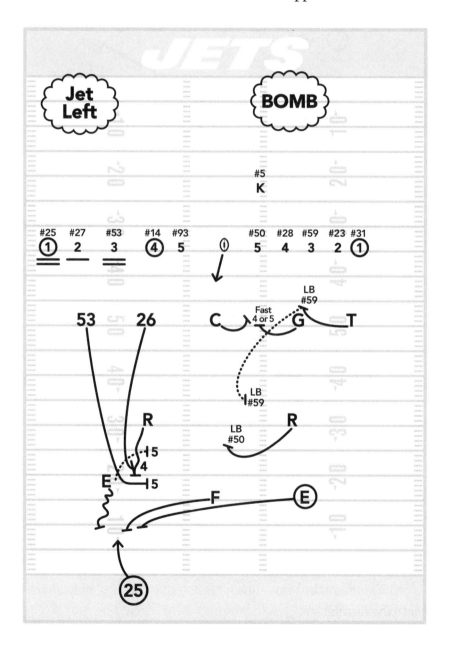

Most of my game-plan drawings looked something like this. I wanted everyone to be aware of exactly who we were going against.

Lee Corso taught me some valuable lessons. I love what he did for me, and I will forever be appreciative. No tuition help and a construction job to get some money, but the absolute greatest opportunity.

Thanks, Lee!!!!

Woody Hayes

As a graduate assistant with Coach Corso, I was helping coach the freshmen and going to graduate school, working on my master's degree. We previously had a coach there named Howard Brown. He was somewhat of an Indiana University legend: football captain on the 1946 and '47 teams, second-team All-America in 1945, played professionally for the Detroit Lions for three years. He went on to become an assistant coach at Indiana from 1951 to 1975. He was a great gentleman and an excellent coach, and he became somewhat of a mentor to me. I always appreciated and respected my relationship with Howard Brown.

Howard died in 1975. Following his death, Lee Corso came to me, handed me the keys to his new car, and told me that he needed my help for two days. Woody Hayes, the great Ohio State coach, was coming over from Columbus, Ohio, to Bloomington to attend the services and funeral. I was to be his chauffeur, host, and his guide. I would drive up to Indianapolis and pick him up, then take him everywhere that he needed to go.

It was an incredible opportunity for me, and I was more than excited to be alone with Woody Hayes for nearly two days. I took him everywhere, and I was a very gracious and happy host.

During my time with Coach Hayes, he never stopped talking to me. He wanted to know my family background and my playing history in high school and college. He specifically was interested in my psychology degree and how I would apply it to coaching. He was very smart and challenged me to challenge my players both physically and intellectually.

Woody was an historian and lectured me on the area, the university, and, of course, football. For a day and a half, he coached me, teaching me then questioning me; he never stopped. He was the ultimate teacher.

He talked to me about being both flexible and demanding, and always setting a high bar.

"Never accept anything mediocre," was his mantra.

One of the things that I learned from Coach Hayes that day was it takes a lot more than just knowing football to be a great coach. Coach Hayes was a well-rounded man and well read. And he seemed to care a lot about people. I believe that his completeness as a person helped him become a great teacher and coach.

As we were leaving Howard's funeral, we were headed back to the airport in Indianapolis about an hour's drive north of the university. Coach Hayes said to me, "Coach, we spent a lot of time talking over these last two days, and you enthusiastically have discussed conditioning and weightlifting. I can see that you've done some weightlifting yourself."

I said, "Yes sir, I certainly try."

He then said, "Well, I want you to remember something about weightlifting and conditioning. I never saw a weightlifter that was a football player, but I've seen lots of football players that become better through lifting weights. Make sure in your evaluations you know the difference between a football player and a weightlifter. Don't ever let a 'number' positively or negatively get in your way of determining if a young man is a football player."

Throughout my entire career, I remembered that advice. I was never going to let a number determine my final decision on a football player.

Bear Bryant

Another incredible event occurred in my coaching journey during the summer of 1979. So here I am, sitting on a curb under a tree in the middle of Alabama's campus with Bear Bryant. How did this ever happen?

During my summer vacation while coaching at Northwestern in 1979, my wife and I drove down from Chicago to Santa Rosa Island on the Florida panhandle. On the return trip, I serendipitously experienced the surprise encounter of my lifetime.

As we were driving north through Alabama, I said that I had always wanted to visit the university and that we should detour slightly and visit the campus. Following my freshman year at Wyoming in 1966, I had considered transferring to Alabama. I had admired Coach Bryant, and they were playing a type of "small ball." Their players had been instructed to lose excess weight and be in excellent condition and to be as fast and quick as possible. This was perfect for me at 6-1 and 230 pounds. I could have competed at several positions. I am not sure I would have been good enough to play at Alabama, but I was a good player for a certain style of football, and I would have figured out something. I believe I could have played.

We drove through the campus and finally found the field house. It was a classic old building located in the middle of the new, beautiful facilities.

Actually, following my last coaching year in 2019, when I was with the New Orleans Saints, Alabama brought me in to speak at a clinic the school was having and explain my kickoff return scheme. When I had first retired in 2012, I started a business in which I would travel to various colleges and install different parts of my kicking game. I am not aware of any other coaches who have done it this way.

I loved doing this—working with the college coaches and seeing them vastly improve their kicking games. I had top schools. I started with LSU and then had Texas A&M, Penn State, Notre Dame, West Virginia, Clemson, and Alabama. There were numerous other schools waiting, but the rule changes that have been adopted by the colleges ended my consulting career.

In 2019, from Alabama's beautiful football offices, I looked out at the old field house and relived that wonderful experience four decades earlier.

I parked that car near the field house, told my wife I would return shortly, and went inside. The building was dark and filled with reminders of the Crimson Tide's great history. It was empty and quiet; most everyone was on vacation.

I noticed a light coming from an office, and I walked in that direction. I stopped in the hall and looked into the office. Sitting in the back at his desk, all by himself, was Bear Bryant. He had on a short-sleeve white shirt and a tie. He noticed me and looked up and said, "Can I help you?"

I walked into his office and introduced myself, telling him I was a coach at Northwestern and I had always wanted to visit Alabama. He told me to come in and have a seat. He said all the coaches were on vacation and that he was just going over some paperwork.

We talked about my job at Northwestern and my football background and educational history. I told him about my interest in 1966 concerning my transferring. He said he knew that Wyoming was playing good football at that time, having played LSU in the Sugar Bowl.

Alabama was playing that type of "fast ball," and he would have given me a chance.

I have never looked back on my life and second-guessed any of my career decisions, but I wish I would have transferred to Alabama. I might not have played a play, but I believe that I would have *figured it out* and had an opportunity to play for Bear Bryant.

He then asked me if I would like to take a look around. He got up and went over to a coat rack and grabbed his hat. Yep, he grabbed his famous houndstooth hat.

We walked through the athletic facilities, and Coach Bryant showed me the tower where he did most of his coaching. He said that as he got older, he didn't do as much on-the-field, close-up work.

As we walked through the campus, he proudly showed me the building additions that money from the football program had helped fund. He would say, "See that new addition, the library? We helped build that."

His pride in his football program at the university was incredible, and it was an honor for me to witness. We walked a little further, and he asked if we could stop for a while. It was a hot day, and he stepped down and sat on the curb under a large tree. He took off his hat and wiped his brow with a handkerchief. He told me that as he had gotten older, he got tired, and he just didn't have quite the same stamina.

There I am, sitting on a curb on a quiet street in the middle of Alabama's campus with Bear Bryant. It can't get much better than that.

He then told me, "Coach, I learned two lessons in this business that I am going to share with you:

"Never be afraid to change. Don't get stuck in a rut. Accept the challenges and make the change. Always look for a better way.

"Also, make sure that the players are doing things the exact way that you want them done. Demand an exact level of excellence. Don't settle for anything less. They want to be coached. Coach them."

I helped him up, and we returned to his office. He asked if we would be driving north through Birmingham. I told him we would be. He told me that we had to stop for dinner at a barbeque place. He told me the name of the restaurant and the street exit from the highway, and he called the owner—telling him that a coach from Northwestern and his wife would be stopping and to put our dinner on his tab.

Bear Bryant was buying me a barbeque dinner. A day can't get much better.

When I got back to the car, my wife asked, "What happened to you?" When I told her what had happened, she was very happy for me. She thought it was incredible.

I wrote Coach Bryant a thank-you letter when I returned to Northwestern. I will always remember my visit with a coaching icon and the wonderful hour or so I got to spend with Bear Bryant. I not only remembered his coaching advice, but I followed it throughout my career.

Those two pieces of coaching advice became my signature mantras and helped me attain a level of excellence.

A chance undertaking turned into the experience of a lifetime.

CHAPTER 4

From a Hoosier to a Flyer

I n 1976, following my graduation from the University of Indiana and receiving my master's degree, I accepted a full-time job as the offensive line coach at the University of Dayton. Ron Marciniak was our head coach: an old-school, hard-nosed coach, but a hard worker and a genuine individualist.

We were a small Catholic university with a very limited budget trying to play Division I football. Dayton was a strong basketball school and went to the 1967 NCAA championship game, where the Flyers lost to UCLA with Lew Alcindor (later, of course, Kareem Abdul-Jabbar).

As for football, it was a tough row to hoe. We were always behind the other schools we were competing against. I'm amused when I see young coaches today accepting head coaching opportunities in the NFL and describing their hard time when they worked for, say, another NFL team as an analyst, slaving away in front of a computer. How much different my introduction was to coaching as a profession.

We only had four full-time coaches at Dayton. I was the strength coach and offensive line coach—real glamorous. During the winter, after the players had finished lifting weights, I cleaned the weight room, cleaned the locker room, and put soap in the showers and toilet paper in the stalls.

I had signed a contract for what I thought was $12,000. After getting my first paycheck, I quickly realized it was toward a salary of only $11,000. I went to the head coach and asked about the discrepancy, and he assured me that I was going to be paid $12,000: $11,000 from the university, and, during our one-month summer break, I was to work driving a beer truck that delivered to various bars in Dayton. Then I would be paid the extra thousand.

Welcome to football in Dayton, Mike.

A strange and somewhat awkward thing happened to me at Dayton when we traveled to play Marshall in West Virginia. After we arrived, each player was given a T-shirt to wear in the hotel for our meals. It was a white T-shirt with a red stripe around the collar and the sleeve, and it said University of Dayton Football. One of my jobs when we arrived at the hotel was to open the trunk containing all of these shirts, with each one on a hanger with a number—the player's number. I was to pass them out after we arrived at the pregame hot meal on Saturday before our game. I would collect the T-shirts before the game and put them back on the hangers and back into the trunk.

Our pregame meal—we didn't have a lot of money at Dayton— was a simple but certainly a good enough meal of pancakes. Before playing Marshall, I was downstairs early as usual, collecting all the T-shirts as the players arrived for the meal. When I was finished, and I put everything away, I sat down to eat. Most everyone had left and gone to their rooms to prepare for the trip to the stadium and the upcoming game.

The waitress came by and informed me that there was nothing left. The pancakes were all gone, and there was no breakfast for me. She then said, "Just hold on a minute, there is a group in one of the other dining rooms that has finished breakfast." A small group with some people who either didn't eat their meal or didn't eat much.

She went over to a cart filled with empty breakfast trays, picked one up, and took off the lid. It was a partly finished breakfast. Someone had not eaten everything. She brought it over and asked me if it would be OK. She took the partly eaten breakfast, warmed it up, and I ate that little bit of someone else's scrambled eggs and bacon. I didn't think anything of it. It wasn't terrible, and I ate it.

We lost that day to Marshall. We got beat by a better team. We played well and hard, and we gave a great effort.

The next day at work, Coach Marciniak was very cold to me—abrupt and short. I didn't understand what I had done wrong. My guys played fairly well, didn't make many mistakes, and had very few penalties. We had represented ourselves fairly well.

On Monday, I went into his office to ask what was wrong. He looked at me and said, "We don't have a lot of money here, and we try to make the best of it. But I guess that is not good enough for you. You have to order your own breakfast of bacon and eggs."

Stunned, I said, "So that is what you think happened."

I then told him the story about eating someone's unfinished breakfast. He became very emotional and started to cry. Ron was a big, tough man, and to see that emotion coming from him, well, I always held a very special place in my heart for him. It kind of formed a bond between us.

Following that season, Dayton decided to drop to the Division III level. It was a smart and prudent decision. It was just too difficult to compete financially at the Division I level. I was very interested in getting that head coaching job, and I tried very hard. The university made it clear to me that they were looking for an experienced Division III coach who could lead them down that path, though.

So, there I was with one month left on an $11,000 contract and in need of a job. I packed up my resumes and headed to Florida for the coaches' convention. Lee Corso had told me he had talked with Earle Bruce, the head coach at Iowa State, about the openings on his staff. Lee had recommended me very highly.

There were three openings on the Iowa State staff, and I believed I could get one. I was very excited to meet Coach Bruce and have the opportunity of interviewing for the job. We met in the lobby of the hotel, sat down, and began to talk. We discussed my playing experience, my master's degree at Indiana, and my coaching experiences.

He then told me that we would go up to his room. He had a blackboard up there. I would use the blackboard, and we would discuss football and he would interview me. As we were getting ready to leave, he saw a gentleman come into a small lobby bar and said that was a good friend of his, an NFL scout, and he was going to take a few minutes to see him and talk with him. He suggested I should wait right there.

I was OK with that, and I sat there and waited—for nearly four hours.

When he returned, it was obvious that he had been drinking with his friend and having a good time, not thinking much about me.

He then told me to follow him up to his room where we would continue the interview. We got off the elevator and walked down the hall to his hotel room. He opened the door and stepped inside. As I prepared to follow, he turned around and said, "You know, I probably have to interview some people in my state. When I am finished, maybe I'll give you a call."

He then closed the door right in my face.

I was stunned, but what could I do? I'm a young guy with very little experience and no job. I went back to my room, changed into shorts and tennis shoes, and I went out to run. I jogged along a path right near the ocean.

When I came back to the hotel, I went up to a small weight room located at the top of the hotel and did some weightlifting. When I was finished, I noticed that there was a small sauna in the corner of the weight room. I went over to it, thinking I'll just go ahead and sit down and relax for a while. I opened the door and stepped in to find in there all by himself was Frank Kush, the head coach at Arizona State.

I introduced myself and sat down. He told me that he remembered me from when I was playing. I'm not quite sure he did, but he was being kind, and we talked about my playing experiences, my master's degree work, and coaching at the University of Dayton—and how I would give anything to have that opportunity again.

He then asked me what I was doing, and I told him I was trying to get a job. He asked what I had experienced so far.

Naturally, I told him about my incident with Earle Bruce. Coach Kush looked at me and said, "Why are you talking with him?" I said he has some openings on his staff, and Coach Kush said, "That jackass. He did that to you?"

I said yes, I think he had a few drinks and was not that interested. Coach Kush then said, "I'll tell you what, Mike. I don't have a job, but someday I will. I know who you are, and I'll call you and interview you."

Now sometimes you hear that kind of thing and nothing comes of it. You try not to get your hopes up too high, but you still have to keep those hopes alive.

Coach Kush's word was good. Six years later, he got the head coaching job at the Baltimore Colts. He called me, and I got the job. He wasn't even sure what the job would be, but he interviewed me and gave me a job.

I became the strength coach, special teams coach, tight ends coach, assistant offensive line coach, and assistant to the head coach—and I helped make our travel arrangements. I don't think I did any of the jobs very well, but it gave me a chance. I got my opportunity to get a start in the NFL from a meeting with Frank Kush in a sauna after what had been one of my very worst experiences.

Let me add a footnote to the story.

I believe that there is some type of life after death, and I hope someday I can get up to heaven and someone will say to me, "You know, Mike, every once in a while, we let someone go back to a point in their lives to relive a moment that may have been a wonderful experience. Or maybe an opportunity to change something you wish you had done differently, or to say something that you wish you could change."

I'm going to take that opportunity, and I'm going to go back to that hotel hallway. When Earle Bruce goes to close that door in my face, I'm going to beat the shit out of that little twerp. Back in those days, I could have done that with my eyes closed. I guess I hope I have that opportunity.

Earle Bruce went on to be a very good coach at Ohio State, and I am sure that he was a good man. But on that day, he wasn't. He was a complete jackass. I would love to have that moment over.

CHAPTER 5

On to the NFL

In January 1982, while I was offensive line coach at Texas Christian University, I received a phone call from Frank Kush. He had just been hired as coach of the Baltimore Colts. After being fired from Arizona State following a very successful but somewhat tumultuous career, he had spent one season with Hamilton of the Canadian Football League and now was heading to the NFL.

Six years earlier, in that sauna in the Diplomat Hotel in Hollywood, Florida, site of the National College Football Coaches convention, Frank Kush had promised me if he ever had a coaching job, he would interview me. He was good to his word.

I flew to Baltimore and accepted the strangest coaching job.

Frank wasn't sure where I would fit. He needed a strength coach, a special teams coach, a tight ends coach, and someone who could help the offensive line coach. He wanted an assistant head coach and someone to be a buffer between the coaches and the front office. I told him I could do all of them.

ALL of them.

He looked at me and laughed, but then he said, "OK, you have it, we'll see what happens."

I went back to Fort Worth and talked with the TCU coach, F.A. Dry, about my leaving for Baltimore. He was unhappy about my decision and tried to talk me out of it. What started as a plea to stay turned into a violent argument about how was I going to take a lowly strength coach's job? When I wouldn't relent, he demanded my car keys; part of our contract was the use of a car the athletic department provided.

Dave McGinnis, who was on the TCU coaching staff—he went on to a long and successful NFL career with the Arizona Cardinals both as an assistant coach and head coach, then had very long hauls with the Titans and Rams—loved to tell the story about after hearing the argument between me and Coach Dry, he looked out the window and saw Mike Westhoff hopping onto a bicycle to begin his ten-mile ride home. Mike's first day headed to the NFL, and he has no car—only a bike to get home.

Welcome to the NFL, Mike.

The 1982 Baltimore Colts were a mess. Their once-brilliant quarterback, Bert Jones, had suffered a career-ending shoulder injury. The offense had a handful of competent players in running back Curtis Dickey, fullback Randy McMillan, center Ray Donaldson, and wide receiver Ray Butler. The defense had gotten old and would have to be rebuilt. We had a tremendous amount of work ahead of us and would basically be starting from scratch.

Frank put together a diverse, and what would turn out to be an incredible, coaching staff. Most of us, including Frank, were college guys and had never coached in the NFL. He did start out with two very experienced and well-qualified NFL coordinators, though. On defense, he hired Bud Carson, a Pittsburgh Steelers veteran and one of the NFL's greatest defensive minds—the architect of the Steel Curtain defense. In 2019, the Pro Football Writers of America gave to me their very prestigious "Dr. Z" Paul Zimmerman Lifetime Achievement Award. There had been only a handful of recipients, and Bud Carson was one of the original winners.

Frank also hired to his first NFL coaching job as defensive line coach Gunther Cunningham, who along with me in 2019 received the Dr. Z award. Also on defense, Frank hired two first-time NFL coaches in Rick Venturi and George Catavolos, who both went on to long and very distinguished NFL careers.

On offense, he hired Zeke Bratkowski, Bart Starr's longtime backup quarterback who later was an NFL assistant coach. Also in their NFL job debuts were offensive line coach Hal Hunter, who would go on to a successful career with Pittsburgh and Carolina, and Richard Mann, who became one of the finest receivers' coaches in NFL history. The offense that I learned from Richard helped me build the foundation to enhance my career as the tight ends coach for Don Shula with the Dolphins.

Frank Kush, out of nowhere, put together what was, in my opinion, one of the NFL's most-qualified coaching staffs. Frank's coaching brilliance was mostly unknown on the professional level—and greatly underrated.

Still, we had two NFL coordinators, but the rest of us were NFL rookies. We had lots of enthusiasm and much to learn.

My first NFL season was the 1982 strike-shortened campaign. We started 0-2, and then the players went on strike. The coaches started out, as normal, forming game plans and preparing as if we would be playing each week. But it quickly became obvious that the strike was going to last, and our workload dramatically changed.

Much of the team's personnel were furloughed. Coaches, to continue being paid, were sent on college scouting trips. For several weeks, we assumed the roles of our scouts. We would travel to a region and visit the various colleges in that area. We would study the film and, if possible, watch the practices. The scouts gave us a list of the players to study, and we would write reports on

each player. When possible, we would talk with the college coaches to discuss the various players. On most weekends, I would go
to a college game to observe the players that I was scouting, and it
would aid in my evaluation.

After several weeks of traveling, we came back to Baltimore to
re-landscape the entire facility. We planted flowers and shrubs,
raked mulch, and picked up every scrap of paper. Having an entire
coaching staff on the road, I believe, was probably an expense the
team did not need during a strike, so the Colts brought us home
and gave us another job. We painted the entire inside of the building. We worked as a team, moved the furniture, and painted the
walls and ceiling. Being the youngest coach, it seemed as though I
spent all my time on a ladder.

Please, Could We Get Back to Football!

After six weeks on strike, the players returned, and the schedule
was reduced to nine games. We were terrible. We tied one game,
and my first NFL year ended with an 0-8-1 record. But it greatly
improved my landscaping and painting skills.

I had started my NFL special teams coaching assignment
completely by accident. I was the happiest and luckiest guy in
town to be working for the Baltimore Colts. I was the strength
and conditioning coach, the tight ends coach, the assistant offensive line coach, and I was Frank Kush's administrative assistant.
Helping Hal Hunter, well, the offensive line was an area in which I
had some experience. At everything else, I didn't know shit. I was
stumbling around, just trying to *figure it out*.

Frank was an old-school, hard-nosed coach, and it was also
his first year in the NFL. He didn't know much about the NFL, but

he had been very successful at Arizona State because he believed in fast, athletic players, solid fundamentals, and hard work.

Zeke Bratkowski and Bud Carson were both great NFL minds and great leaders. They constantly reminded the rest of us how little we knew as NFL coaches. Hal Hunter had a sign in his office that said "... in this league." In other words, "Yes, I know, we don't know crap about the NFL."

For me, it was a great learning environment, and I was a gigantic sponge and tried to absorb every drop.

Coach Kush will never get enough credit for what he was putting together with the Colts. Bud Carson was one of the top three or four defensive coaches in NFL history. Hal Hunter was an excellent offensive line coach working with the Steelers, then finishing his career in personnel with the Carolina Panthers. George Catavolos coached with several NFL teams and retired after a stint with the Buffalo Bills. Rick Venturi was an outstanding pro coach with the Colts and Saints, working with the secondary and also as a defensive coordinator and a head coach. Zeke Bratkowski brought Super Bowl rings and experience with Vince Lombardi. Richard Mann, who played for Coach Kush at Arizona State, excelled with the receivers like few others. Tom Zupancic, who thank goodness took my place as strength coach, became one of the NFL's best in that role.

If we had been able to stay together for a few more years and not been hindered by administrators who pushed their own agenda—such as drafting John Elway in 1983 over Dan Marino—I believe we would have put together a very good football team. We were a damn good group of coaches who went on to outstanding levels of personal success throughout the league.

So here I am trying to figure out my various jobs. I had gone out for my daily afternoon run. I was jogging on the back road in Towson, Maryland, when I came across Coach Kush. He stopped me and told me to walk with him. He talked for a while about our first two games and his thoughts on the direction of the players' strike.

He then brought up our special teams and Bob Valesente, a college coach from Mississippi State who was helping Bud Carson with the defensive backs as well as coaching special teams. Frank told me he thought Bob was terrible and was going to fire him if he could find a replacement. I told him that I would take over the special teams and not to fire Bob.

I said that working for Bud Carson was very demanding and to let him just concentrate on defensive backs. I would handle the special teams.

Way to go, Mike! Just seeing if you can put your ass even further out on that limb.

Bob never did learn that I had done that for him, and I would repeat it a year later when the Colts were preparing to leave for Indianapolis and Frank wanted to fire him again. I talked him out of it and convinced him to let Bob decide whether he wanted to go to Indy.

Bob decided to go to the University of Kansas, where he would stay for several years before becoming the head coach. As he was taking over that job at Kansas, I was out of a job and we talked about my joining him. For some reason, though, his sorry ass never called me back.

It worked out pretty well for me, though, as I got hired by the Miami Dolphins. Where would you rather be? At Kansas with Bob Valesente or Miami with Don Shula?

When I think back about not receiving a phone call from Bob, I should have let his ass get fired. I don't do a good job of forgiving and forgetting, but for me, the whole thing worked out great.

Now the question was, how do I become a special teams coach? I really didn't know the first thing about that part of the game. Thank goodness I had the rest of the strike to try to figure it out.

During the strike, when I wasn't on the road scouting or back at the complex planting flowers and painting, I spent every minute reading the rules and watching film of every possible NFL special teams play.

The only notebook I had was Valesente's from Mississippi State, and it was terrible. It was better than mine, though; I didn't have one.

I spent weeks going through every word and drawing. I rewrote, reconfigured, and redrew everything. As I rewrote each section, I made sure that the rules pertaining to that specific area were incorporated into my description of the play.

The first part of special teams that truly resonated with me was the punt. Initially, it might as well have been written in Chinese. It made no sense and was way too complex to communicate simply and quickly. I figured out that an easy way was to number the defenders and design a blocking scheme that was based on man-to-man assignments within a zone-type protection technique. The punting team would form a protection cup around the punter, quickly block and still be able to release and cover the punt.

In the NFL, only the two players on the end of the formation can release downfield when the ball is snapped. Everyone else can go when the ball is punted. In order to accomplish both blocking and covering, I had to address stance, alignment, assignments, and technique.

The center, now a specific job as long snapper, had to learn how to snap and block, one of the toughest jobs in football. Because his assignment is the most difficult, he needs the most help.

Where, exactly, does the personal protector take on his blocking assignment? Most NFL teams still don't know the answer to this. And how do I teach a wing to block one of the best "rushers" in football?

It seemed like I had a million things to figure out, and I hadn't even written an introduction. Way to go, Mike! Strength and conditioning coach, offensive line, tight ends, Kush's assistant, and now special teams. And I kept someone from getting fired.

The next time, jog faster and shut up.

As I look back on developing as a special teams coach, two distinct things stand out as having a profound influence on me. First was designing any type of kick return or coverage. I leaned back on my experience as an offensive line coach and related kick returning to the principles and concepts of offensive running play design. Kick coverage philosophies I designed based on principles of defense, particularly blitzing. I wanted my special teams units to be based on the philosophies, concepts, and techniques of offense and defense.

I knew that everyone did this to a degree, but I wanted it more specific than I had ever heard anyone explain and compare it.

The first thing I did was to go into Bud Carson's office and ask him to explain his philosophy of blitzing. Bud was a defensive genius. He told me about creating an overload, confusing blocking schemes, and establishing edges. How to stack rushers and get a safety in position. Bud showed me how to present various problems from the same look. I was going to design and implement my kickoff coverage based on the precepts of a Bud Carson blitzing defense.

I believe if you asked anyone who went against me back in the day when movement and variance were legal in kickoff coverage, they would tell you that I presented the most complicated defensive problem they ever faced.

I wanted my kickoff return to look like an off-tackle power running play. There would be a double-team with either a trap or kick-out block. The back side of the play would be secured by a "running wall" to cut off the back-side pursuit. There would be lead-blocking principles and a very specific read. Distances, spacing, and timing would be incorporated, as well as climbing up to stop a safety from filling over the top.

I then took each one of these assignments and designed very precise techniques, position on the field, and an exact timing and path of the ball carrier. The more exact that the return mimicked the running play, the more I realized how difficult it would be to defend. Coaches had been designing football running plays since Knute Rockne—now all I had to do was to properly transfer them and, then conversely, to apply the same principles of defense to my coverage units.

Bill Callahan, one of the NFL's great offensive line coaches, knew I *figured it out.*

"I coached with Westy for four seasons (2008-11) with the New York Jets," Callahan said, "and what I admired most about him was his old-school coaching traits. He was compellingly principled in his philosophy of coaching. A lot of what he stood for as a coach was derived from his experience of being on Don Shula's staff with the Miami Dolphins in the 1980s and '90s. He was extremely knowledgeable about schematics, tactics, and the rules of the game.

"Mike also had a unique expertise in coaching special teams techniques because of his background as an offensive line coach."

Figuring out all of this started during the players' strike with a notebook that should have included crayons. But it slowly developed into a philosophy that helped me formulate some of the very best special teams units in NFL history.

The second-most helpful area for me was to study the somewhat small group of successful special teams coaches. Special teams in 1982 was not a dominant part of the game, and only a few coaches seemed to me to stand out: Frank Gansz in Philadelphia, Wayne Sevier in Washington, Rusty Tillman in Seattle, and Alan Lowry in Dallas.

I am sure there were some others, but those four stood out to me, and I studied every thing that their teams did.

Each of those coaches had something of a blueprint. Frank Gansz's teams were the most disciplined. They were exceptionally well coached and fundamental, and always seemed to be the least penalized. His teams were basic and, frankly, not very innovative, but they were always exceptionally prepared and hard to beat.

I can remember early in my career that we played very well against one of his teams and had definitely won the special teams battle. I felt that I had arrived; it was the first time that I really felt special in the NFL.

I am sure that over the years there were a few coaches who felt the very same way after having gotten the best of me. Not too damn many, though!

Rusty Tillman was easy to categorize. His teams could rush the punter and really cover kickoffs. They were aggressive, fast, and relentless. I never thought that his return teams could run across the street, but his coverage teams could swarm you and dominate an opponent.

Wayne Sevier in Washington could do everything. His teams were innovative. You had better be prepared for anything and everything. He wasn't going to beat himself; you had to beat him. In my opinion, his special teams positively contributed to his team's success everywhere he coached.

Alan Lowry in Dallas early in his career fit right in with the solid, fundamental, exceptionally disciplined, and prepared teams of the Tom Landy-coached Cowboys. Later in his career while at Tennessee, he was creative and stayed at the top of the special teams game for a long time.

These were good coaches to study in the early years of my career. I learned, borrowed, and stole a little from each of them. I never gave any of them credit—and I still am not—but these guys were special and helped me like you will never know.

To prepare for the 1983 season, we gladly volunteered to coach the Senior Bowl in Mobile, Alabama. The Senior Bowl then was a much different event than nowadays. Today's game, in my opinion, is a media event. Back then, only coaches and scouts were at the practices. Two of the week's practice days were double sessions. You can't even imagine that happening today. During those practices, coaches and only coaches were allowed on the field. Not even the scouts could be on the field.

With the exception of the two Super Bowl teams, every coach in the NFL spent at least three days at the Senior Bowl and attended every practice. One of my early NFL "moments" came during a Senior Bowl practice. I was coaching a blocking drill involving our tight ends and tackles. I was in the corner of the end zone preparing to start when I looked up and standing together right next to my drill were Don Shula, Tom Landry, and Chuck Noll. I knew that they were there to watch the players but also that they would hear every word that I said. My pulse quickened, and I made sure that I had my "A" game fully in gear.

In 1983, the NFL was dominated and controlled by very powerful and successful coaches. Standing on the field every day and working in front of such a distinguished and intimidating audience was a great growing experience. I went through the next three decades of my coaching career reminding myself that every word I said on that field was in front of Don Shula, Tom Landry, and Chuck Noll. I made sure that I brought my "A" game to every practice through three decades, too.

Our staff had the North team, and Bum Phillips and the New Orleans Saints coached the South. Following the afternoon practices on both Tuesday and Wednesday, our staffs would come together to have a few beers and mutually discuss our personnel. We each would take a few minutes to discuss what we had observed in practice and how we felt about the individual players.

In one particular meeting, the linebackers coach for the Saints was talking about the great linebacker/defensive end from Arkansas,

Billy Ray Smith. He was describing how tough Billy Ray was and how much fun he seemed to be having while at practice.

Bum Phillips abruptly interrupted him, saying, "You would be having fun, too, if you were beating the shit out of everyone. Move on to the next guy."

I was learning what the real NFL was like. The real NFL was all business—being tough and physical was very much the norm. Grown men play on Sunday.

We won the game, and our young quarterback, a guy named Dan Marino, was the Senior Bowl MVP. We loved him as both a player and a leader and thought he would present an interesting dynamic in the months to come. We were right.

The 1983 draft was what would become known as the "QB Draft." There were six exceptional quarterbacks drafted in the first round. John Elway from Stanford was selected first by us, the Colts. Todd Blackledge from Penn State was selected by Kansas City with the seventh pick. Jim Kelly was taken next by the Buffalo Bills with the fourteenth pick, and next up was Tony Eason of Illinois, taken by New England. With the twenty-fourth pick, the New York Jets took Ken O'Brien from California-Davis.

And the last of the quarterbacks selected was Dan Marino of Pittsburgh, by Don Shula and the Dolphins. Marino went twenty-seventh overall. Certainly, the best twenty-seventh pick in NFL history.

Elway was ranked first by most everyone in the NFL. Many had Marino second, but some questions about his off-field life and some rumors about off-field problems that were totally unfounded dropped his ratings. Not one of the questions about his character was accurate, of course.

We had the No. 1 pick, and Ernie Accorsi, the Colts' general manager, was adamant about selecting Elway. "I simply picked the best player in the country," Accorsi said. "If the Baltimore franchise was good enough for John Unitas, the greatest quarterback in the history of the league, it was good enough for John Elway."

Not according to Elway. He had made it clear he did not want to go to Baltimore. He gave lots of reasons; I believe not playing for Frank Kush was one of those reasons.

Elway had been selected by the New York Yankees and threatened to forgo football for a baseball career. None of us believed he wanted to do that, but our team leaders were faced with a dilemma. Frank was very upset with Elway, and we as coaches had discussed drafting Marino with our first pick. Five of us were from the Pittsburgh area and loved Dan from the Senior Bowl. It wouldn't have taken too much for Frank to insist we draft Marino.

But it was made very clear that the owner of the team, Bob Irsay, and Accorsi were going to make Elway our No. 1 pick no matter what Frank threatened.

So, how well did that decision work out? Ernie said later that he would never have traded Elway; maybe he should have worked that out ahead of time.

We traded the rights to Elway to Denver for Chris Hinton, an offensive tackle/guard who was a great player and one of my personal favorites, and two high future draft picks. We only signed one of those. From the Baltimore side, that was one of the worst trades ever in the NFL.

One person who probably benefited from the whole mess was, yes, Dan Marino. I am certain that had the coaches been given the freedom to make the pick, we would have drafted him. He somehow slipped all the way down to Miami, which was coming off a Super Bowl loss to Washington. Under Don Shula, Marino went on to Hall of Fame greatness.

After spending thirteen years in Miami with Dan, I firmly believe he is the best quarterback to ever play in the NFL. I know that he didn't win a Super Bowl, but he is the person least responsible for that negative fact—myself included.

One of the greatest experiences of my life was being there every day with Dan Marino. Sometimes I think that maybe I am the luckiest guy in the world.

1983

My second season in the NFL was for me a profile in courage. I had boldly taken on all of the jobs that now I had to do and execute for a full season. I was coaching the tight ends, helping with the offensive line, trying to learn what special teams were all about, and handling being the strength coach. The only job I handled well was coaching the tight ends.

We had two good young players, Tim Sherwin and Pat Beach. They both grew and developed as players. Their blocking and receiving skills improved, and both had productive years. I felt good about my coaching performance in that area.

Now, if I could only figure out the rest of this mess.

Approaches to special teams in 1983 were relatively simple. Most teams did not have a specific special teams coach. The various roles were divided up among the staffers, and things were kept somewhat basic. My special teams journey as a coach was emblematic of that. I know that I started out at the very bottom and ended up at the top. When I started, I was stunned to realize the complexities of the NFL rules pertaining to the kicking game. I remember doing a study that showed over 20 percent of the rulebook in some fashion referred to the kicking game. I studied hours of film trying to understand all the aspects of special teams.

Kick coverage was simple, and there were only one or two schemes for kick returns. There was no formation variance, and one team pretty much looked like the other. The more I studied, the more my interest piqued.

I started by moving players around in the formation to gain a mismatch. Rather than have one kickoff return, I always had four. I recognized that, unlike offense and defense, because of the change of possession, we, in essence, had a timeout before most of my plays. Therefore, on every kickoff coverage or return, we would be together on the sideline and huddled before the players went on the field. In the huddle, I would show a drawing of the play. I covered everyone's exact assignment, so we could run different plays and formations due to the ability to use the drawings before every play. Offense and defense can't do this.

The more I did this, the more I perfected it. I was having a miniature meeting before nearly every play in a huddle on the sideline. When I started this, it was primitive, but over the years it evolved to somewhat of an art.

One area I knew I needed help in was being the strength coach. I talked with some of the most experienced strength coaches, trying to gain some insight and knowledge. Fortunately for me, two of them were very successful at their craft: Boyd Epley, who was from Nebraska, and Clyde Emrich from the Bears were most helpful. They taught me some basic training routines and some of the testing procedures that would help me survive as a strength coach.

It was one of the jobs I least liked; I longed for the day I could turn it over to a full-time—and qualified—strength coach.

We finished the 1983 season 7-9, an outstanding effort for a team with an average talent level and a coaching staff that was learning what the NFL was all about. We narrowly missed getting into the playoffs. We gave up a 19-point lead in the fourth quarter to Denver in what was the first of Elway's many, many come-from-behind drives to victory.

That game made me wonder: is anyone with the Colts happy with the draft pick we made and the subsequent trade?

Though 1983 certainly was challenging and educational, it was nothing compared to what would take place in the upcoming offseason.

The Baltimore Colts were in trouble. The stadium where John Unitas, Lenny Moore, Gino Marchetti, and Raymond Berry had starred was old and generally falling apart. There was no way the team could generate any real money. Other NFL teams were moving into new stadiums, and the Colts' situation seemed hopeless. The city had fallen on some hard times. Some of the major industries—steel and textiles—had begun to shut down their facilities.

Rumors started that the Colts were looking to move. Every week, a new city was in the news as the future destination of the franchise. Memphis and Jacksonville were early contenders, but the one with the most steam was Phoenix.

Frank Kush had a number of connections in Arizona from his college days at Arizona State. One time, he told me that he believed Irsay would sell the team to the Arizona investors and the Colts would move to the "Valley of the Sun" under new ownership. I don't know if Irsay even seriously considered selling the team. I personally don't believe so, but I knew he was looking to move.

The next city mentioned as a landing spot was Indianapolis, which was perfect for the franchise. The large drug company Eli Lilly had built a domed stadium in downtown Indy with the goal of luring an NFL team. They made an offer the Irsays couldn't refuse. A beautiful new stadium and a financial deal to move the team from the bottom of the non-television money list to close to the top? We all heard the rumors, and this one seemed too good to be true.

But the Colts had one major problem. The mayor of Baltimore, William D. Schaefer, didn't want to lose the Colts and believed he would have one last chance to work a deal to keep the team in Maryland. And he had an ace up his sleeve: the training complex in which all of us worked was owned by the city and leased to the

Irsays. If they were going to leave, it might have to be without all the office supplies and equipment.

None of us working there really knew what was happening, and without our knowledge, the deal was completed for the Colts to move to Indianapolis. The moving plans were in place. Mayflower, the moving company, was contracted to gather numerous trucks at a Pennsylvania Turnpike rest stop. Then, after procuring some workers, the trucks would head into Baltimore and begin the "midnight move" to Indy.

At about 4 p.m. on March 27, Jim Irsay, the owner's son and the acting general manager, came into my office and told me to stick around for a 6 p.m. meeting. Most of the people in the building left at their normal 4:30 or 5 p.m. quitting time.

At the meeting were the coaching staff, three trainers, three equipment employees, and a handful of front-office workers, plus our two film guys. We were informed that we were, indeed, moving to Indianapolis and that the trucks were on the way. Boxes would be brought to our offices, and we were to pack everything and label it with our names.

"Take everything; leave nothing," we were told.

I lived only two miles from the offices, and I drove home to grab some dinner and to tell my wife and three-year-old son that "the fat lady had sung." We were leaving for Indianapolis that night. That was the time frame I was given—and it's exactly how it would happen.

My wife and I were excited for a move; we had no ties to Baltimore. But we recognized how wild and hectic this could be.

I returned to work and packed. I was also the strength coach, remember, and had to completely disassemble and pack the weight room equipment. It was lightly raining that cold night, and all my weights got wet and ruined.

It was dark when the trucks began to arrive like a swarm of locusts. Everything was packed and labeled—and moved. Every piece of furniture and all the files and pictures in the building were taken. When a truck was loaded, a new one took its place.

The filled trucks left Baltimore and returned to the truck stop on the Pennsylvania Turnpike. When the task was completed, they were met by the Indiana State Police and escorted to Indy.

The only things left behind were the telephones. Seeing the empty offices was a stark harbinger of what was ahead for most of the employees.

The next morning at the deserted offices was a fiasco. Employees who had spent years in their offices walked into emptiness. Everything—even their personal items—was gone. There was lots of anger and plenty of tears.

Sure, it was an excellent business move for the Irsays. But there were some harsh results from it.

Severance packages were awarded, but the reality of seeing a job, or a career in some instances, end in such a fashion was devastating. The Colts were gone from Baltimore and had landed in Indianapolis.

CHAPTER 6

Adjusting to Indy

Picking up everything and moving to Indianapolis on a moment's notice was quite an ordeal. The people in Baltimore were furious, feeling both deceived and cheated. The safest place for a Colt was to be heading to Indianapolis and nowhere near Maryland.

Zeke Bratkowski, our offensive coordinator, wanted to drive his personal car to Indy and asked me to drive with him on the day after the "midnight move." I told him I would, but it would have to be two days later, as I was going to watch *The Wizard of Oz* on TV with my three-year-old son John. Nothing was going to keep me from having that very special time with my son.

When we did set out for Indianapolis, I left Baltimore for good. My wife, Marilyn, handled the move, and we sold the house. Indeed, about a month or so later, we bought a house, and within a relatively short time were a family setting into life in Indiana.

When Zeke and I arrived in Indianapolis, the town was ecstatic. The people opened up their hearts and doors to each of us. About ten years earlier, I had lived in Bloomington, about fifty miles south of Indianapolis, where I coached under Lee Corso at Indiana University while I attended graduate school and earned my master's degree. Indiana is an excellent school, and I was very proud of my educational achievement. I completed my requirements in one calendar year and received all A's, with one B.

Evolving from being a relatively poor and somewhat intimidated student to one who could receive A's and complete a prestigious master's degree from a great university was a totally rewarding experience.

As a football team in our first year in Indy, we temporarily moved into an abandoned grade school. The Colts would eventually build a beautiful new facility and practice fields that they occupied for decades. We turned the grade school into NFL offices, meeting rooms, and practice fields.

When we arrived, there were boxes everywhere. Construction crews reconfigured the facility and built a shower and locker room. A playground and gym were turned into NFL practice fields. I took the gym and converted half of it into a weight room. I hired some high school students to help me clean and paint all of our "Baltimore Midnight Move" rusted weights. I bought some new racks and machines and put together a functional and attractive weight room.

The auditorium became the team meeting room, and an area was set up to conduct the "war room" for the draft.

By the time the players arrived for the spring minicamps, we had a serviceable NFL facility.

Aside from my assignments as special teams coach and tight ends coach, I was going to be made responsible for beginning the process of finding a training camp site. First, though, I was going to pursue finding a full-time strength coach. I told Frank Kush the job was too much for me. I loved the testing part of the job and thought that I did it well, but the rest of it, well, we needed help.

Frank said: "OK, you want it, you go find one."

Yep, another job, Mike.

I put the word out to several colleges and my few (very few) NFL connections, knowing that it would spread rapidly that the Colts were looking. It did: letters and resumes quickly arrived, and the process was quite simple. Each day I would review the letters and categorize them according to a level of excellence that I—and no one else—had developed.

One day I received a letter from Dan Gable, the University of Iowa's wrestling coach and not only a former NCAA champion but one of the best Olympic champions this country has produced. Dan was probably the greatest wrestling figure not only in America but in the world. He talked about a young man he was coaching in the Olympic trials—a heavyweight freestyle wrestler who was for some reason disqualified during a mishap in a match.

Dan said he believed that it was a mistake and that he felt that the young man possibly could have won a gold medal. He kept him on his squad as the strength coach to help train the U.S. Olympic team.

Tom Zupancic was not only a big and powerful man who also happened to be from Indianapolis, but he had earned Dan Gable's complete confidence to work with the Olympic team. To me, it was a no-brainer.

I interviewed Tom and loved him. He was qualified, personally powerful, and tough as nails. He was intelligent and well-spoken and even had a somewhat genteel, calm manner about him. I later learned that calm manner was part of a Jekyll and Hyde makeup. He was a character in every sense. He could thunder with the best of them.

I took him in to meet with Frank, who interviewed him. After the interview, Tom left the room and Frank told me: "No way. This guy is not cut out for the NFL. He doesn't have what it takes for the NFL."

I told Frank that he was wrong and not only was Tom perfectly qualified, but he would easily handle even the most difficult of NFL players.

Frank relented. "OK," he said, "if you want him, you take him. But you are responsible, and it will be your ass on the line."

That hiring opened the door for one of the NFL's all-time great strength coaches—and one of its largest characters.

A few years later while working for the Miami Dolphins, I became very involved in the hiring of another strength coach. When I arrived in Miami, Junior Wade was our strength coach. He was a former athletic trainer who took on the strength training duties and was kind of a "jack-of-all-trades."

Junior and I shared an office at our St. Thomas University training center. If you could see now what that facility looked like, you would even more appreciate what a great coach Don Shula was. To compare that place to a high school would be a slap in the high school's face. The place was a complete dump.

The weight room was under an awning, and when it rained, Junior would leave his home in the middle of the night and run over to "shop vacuum" the water off the floor. Junior helped me coach special teams and helped the trainers tape the players, as well as a million other jobs. But . . .

Following our move to a beautiful new facility in Davie, Florida—with an incredible weight room, by the way—we finished the season on a down note following an injury-riddled year. While discussing our injury problems with Coach Shula, one of our trainers blamed them on our strength program. There was probably an element of truth to that accusation, but don't believe for even a second that the NFL doesn't have its share of chicken-shit people.

I got word that Coach Shula was thinking of replacing Junior. I went to him and asked if I could find a more complete strength coach. Thank goodness, he gave me the job.

Letters and resumes poured in, but one applicant stood out: John Gamble, the strength coach at the University of Virginia. Everyone I talked to raved about him—not only about his professionalism, but also his extremely well-rounded character.

John had been an incredible powerlifter, competing nationally and internationally. He competed in the World's Strongest Man contest, but none of that was the reason I was so impressed. Rather, it was his ability to relate and communicate. He could produce better-conditioned football players, and they loved working with him. He was excellent in every way, and I recommended John to Coach Shula. He got the job.

Junior Wade stayed on as his assistant and mostly worked with rehab. They ended up being a good working pair. A year or so later, when Jimmy Johnson took over, he fired Junior over a contract problem. I just wish it could have been resolved—not my favorite subject.

I think I did pretty well with my choices in strength coaches.

Tom went on to a distinguished career in Indianapolis as not only the strength coach but later as a front office executive and radio personality. John had a highly successful NFL career as a strength coach for fifteen years and as a player program director, also with Miami.

Both were huge, powerful men, and terrific personal weightlifters. But more importantly, they were knowledgeable about their craft and established strong relationships with the players.

Tom's lifting prowess was Herculean. He could easily bench press 500 pounds and was famous for pulling a car attached to a head-and-neck harness. Often in the evening after work, I would go into the weight room to work out before going home. I was proud of my work ethic and was an above-average weightlifter for being in my mid-thirties.

Normally, Tom and I would be the only people in the weight room. He would coach me and push me as if I were a player. He would get me to spot him in some of his lifts, too.

That could be a harrowing experience.

He would be preparing to bench press 500 pounds, and I was to give him a lift—help him to take the weight off the rack—and spot him if he experienced trouble. Like I was going to be of much help; how was I going to lift 500 pounds off his chest?

Before the lift, he might pace around, getting into the right frame of mind. He would break an ammonia capsule in half and insert it in his nose, often drawing some blood. Next, he would drop down onto the bench and prepare for the press. He was incredibly strong and would do more repetitions than I thought was humanly possible.

I was just happy he never needed my "help." I would have been running around pulling weights off the bar, not lifting it off his chest and back onto the rack.

Tom pushed and challenged the players in various fashions and even pulled one on me.

I weighed 195 pounds and was in good shape. I was doing individual dumbbell bench presses with 90- and 95-pound weights. I had never tried the 100-pound dumbbells because I was afraid that I might not be able to complete the lift and they would drop onto my face.

Using 100-pound weights when you only weigh 195 seemed like a lot of weight—and not too smart. Tom had often chided me about not attempting the 100-pounders and reminded me of it each time I did the exercise.

He was fastidious about the weight room—HIS weight room— and everything was exactly in place. Not a single weight was not precisely where it belonged.

One night, I came in to find his neat and orderly dumbbell rack greatly disturbed. One of the 100-pound dumbbells was out of the rack and placed at the opposite side of the room and on the floor.

"You see what happened here? I came in today and heard them talking," Tom said, referring to the dumbbells. "I am not exactly sure what they were saying, but I believe I heard them say something about a pussy.

"I am not sure they were talking about you, but I suspected they were anyway."

I did the 100 pounds that night. Not many times, but I lifted them. It was the most I ever attempted. It was a lot of weight for me, but I couldn't resist. For a 195-pound person to be lifting 100-pound dumbbells in each hand is pretty good.

Tom had gotten to me.

I laughed at what he was doing, but it worked. I overcame my fear and did it. No pussy here.

He had the biggest smile and said that now he could put them together back in the rack. Tom had a great way of challenging you to do your utmost.

One of my favorite times with Tom occurred at the NFL's scouting combine in Indy. NFL prospects from the college ranks would come together for a week of physical and psychological exams. One of the tests was with the bench press: a player sees how many times he can bench press 225 pounds. Over thirty is good, under twenty is very average. Fewer than ten? Go home.

After the workouts were completed, I was in the weight room with most of the NFL's strength coaches. It was Tom's first year, and the guys didn't know him too well. I knew he had incredible bench press strength, and I couldn't wait. So, I asked him what was the most reps anyone had done? He said thirty-seven or thirty-eight by a lineman, I think from Nebraska. I asked Tom how many he could do.

"I can do fifty without taking a breath," he claimed.

I told the other strength coaches that "my man" could beat the best by ten and was willing to bet each of them twenty dollars. At only twenty dollars, everyone got in.

Tom rattled it off easily. I laughed and collected my money and gave half of it to Tom. Needless to say, I only got to play that trick one time.

But my favorite time with Tom came on a cold winter night when he asked me to accompany him about an hour's drive from Indianapolis to a high school for a "wrestling match." These guys were professionals, but not the veteran Hulk Hogan types. These guys were at the beginning, working their way up the ladder.

Tom, who was a great wrestler himself, was there for a different reason. Part of the show was for someone to wrestle a bear. I was his acting manager, and he was going to fight the bear. If I had thought I had seen it all before this, well, I guess not.

The bear was handled by two guys from Australia. They were big hustlers. They were as carnival as you could get. And they made it clear how this match would be conducted.

The bear wore a muzzle. Tom was told to grab and push—generally a bullshit fight. Tom had none of that in mind. He was determined to all-out fight the bear. The match lasted about two seconds and then pandemonium erupted. Tom punched the bear so hard in the ribs you couldn't believe it. The bear howled, and the fight was on.

Or not.

The carnival trainers jumped into the ring screaming at Tom and grabbing at him. I couldn't let my friend be accosted, so I jumped in next. Lots of pushing and shoving ensued—not with the bear—and finally everyone was separated.

No one was particularly happy with the whole "bear wrestling" show. Tom and I were escorted from the gym by the local police. Thank goodness they knew we were Colts coaches.

The whole thing was crazy and funny. We were instructed to go back to Indianapolis and stick to football. And we did.

The city of Indianapolis was great to us. The people met us with enthusiasm and warmth. When we arrived, we were each given new cars for our personal use, and a beautiful two-bedroom condo in which to live with our families. The renovated grade school rapidly became our NFL offices and working facility.

Now that we had hired a full-time strength coach, I could devote my time to working with my tight ends and learning as much as possible about special teams. There were no real great NFL special teams units or coaches back then, so I studied film for hours and tried to piece together the best components of each unit. I had a good start with my group in that we were blessed with a very good backbone: Rohn Stark, a left-footed Pro Bowl punter, was at the top of the league.

Stark, who would spend sixteen seasons in the NFL, was an explosive punter and one of the NFL's most-gifted athletes. A former high-jumper from Florida State and our first pick in the second round of the 1982 draft—yes, we grabbed a punter at the top of the second round—I used to describe him as one of the few people in the world who had four very special skills:

He could dunk a basketball like Michael Jordan.

He was a legitimate seven-foot high-jumper.

He could bench press 400 pounds.

He was a scratch golfer.

Rohn Stark had a great punting career, but at the very end, he was a free agent and was looking to extend his career for an additional year or two. I was at Miami and very much wanted to see him finish with me. Pittsburgh was also in the competition, but Rohn made it clear to me that we were at least a 90 percent favorite.

For me, it was a very difficult time medically. Having been cancer-free for more than five years, the last thing I expected was a recurrence. Following a yearly CT scan, they discovered a metastasis in my lung. I was headed to Massachusetts General Hospital for a somewhat complex surgery to remove the tumor and part of my lung. Over the years, players would tease me that they wished maybe doctors could have removed just a little bit more of that lung.

Fortunately for me, a very talented—unlike most any of the other physicians who examined me—thoracic surgeon named John Wain was able to perform this surgery with a scope. It was very non-invasive and very successful. I will never forget waking up in the intensive care unit and my wife saying, "The good news is that the surgery went great, they removed all of it, and you will not need any follow-up treatment."

Then she added: "The bad news . . . Rohn Stark signed with Pittsburgh."

What happened to 90 percent? He was full of shit. To this day. I am still angry about it. I have never been able to let things go, and I am not letting go of this one. He was a great punter, but his years at Pittsburgh were nothing special. He should have come to Miami.

At least the surgery went great.

In Indy, Stark's explosiveness was off the charts, and we were always going to be at the top of the league's punting stats. That was a real blessing in many ways, because our offense was terrible. We punted a million times.

Our placekicker was rookie Dean Biasucci, who like Stark would be in the NFL for a long time, eleven seasons. He was very accurate, with a powerful leg. Dean was a very good-looking guy who aspired to be an actor. He had a very impressive array of extremely attractive girlfriends. You could say the rest of his teammates paid close attention to his constant accompaniment of women.

There were no long-snapper specialists back then, so one of our tight ends, Pat Beach, was the long snapper. He was very good. I had a solid foundation for my units, but there was something major that was missing. I needed a return specialist.

Oh yeah, I also needed to gain some knowledge about how to build an effective NFL special teams unit. I knew absolutely nothing.

Remember, I also had other jobs, one of which was as assistant to the head coach. Shortly after arriving in Indy, Frank had put me in charge of finding a training camp site. First off was to meet with all our department heads and gather a list of their specific needs. Our training and medical staff, equipment and locker room staff, guys who worked with film, the media, our strength coach, and our assistant general manager had their own needs.

We had to determine housing and eating needs for the entire team and staff.

Once I had their requirements, I could begin my search. I sat down and drew a circumference of the area in which I hoped to locate a facility, adding a list of the colleges and universities. I reached out to them, and if they expressed interest, I would send them that list of specific needs and rate them according to their being able to fulfill each area. In some areas, we could help, such as turning a gym into a locker room and weight room. Our groundskeeper could help groom and maintain practice fields.

But we needed seating for fans to watch practice and proper parking for those fans.

Dining and sleeping arrangements were most important—there wasn't room for error in those areas—and security was also thrown into the equation.

If you think putting together a game plan is complex, well, matching up all the needs for training camp is like building a dozen game plans.

Several universities withdrew, as their own issues were overwhelming. A number of schools really wanted us—and the publicity of housing the Indianapolis Colts—but they just didn't have the facilities. We narrowed our search to several schools, and then an interesting dynamic developed.

Our department heads and I visited our top picks and worked on making a decision. We had two finalists: Ball State in Muncie, Indiana, and Anderson College in that city. Anderson had the edge in location and housing, and the other areas could be adjusted to make our needs fit.

When we decided on Anderson, I remember an unhappy representative from Ball State complaining to me. Hey, he said, they were a Division I program, and Anderson was a Division III school. I made it clear to him that we were looking for a training camp site, not a playing opponent. Ball State was probably a better football team than Anderson, sure. But they were not going to be on the Colts' schedule.

You know what. Looking back at the 1984 season, I kind of wish Ball State had been on the schedule.

For carrying out a job that I really had no qualifications for, I believe I handled finding a training camp site darn well. Anderson College was an excellent decision—the right decision—and remained the team's training camp site for many years after 1984.

As well as the training camp search turned out, the regular season was the opposite. We went 4-12 and lost the head coach before the final game. Frank Kush was an old-school coach who was very tough and demanding. The practices were always in full pads and very physical. In my opinion, Frank was a good coach, but he did not adapt well to the NFL. At Arizona State, he was used to winning by recruiting superior athletes, getting them in better condition, and dominating opponents physically. Those qualities are somewhat evened out in the pros, due greatly to the draft and salary restrictions. And, don't forget, the excellent talent and physical abilities of each NFL player.

Most of Frank's winning philosophies were somewhat minimalized in the complex NFL.

Frank pushed the team hard, and now—in his third year—despite his overcoming the adverse circumstances of moving and adjusting, he soon fell out of favor with the players. We just weren't very good, and we struggled weekly. We were headed toward a meltdown, and when it happened, in all my years in the NFL, it was the most disappointing and ugly situation that I ever encountered.

Early in the season, Frank hired a chef to cook dinner for the coaches on Tuesday night, which was the night we'd work late on the game plan. He was an excellent cook, and the late-night sessions took on special meaning.

The week before Thanksgiving, Frank came to me and asked about my plans for the holiday. I told him that my mother-in-law was in town, and with my wife and three-year-old son, we were going to have a quick dinner at home and watch some football. He then asked me if I would attend a team dinner if we had one. He said that so many of the staff and players had been abruptly moved from Baltimore to Indianapolis. They were not very settled yet and it might solve some unfinished dinner plans.

I said it was a great idea and would be very special for everyone and my family, and I would certainly be a part.

On Monday before Thanksgiving, Frank told the team that if enough people were interested, he would have a Thanksgiving dinner. He had a convenient location and would provide a great menu with a seafood bar; turkey, ham, and beef carving station; every possible side dish; and dessert. We couldn't have liquor, but there would be beer, wine, and soft drinks included. Plenty of seating would be available, and TVs and a kids play area would be provided.

He made it clear to the team that everyone could come and go at any time and could bring as many guests as they wanted. He just asked that they sign up and include the number of family members or guests who would attend. Frank asked the team to sign up by Tuesday after practice, so that if there were enough interested people, preparations could be made.

About thirty players signed up, and most of the staff accepted. Frank told me he felt it would be beneficial for the team and maybe help bring us together to finish the season on a positive note.

After an early Thanksgiving morning of meetings and practice, I went home, got dressed up, and took my family to the dinner. The scene was tremendous. The hall was beautifully decorated, and everything was in place. Televisions were everywhere, and the play area was perfect. The tables were plentiful, and the food was beautifully presented.

The staff had arrived and shared drinks and appetizers, but where were the players?

I remember Frank coming over to my table and telling us we should begin eating. But where were the players?

I told him I guessed they could be haphazardly late, and we would begin eating, and they would catch up. I couldn't have been more mistaken.

As a staff, we all began eating, but a tension hovered over the room. I saw the Colts owner, Robert Irsay, and Frank huddled together, and the conversation did not look like a pleasant one.

It is one of the worst and ugliest memories of my more than three decades in professional football. Not one player showed up. Not even one!

I can't be sure of the total number that actually signed up. I can't prove it, and I am no tattletale, but I believe one particular player led the group boycott. I would bet my boat that I know who led it, but I don't know who signed up, so I can never be 100 percent sure.

It was a slap in Frank Kush's face. On Thanksgiving, yet.

The players were telling him they no longer believed in him or his methods, and this was a way of showing the ownership their displeasure. Irsay spent a lot of money and did a very good thing; in no way did he deserve this. But the actions were directed, in my opinion, toward Frank. In all my years, I thought it was the most chickenshit thing that I experienced in the league. Any player that signed up and did not show should've been ashamed.

Following the dinner of "no shows" the team was more of a mess than ever. We played terribly and lost the rest of the games after the Thanksgiving bullshit.

Naturally, Frank was devastated. He knew it was the end of his time in Indy, even though we had a few games remaining. He resigned with one game left in the season and later signed on with the Arizona Outlaws of the USFL. It was a very sad way for Frank to finish those very tumultuous years.

Frank Kush wasn't perfect for the NFL, but he was a good man and put together an excellent coaching staff. With some redesigning of the team, he would have been successful in the NFL. For me, I look back and know with great pride that Frank was one of "my guys."

CHAPTER 7

The USFL—and a Call from Coach Shula

Following an awful season in Indianapolis, Frank Kush accepted an offer to join the Arizona Outlaws of the USFL. The league was entering its third year of playing in the spring and was constantly raiding and generally irritating the NFL.

The USFL in its own draft had taken a number of very good players away from NFL pursuers, most notably Steve Young and Reggie White. A number of veteran NFL players received some extra money and a chance to extend their careers in the USFL.

Jim Mora led a group of very solid coaches who were making the USFL a competitive NFL opponent.

Donald Trump, one of the team owners, in an expected fashion was ready to battle the NFL to force some type of merger or acceptance. The new league was an interesting alternative to the NFL.

But the USFL did not have the financial backing needed, and that eventually led to its downfall. Not before presenting that challenge to the established NFL, though.

Frank Kush immediately accepted the offer to return to his hometown of Phoenix and asked me to accompany him as the offensive line coach. I had really no connections in Indianapolis; I was completely one of Frank's guys. I accepted his offer and was joined by Roger Theder, the Colts' running backs coach and a brilliant offensive mind. He was the former head coach at the University of California and would become our offensive coordinator.

We also were joined by Skip Stress, one of Roger's former assistants and a person who became one of my best friends—and maybe the smartest coach I ever worked with.

The last member of our staff was one of Frank's former Arizona State players and a longtime NFL receiving star who had a brilliant career with the Philadelphia Eagles. Benny Hawkins coached our wide receivers and became my roommate and one of my very good friends.

Frank put together what I believed was an excellent offensive coaching staff to join the defensive staff he kept from the previous head coach, George Allen. Yes, that George Allen, the Hall of Famer.

We moved into a dump of a facility to meet players we knew very little about, put together a new notebook, and prepared to start training camp and begin the season. We had about a month to accomplish all of this, and it was a schedule as brutal as any I have ever encountered.

I lived for one month in an equipment cage in the back of our locker room. Many of today's coaches talk of the obstacles of today's job as they slave away in front of their computers doing analytics while living in a nice hotel. They make me want to throw up.

Everything was accelerated. We put together a notebook and practice schedule, and, seemingly out of nowhere, we were in training camp. I had a few weeks to put together an offensive line capable of playing professional football. Fortunately for me, I had an excellent group to work with.

We started off slowly, but before long we were playing very good football. I ended up with a terrific offensive line headed by three really good players. Our center was Gerry Sullivan, a thirty-three-year-old NFL veteran who had played eight seasons with the Cleveland Browns. He was smart, exceptionally strong, and a real tough guy.

Tom Thayer, a first-year guard from Notre Dame, was basically stolen from the Chicago Bears by the USFL. Following my one season with him, he returned to the Bears, who had drafted him, and he started on their world championship team. He had an excellent nine-year career in the NFL, including eight seasons with Chicago.

Tom Thayer and Gerry Sullivan were top offensive linemen in any league, but the real star was a relative unknown guard from Winston-Salem State, Alvin Powell. At 6-5, 294 pounds, Alvin was one of the most talented O-linemen I saw in my coaching career. He was an incredible athlete: big, strong, and very fast—the best pulling guard I have ever seen. He just ran defenders over. When he pulled, he didn't just block one defender—he blocked everyone.

For two years of my retirement, I did a weekly radio show with Stephen A. Smith of ESPN. Stephen is a Winston-Salem graduate, and I asked him about Alvin Powell. I knew they were in school at vastly different times, but when Stephen didn't know him, I kind of wanted to check Stephen's degree.

Following his time in the USFL, Alvin played two seasons with Seattle before spending some time working with me at the Miami Dolphins. Some off-field issues slowed his career and helped bring it to an end, but not before he made an incredible impression on me as a coach. He practiced and played at a level of excellence few NFL players achieve. Watching him play each week was a thrill.

The season seemed to go by in a flash, filled with highs and lows. One of my favorite experiences was working every day with our quarterback, Doug Williams. Doug would become a Super Bowl MVP with Washington and was a real pro. Doug could throw the ball with anyone and was a special talent. He became a friend and was someone I appreciated working with.

Following the season, the USFL was locked in a lawsuit against the NFL, claiming the NFL held an illegal monopoly in pro football. The USFL won the suit and collected one dollar for its trouble. Actually, the court awarded triple compensation. So, the USFL got three bucks. And folded.

I had talked with Bob Valesente, whose job I had twice saved. He was going to Kansas University and promised to call me. I am still waiting.

Following the 1985 season, the Miami Dolphins staff was coaching the AFC in the Pro Bowl after having lost to New England in the AFC title game—losing out on a rematch with the Bears, who they had given their only loss during the season in one of the greatest *Monday Night Football* games.

Coach Shula was looking for a special teams and tight ends coach, and during Pro Bowl week talked to Rohn Stark, the punter from Indianapolis who I had drafted and coached. Rohn was very complimentary about me, and Coach Shula became interested. He gave me a call the next week and brought me to Miami for an interview.

Actually, there wasn't much to the interview. Coach Shula knew how he wanted things to be done, and that was pretty much it. I added a great deal as time went on, but at first, I was just presenting his program. It wasn't much about what I knew, but rather how well I could present what he knew.

Still, this was a chance—and thrill—of a lifetime. The opportunity to join Don Shula in Miami, or wait for the non-call from

Bob Valesente of Kansas? Guess who won that. Sometimes I have been the luckiest guy ever.

Looking back at various aspects of our lives, it is interesting what resonates. My time in Arizona was highlighted by several aspects. I enjoyed every minute working with the players I coached. They were doing everything possible to have a pro career, and I loved my relationship with them. Frank Kush became one of my favorite people ever, and what he did for me in several ways will always be remembered and cherished.

But one crazy thing sticks out. I moved my family into a small house with a swimming pool. I wanted us to enjoy Arizona's great weather for the short time that we would be there. What stands out was that I was able to teach my son John how to swim. It wasn't easy, but we *figured it out.*

After that, moving to Florida for his elementary, high school, and college years, he lived in one house with a swimming pool. My time teaching John how to swim in Arizona was one of my favorite parts of being a father.

There aren't many NFL coaches' children who get to spend their entire school years in the same home. John was an excellent student who went on to an Ivy League education and have a very good athletic career in high school and college—and he learned to swim. My coaching career was blessed in a hundred different ways.

CHAPTER 8

A Miami Dolphin

My time with the Miami Dolphins and Coach Shula was a constant learning experience. I was working for and with, in my opinion, the greatest NFL coach ever. I was the special teams coach, the tight ends coach, and I helped with—and on several occasions took over due to illness—the offensive line coaching duties.

Tight ends and the offensive line were easy and fun. Why? Dan Marino was our quarterback, and every resource possible was put into that part of our team. Being around Dan Marino every day was the experience of a lifetime for someone like me. And Dan was the league MVP, by the way.

Dan Marino

I first got to know Dan when I was working for the Colts and we were coaching the Senior Bowl in 1983. Dan had graduated from the University of Pittsburgh and would become part of the NFL draft's all-time greatest quarterbacks class—yet somehow, Dan slipped to the bottom.

Don't forget, as I previously mentioned, had it been up to our coaching staff in Baltimore and not our owner and general manager, Dan Marino—not John Elway—would have been selected with the first pick in the draft.

Everyone knows how well that worked out for the Colts.

As coaches, we got to know Dan during Senior Bowl week, and we loved him. He was great in practice all week and led us to a victory over the South team.

As a coach, it was my first of three Senior Bowl victories; I wonder how many coaches are undefeated in the Senior Bowl and have at least three victories.

Dan was a player that anyone would have loved being associated with. Everybody knows how talented he was, but what was incredible was how hard he worked at improving his skills. He had a sign in his locker that read: "I am going to practice every day and play every play." I read that sign to my players in training camp every year of my entire career. I wanted them to understand what greatness in the NFL was all about.

Until Dan tore his Achilles tendon in Cleveland, he never missed a play or a practice. NEVER!

Dan performed in practice like it was a game. He tried to make every play perfect. Being on the practice field and then sitting in a film session with him and listening to him talk with his teammates about what they were watching was a complete learning experience. Dan demanded perfection from himself and everyone on the field with him.

Each week, I watched Dan work in two specific areas that I believe helped him develop and enhance his abilities. Every Thursday after practice, Dan and the receivers would work against the Dolphins' defensive backs in 1-versus-1 or 2-versus-2 passing drills at the goal line. The ball was placed at either the eight-, five-, or two-yard line, and the drills were extremely competitive. Score was kept, the drill was officiated, and each play was worth twenty dollars.

Dan covered the offense for the money—and usually won.

Dan believed that you couldn't cover a perfect pass, and he tried to fit one in on every play. It helped Dan develop his lightning-quick release and pinpoint accuracy. The timing was superb.

Also, every Wednesday and Thursday during practice, the offense was going 7-on-7 with the defense, in which the receivers, tight ends, and backs would compete against the secondary and linebackers representing the upcoming opponent's defensive schemes. The second 7-on-7 period was conducted for the Miami defense versus the scout-team offense portraying the opponent's offense. While this was going on, Dan would go with the linemen who were working against one another on the various pass rush games.

Dan would call a play and a particular protection. He would then take the snap and move around in the pocket and feel for a throwing lane. He would then throw to a receiver running the last two or three steps of a called pass route or dump off to a check-down. It helped Dan improve his maneuverability in the pocket and his quick release. I am very familiar with this because for several years I was the receiver running the last two or three steps—and catching a Dan Marino pass.

Before all my surgeries, I was athletic and could do this very well. I only had to run several steps, thank goodness, but I loved being a small part of the development of, in my view, the NFL's all-time best quarterback. Yes, I know without a Super Bowl win you can't be considered "the best." But believe me—and I was there—Dan Marino was the person least responsible for that shortcoming. Dan could have won a Super Bowl with twenty different teams. I watched him every day and in nearly every game. Dan was the best ever. I was privileged and honored to be on the field and in the classroom with Dan Marino.

As a young coach, I enjoyed being athletic enough that I could participate in, and in a very small way contribute to, the practices. I am sure that every one of my peers—the ones who only know me as a person who walks with a cane and is barely able to get around—would not believe a word of this. Believe it or not, during my first three years in the NFL while with the Colts and at the NFL Scouting Combine working with Zeke Bratkowski, our offensive coordinator and the former Green Bay quarterback, I helped coach the wide receiver drills on the field. I, along with Zeke, threw in the receiver drills. Not the actual pass routes the quarterbacks throw but the drill work. Yes, I threw the receiver drills at the combine. Remember in the 1980s we had coaching staffs of nine or so. Today they have twenty-seven. We all had to do extra.

I had an excellent arm and could throw the ball very well. I loved having that small role and took it very seriously.

My surgeries ended all of that, and who would have believed that Mike Westhoff was on the field and throwing to future NFL receivers? They know me as a cranky, old, cane-using pain in the ass. Not as an athlete who could throw in an NFL drill.

But I loved it and am proud to have done it.

During my years with the Dolphins and Coach Shula, finding a solution to one of my biggest problems opened the door to an area of my greatest success.

The Dolphins in the 1980s were a team wrapped firmly around Dan Marino. The "Killer Bees" defense of Betters, Bokamper, Baumhower, Brudzinski, and the Blackwood brothers had gotten old and had faded. Dan was the most explosive QB in the NFL, and with the help of tight ends Bruce Hardy and Joe Rose, running backs Tony Nathan and Jim Jensen, and, of course, wide receivers Nat Moore, Mark Duper, and Mark Clayton, this group was dominant and could score on any possession. But what we surely weren't was a complete team.

We couldn't run the ball or control the clock at all. Our short-yardage offense was mediocre at best. Our defense could not rush the passer without blitzing, and if we did blitz, our cornerbacks could not stand alone in coverage.

The Dolphins had basically struck out on defense in the draft. For the most part, all of our highly selected players had failed. Either from injury or they just weren't good enough. One thing was for sure: our defense didn't scare anyone. Everyone could score on us. The only question would be: could Dan Marino score more?

My Guys

My problems as a special teams coach were multiple. Dallas and Jimmy Johnson had come along and changed the blueprint for special teams in the NFL. Jimmy couldn't have cared less about kickers, being average was good enough for him. But the rest of his units were outstanding. Jimmy kept great special teams players. If they could play offense or defense, OK. But it sure wasn't necessary.

He made the kicking game a true one-third of the sport and was going to win that segment every time. Brock Marion, Bill Bates, Darrick Brownlow, Joe Fishback, Matt Vanderbeek, Kenneth Gant, and Elvis Patterson were all great special teams players, and only Brock Marion went on to a level of prominence as a starter.

Dallas had captured the top special teams ranking, and I had to figure out a way to catch the Cowboys. I believed that I was smarter and would become more creative, and I could certainly work harder. I just had to *figure it out.*

I was only going to have a few really good special teams players available. How could I take a good player and make him great? And how could I take an average player and make him good?

I believed if I could present very complex problems to my opponents, I could even the playing field. I had to put players into roles in which their talents were maximized. More importantly, their inabilities would be minimized. Every single thing I did had to be designed a hundred different ways. I had to present problems, hide deficiencies, and greatly promote strengths.

So, I became creative.

"We had very informative and detailed meetings, and you had to pay attention or, oh man, you could really be embarrassed," recalled Louis Oliver, our star safety who also played for me. "Once he showed it to you twice, that was it. No more than twice. We'd be in meetings and he'd be the only one talking, and he would go over a scheme, and if you didn't know it, he would get someone else in there and get your ass the hell out of there.

"On film, what better way than to make a correction? He'd run it, everyone would see what you did wrong, and you knew you had to fix it, not make that mistake again.

"But I always felt Mike was one of your teammates; that is how he came across. He treated you like best buddies as long as you did what he wanted you to do. As long as you were going 1,000 mph and knocked the shit out of somebody, you were one of his guys.

"When you've got a coach putting his all into helping a team win and putting the right guys in the right places, you give it all you can, too. He is giving you all he can. The players, we had all felt that way.

"When somebody is laying out a great plan and he's all about wanting to make you the best player you can be—he knew we were aggressive and he let us be as aggressive as fuck, as aggressive as you have to be to win the ballgame—and that is what we did.

"We would bring in a guy into camp for two or three days, and he had to play on a Sunday, and Mike is meeting with the guy until nine, ten at night to get the guy ready to play. He didn't have to coach at night, but he did.

"He got you so prepared that when it came time to make a play, we had a shot to win some ballgames because of special teams. And we had some great special teams."

Because we got creative.

I took kickoff coverage from ten guys running down the field to what seemed like 1,000 running from everywhere. I shrunk the field and used the side-

Louis Oliver

line as an extra player by always kicking into a corner. Ten screaming guys coming at you from everywhere, running in levels and stacked behind each other, then funneling into a small area where it was a lot more difficult to block than ten more skilled players spread out covering a kick in the middle of the field.

I found ways to hide my poor players and accentuate the strengths of my best players. If your kickoff return called for a double-team, you had better be flexible or you were going to be double-teaming my worst player who couldn't make the tackle anyway. And my best player would be right next to him and knock your player on his ass at the 15-yard line.

I was going to try to destroy your best player and make his life miserable—and give him a headache for a week. Those guys never wanted to play us. I greatly respected them, and I often told them so, but I was going to kick their ass. I would double-team them so often they would think we were playing against thirteen guys.

"If we were on punt return, he was studying and figuring out schemes where maybe we could make a big play to block a punt or a return one," said Louis Oliver. "Or block an extra point. He never stopped thinking."

Louis Oliver's partner on my teams, Kerry Glenn, was drafted as a defensive back by the New York Jets in the tenth round in 1985 out of the University of Minnesota. He then came to the Dolphins and became my first of many special teams aces. Make that ACES.

Kerry became my "Playmaker," my "Shark," and my "Cheetah." Those were all my pet names I used to describe my top players.

At 5-9 and 180 pounds, Kerry was the "Little Guy." Until he took his shirt off, and then he looked like Arnold Schwarzenegger. Pound for pound he may have been the strongest player in the NFL. He was fast—ran a 4.3 in the 40—and he was very smart and extremely tough. He loved special teams and never stopped working to perfect his craft. It didn't take much for me to love him.

Kerry Glenn

"There is a reason 'special' teams have 'special' coaches. Mike Westhoff is one such coach," Kerry said. "In my experience as someone who played for him when he was the special teams coach of the Dolphins, he was able to get the best out of me, and from my observations, everyone he coached.

"As relationships progress, it seems as if you either grow to like and respect a person more, or you like and respect a person less.

The more I got to know and work with Mike, the more our mutual appreciation and respect for each other flourished.

"Tuesdays were the players' day off, but I was often at the facility with Mike to assist him with the game plan. We would typically view film together, determine strengths and weaknesses of the opponents, and then create a plan.

"We had strengths and weaknesses on our team, too. One day, I came into the complex and Mike stopped me to say the 'Big Guy' (Coach Shula) wanted to see linebacker Eric Kumerow, a first-round pick in 1988, on the field. This meant he would be on special teams.

"We were trying to find a position for him on our kick coverage team. He had never done this and wasn't at all prepared for the skill or technique involved. I suggested to Mike we talk about this after we looked at the film.

"We looked at the film and saw that our opponent typically double-teamed the R4 position, which was sometimes where I usually played. Our discussion led to the idea of putting Kumerow in that position. This served two purposes:

—"it got that first-round pick on the field;

—"it set him up to be double-teamed, thereby freeing me up. I assumed the R2 position.

"During the game, when we kicked off for the first time, I went down and made the tackle. Mike asked Kumerow how he did. Kumerow responded, 'Well, I got double-teamed.' To which Mike said, 'You have got to fight through that' and reminded him how to defeat the double-team.

"The offense scored, and we kicked off again. The scenario was familiar. Mike asked Kumerow how he did, and he responded again that he was double-teamed. Then Kumerow asked Mike, 'Is there a reason they are double-teaming me?'

"So Mike told him: 'Eric, you are a first-round draft pick; they know who you are. They are scared to death of you. You are going to get double-teamed. Don't worry about it, just try to hold up. If they are doubling you, someone else is going to be free.'

"He then came over to me and gave out a knowing chuckle.

"What I learned about Mike during our planning time together is that he saw the big picture, was not hesitant to collaborate, was facile, and he knew how to use anyone as bait. He was able to build the special teams plane, if you will, sometimes when we were flying it. With Mike at the helm, there was no fear of plunging into the Atlantic.

"When I came to the Dolphins, Mike lined me up as the 'flyer' on the punt team. The flyers line up as the outside men on the punt team and are the only two players who can release to run down the field to cover the punt when the ball is snapped. Everyone else must wait until the ball is punted.

"As the flyer on the punt team, I was designated to make the tackle. I now had the chance to work with Reggie Roby, one of the greatest punters to ever play the game. I would always tell Reggie to punt the ball my way so I could make the tackle. Reggie would blast the ball and I could cover it; we were always at the top of the NFL net punting averages.

"One of my favorite roles on special teams, though, was working with my partner Louis Oliver in what we called 'Double-Vise.' Two of us were assigned to block the punt team's flyer when our opponent was about to kick the ball to us. We always picked their best guy and would mirror him anywhere.

"One, uh, special memory is from our preseason game against the Raiders in Tokyo. We were over there for a week and every practice versus each other every day was highly competitive. At the end of one practice, we transitioned to special teams work. On this day, it was our punt return team going against the Raiders' punt team. That meant our double-vise was on the field. That also spelled trouble for the Raiders.

"Louis was 6-foot-3, 225 pounds, a No. 1 draft choice as a safety from the University of Florida, and we were the best pair in the NFL."

Louis proudly agreed with that assessment by Kerry—and one I am certain is true.

"I was always put on for kickoff team, always the safety in case a guy broke one," Louis said. "Mike would have a guy who could chase him down and stop him from scoring. So I knew I would play kickoff.

"On punts, if they had a good guy coming off the corner against our punt teams, I knew I was the blocker. Special teams were my mindset that I would play.

"I do recall one preseason game at Denver, and they came out after we kicked off in two-minute offense and went 80 yards and scored. They went no-huddle, and the defense was out there for fifteen, eighteen plays in the altitude. And once I came off the field, I thought, 'Fuck that, I am saving all my strength for defense.'

"So I told Mike, 'This is a preseason game. I ain't playing no more special teams.' At times, I was on all the teams, even kickoff return teams. But I tell you what: it allowed me to hit some more people, and I liked that.

"Not only was Mike an aggressive coach, but Mike should have been our defensive coordinator. He had balls and was all about attacking and all about being proactive as opposed to reactive—my kind of coach. He would always say, 'We've got to make teams react to us.'"

Louis is correct. That's exactly what we did in Tokyo against the Raiders.

"Al Davis, the flamboyant owner and former coach of the Raiders, was on the field and very much involved in the practices," Kerry recalled. "Al Davis directed his flyer to run over the 'little man.' The 'little man' was me!

"And standing next to Louis, it was pretty obvious who they were going to go after.

"The Raiders player made a move to the inside at Louis, and I knew it meant nothing because he was going to come at me. He then changed his direction and came hard at me. I was prepared and attacked him: I grabbed him and easily ran him out of bounds and into his teammate standing on the sideline.

"On the next play, Davis redirected his player to run over the 'little man' again as they set up to repeat the play. This time when he came at me, I locked on to him, ran him out of bounds again, and threw him over the table holding the cups of water and Gatorade. Our team loved it and the Raiders were furious.

"For the first time, I saw Coach Westhoff talk some trash. He asked if the little man wanted to go again. My response was a wholehearted 'Hell, yes.'

"Al Davis was fuming and said, 'NO, NO, NO, NO. This practice is over.'

"Our coaches were amused at what the 'little man' did to their flyer and Davis' abrupt end to the practice. The Dolphins loved the whole thing.

"This was how Mike Westhoff taught us to play. Watching the film that night was a highlight of our trip to Japan, and Coach Westhoff made it clear how he wanted his teams to play. During that exchange on the field versus the Raiders, the 'little man,' relatively new to the Dolphins, got a glimpse of the Westhoff personality.

"It would become one of the more vivid memories as our relationship progressed.

"I was commonly referred to as 'Westhoff's Boy.' Teammates thought I could do no wrong in Mike's eyes. But I was also the MVP of special teams during the 1990 season.

"During one of our games, I was hit in the ear on the blind side and was knocked off my feet. At the next day's meeting, Mike showed the film to the team. It got many laughs at my expense, especially given the perception that I was his chosen one.

"Mike was the perpetual teacher. After the laughs subsided, he said: 'I want you to take a look at what Kerry does now.' He directed the players to focus not on how I went down, but how I got up. And made the tackle!

"In his usual manner of imparting lessons through examples, Mike reminded us that it does not matter how many times you fall in life. What matters is the number of times you get up.

"Louis Oliver and I changed how the flyers came down the field."

The NFL wound up changing the rule dealing with blocking the punt team flyers because of the aggressiveness of Kerry Glenn and Louis Oliver. The rule stated that if the blockers initiated contact in the field of play and sustained it, they could carry that contact out of bounds. Hence, the throwing of the opposing player into his teammates on the sideline, the bench, or the top of the Gatorade table.

"The rule was changed to the blockers (myself and Louis) must release the opponent within one yard after going out of bounds," Kerry added. "Who knows, maybe Gatorade complained about their table getting upended.

"At the time, we were the best double-team vise in the league. We would drive opponents out of bounds to the point where when we did so, the guys on the bench would part like the Red Sea. My philosophy was once I put my hands on you, I will hold on like a spider monkey until you are out of bounds—and over the Gatorade table.

"Louis and I were technical. We measured out every step we took in a game to make sure the flyer would not split us. We knew the flyer would always fake to Louis, but then come back to the 'little man.'

"During a game with the Steelers in September 1990, Dwight Stone was their flyer. Right before the snap, I was yelling to Louis

'Gatorade, Gatorade.' Stone did the usual fake to the big guy and came at me. I took him to the sideline and threw him over the Gatorade table.

"During the next punt, I yelled 'Gatorade, Gatorade' again. This time, Stone knew what it meant.

" 'Oh, hell no, you aren't throwing me into that Gatorade table again,' " he yelled.

"Louis and I laughed so hard that our double-vise was not up to its usual standard.

"So, what does all this have to do with Mike?

"Mike taught us, coached us, and trusted us to make the right decisions under pressure. He knew doing your job and having fun should be synonymous and never in opposition to one another. With his great attention to detail, he nurtured our talents on the field, including the orchestration of our step-by-step technique, which in my opinion often is lacking on the fields of today."

Louis takes it a step further, mentioning a specific meeting with the Colts, my former team.

"One time against Indy," he said, "they've got Michael Ball, a Pro Bowl guy, and I told Kerry, 'This guy better switch sides because he won't get off the line against me and Kerry. He sure as hell had to go to other side, and he couldn't make a play all game. We kept following him. Mike said, 'I don't want to see that mother down the field,' and we made sure he didn't get down the field.

"We fly on the plane going home, with the coaches and the execs and staff up front, and we are in the back of the plane. And on the back of the bus to a stadium or hotel, with all the other coaches in front, where is Mike? In the back with us, laughing and cracking up, gambling and talking his usual trash.

"There's that phrase 'MY GUY.' Mike would always tell us, 'Until you quit, you are my guy.' And guys would get excited about it—especially rookies and free agents. All Mike would tell them is, 'You will be one of our guys if you keep making plays.'

"If you're putting coaches in the Hall of Fame based on particular expertise, he should have been in there already. Ask opposing coaches around the league, and the name they will come up for special teams—there ain't but one name: Mike Westhoff."

Coach Knight

Our Dolphins teams had backup players who, as the supporting cast for Dan Marino, surely were not great special teams players. I was forced to become creative, and I believe I excelled at getting that accomplished.

If I couldn't *figure it out*, I wasn't going to have a chance. You know, sometimes necessity is the mother of invention.

That was something an encounter with Bob Knight reinforced.

In January 1990, as I was preparing to attend the NFL Scouting Combine in Indianapolis, I thought it would be great if I could drive down to Bloomington, the home of Indiana University where I went to graduate school, to attend a basketball game.

While I was a graduate assistant for the football program at Indiana, I got to know Coach Bob Knight, and I called and asked if I could attend a game while I was at the combine. He arranged tickets for IU versus Wisconsin on February 1, 1990. I picked up two tickets at will call for myself and Dolphins strength coach Junior Wade.

Following Indiana's victory, Coach Knight told me to follow him to the locker room.

He took us into a small room and told us to wait while he finished with his team and the media. As we were waiting, Bill Belichick came into the room. At the time, he was the defensive coordinator for the New York Giants. I knew him but not well. We sat and awkwardly talked until Coach Knight returned.

When Coach Knight came back in, he asked me, "Do you know Bill?"

I said yes, I certainly knew who he is.

He then asked if I knew why he was here. I said, "No sir."

He then said, "When I was the head basketball coach at West Point, Bill Parcells was on the football staff, and we became good friends. Coach Parcells asked me if I would spend some time with Coach Belichick teaching him 'how to guard.'"

In the NFL, we would refer to this as teaching defensive backs how to cover receivers.

Coach Knight said, "You guys can't cover for shit. Your technique is terrible, you have no footwork, you grab and hold, and you don't know how to play to your help."

Then he asked me a question.

"Mike, if you were coaching receivers and wanted to run a specific route versus a defensive back, how would you teach it?"

I told him, "We teach the receiver to drive straight at the DB, aiming for two steps, freezing him for a second. Then break hard for a specific point slightly outside of his shoulder. We try to get his shoulders turned in a direction and then break the opposite way."

Coach Knight said to me, "You are pretty smart, but you're not playing us. We will stay in front of you and won't give you a two-way go."

For the next hour he specifically described the details of "guarding," i.e., covering receivers in the NFL. He went through footwork, hand placement, not grabbing and holding, body positioning, and how to guide your man, the receiver, into your help. His detail was incredible: How to take specific basketball skills and relate them to NFL defensive secondary technique.

Listening to Coach Knight—that is always a great learning experience.

The following fall on September 23, 1990, the Miami Dolphins played the New York Giants in the Meadowlands. Final score: New York 20, Miami 3.

We entered the game with the high-powered offense of Dan Marino, the Marks Brothers—Duper and Clayton. We were totally stymied by a completely smothering Giants defense.

The following day, Monday, Coach Shula gave the players off, and we were sitting as coaches having lunch. Coach Shula mentioned to Mel Phillips, our secondary coach and former San Francisco 49ers defensive back: "Mel, this afternoon when you are finished, get our offensive tape and watch the New York Giants secondary. They covered us perfectly. They never got out of position, they never had to grab and hold, they stayed in front of us, never letting us turn them, and they squeezed us specifically to their help. It looked like they were playing basketball."

My heart stopped. I had never told Coach Shula about my experience with Coach Knight and Bill Belichick.

I said to Coach Shula, "Coach, they are playing basketball."

I then told him the entire story. Coach Shula said, "That son of a gun, Parcells. So, he gets Bob Knight to teach Bill Belichick how to teach his secondary how to cover."

So, if you are wondering what makes great coaches, here you have Bill Parcells asking Bob Knight to teach Bill Belichick how to relate basketball skills to football technique. Then, Don Shula figures the whole thing out without any provocation.

Many people aspire to be a fly on the wall. I was a fly on that wall and witnessed exactly why four of the greatest coaches ever were precisely that.

CHAPTER 9

The Biggest Fight of My Life

My medical journey began in July 1987. I was wrestling around with my four-year-old son John and preparing for training camp with the Miami Dolphins. John somehow landed on my left thigh and a pain shot through me like an electrical charge. That bump shouldn't have hurt like it did, and it startled me. I was a runner, and I had played golf all summer. I felt fine afterward, but I did notice some weakness in my left leg.

The good news, though, was that during training camp I would be able to see our team doctor and describe the symptoms.

The doctor told me that the radiating pain and weakness in my leg seemed consistent with the sciatic nerve being pressured by a problem with a disk in my lower back. He also said that if it persisted, we could get an X-ray or MRI and see exactly what was transpiring.

As training camp progressed and the season started, the symptoms worsened. Some X-rays were taken, and the doctor told me there appeared to be some disk damage in one of my lower vertebrae, and that following the season, a small surgery could solve the problem. By the end of that football season, the ache in my leg was nearly constant, and I couldn't wait to have it relieved.

Two days before I was to have the surgery, I was at Dan Marino's house giving him my rent check. Dan was involved in a promotion deal with Arvida, a large real estate development corporation in Weston, Florida. Dan built a beautiful home, and they had given him a three-bedroom house as part of his package. He offered me the use of the home for free, but I couldn't accept that. We worked out a rental agreement. It was a great deal for me, and I lived there for more than two years.

I was telling Dan about my upcoming surgery, and he expressed his concern. He said that our team doctor was not a neurosurgeon but an orthopedist, and he asked if I was OK with this. I assured him that I had only a slight bulge in my disk, and it merely needed to be trimmed up. The doctor had performed this surgery numerous times, and I was comfortable with him.

I didn't know shit about medicine back then. Dan wasn't being critical of the doctor, but he had some surgery experience and felt that a back surgery should be in the hands of a neurosurgeon.

I was expecting about an hour or so of surgery, a two-inch incision, and maybe a day or two in the hospital. I had several tests done on my back but nothing on my leg—where the symptoms actually were. I was to undergo a laminectomy to relieve the pressure of the bulging disk surrounding my spinal cord, in one of my lower vertebrae. The bulging disk material was to be cleared away with a serrated instrument to relieve the pressure.

During the procedure, an accident occurred. Somehow, the iliac artery was nicked. The aorta artery comes from the heart and travels down into the groin area, where it forms the iliac and then splits into the right and left femoral arteries that carry blood to the legs. The iliac is the second largest artery in the body, and even the smallest nick can cause major blood loss.

My blood pressure dropped, and I was in trouble. Some sort of alarm went out to the various operating rooms signaling a problem and asking for help. Dr. Cristobal Viera, a vascular surgeon, came into the operating room and asked what was going on and began to examine the problem. (I now know of these exact procedures because Dr. Viera and I became well-acquainted, and he told me exactly what happened.)

He asked who this patient was, and when told, he said he knew of me from the Dolphins. He tried to find the problem through the incision in my back, but he was unable to do so. He then packed the incision, and they flipped me over and opened me up with an incision from the top of my stomach down into my groin. He then moved my stomach and my intestines, taking some of them out of my body so he could get to the damaged artery.

After having clamped the artery, he went to work on removing the damaged section and sewing the artery back together.

Several days later, as he was describing the procedure, he showed me his hands, pointing out that they were small and perfect for this type of medical work. I will never forget what he said to me: "Mike, I am very good at this. I got it exactly right, and you will heal completely."

He also told me that I was in very good physical condition, with very healthy blood vessels. He knew so because he had looked inside of them.

He told me that the night of the surgery, after he had come into my room in the intensive care unit and awakened me. He told me that I was going to be fine, but I needed to rest and sleep for twenty-four hours and give his work a chance to hold and begin to heal. My wife later revealed to me that Dr. Viera had told her that if in those twenty-four hours the blood vessel didn't bind, I would be in very serious trouble.

"The doctor had nicked an artery," my son John said years later, "and it was really some kind of miracle that there was somebody (Dr. Viera) in the next room who could fix that error.

"He was fortunate to find the right doctors. He has never settled, and he has never been intimidated by them either. He would ask questions. He was respectful of them. His case is so unique, he knew about it as much as anybody."

I woke up with my entire midsection bandaged and tubes coming from seemingly every area of my body. I felt like I couldn't move. I asked my wife what had happened, and she said that they couldn't get it all from the back and had to go in through the front. I wasn't sure what I thought about that, but I kept going in and out of being awake, so it never really registered.

Over the next few days, my mother and father arrived from Pittsburgh, and several of our coaching staff members stopped by for very short visits—with long and concerned looks on their faces. It didn't take much to realize that something very dramatic had taken place, and I was very fortunate.

I somewhat celebrated my fortieth birthday in that hospital and greatly anticipated each new day when a tube would be removed or a bandage taken off.

Through the next thirty years and my many extremely complex medical adventures, I received many acts of kindness from an incredible variety of people, aside from the love and care from my family.

Don Shula came to see me and was very kind, but he didn't handle me with kid gloves. What he did with me was what he did so very well during his entire coaching career. He saw me not as I was that night but exactly as how I was going to be if I pushed and fought hard enough to get to where I could be. He didn't see me as a damaged patient. He saw me as an intricate and successful part of his coaching staff. He was only going to treat me as the person (or player) that he knew I could become. There were times during that next year when it was difficult, but he was not going to let me feel sorry for myself, and he would always demand a certain level of performance. Coach Shula saw people, including me, based on where they could be, not necessarily where they were.

I was released from the hospital after about ten days and couldn't wait to get home and begin returning to normal. But normal was the last thing that was going to happen to me.

Being in good physical condition was helping me to heal and quickly bounce back, but for some reason, my leg still ached, sometimes more severely than before. I was told that, following the back surgery, the nerves in that area were regenerating and could cause the pain.

Dr. Bud Jaffe was a radiologist in Miami and a personal friend who had closely followed the entire experience. A Northwestern grad, he had helped me recruit years before while I was coaching at Northwestern. We rekindled our friendship when I joined the Dolphins. He called me one day, saying he wasn't comfortable with what was going on and had put another plan into action. He had made an appointment for me to see a neurosurgeon in Miami, and he wanted him to have a look at all of this from a slightly different angle and present a second opinion.

I drove from my home in Fort Lauderdale to Miami and met with the doctor. He ran a series of tests on my leg and quickly decided that something was affecting a group of muscles in my left thigh, causing them to only partially function. He then sent me to get an X-ray, an MRI, and a CT scan. I sat in a lounge area for over an hour waiting for the results.

It is amazing to look back on key aspects of our lives and what resonates. I can remember sitting in that doctor's office, and I couldn't believe the size of his desk. It was gigantic, as if he was the president of a bank or the CEO of a major corporation. My life changed that day, and I still think about the size of his desk.

I had never met this doctor, but I will never forget his kindness and sincerity. He looked at me and said, "Mike, this is a whole different ballgame. The blockage in your thigh is being caused by a mass. It appears to be some sort of tumor. We don't have any pathology, but these types of tumors can be many things, including malignant."

I remember thinking: CANCER!

My entire body froze. I felt like I couldn't move.

Me? How? I am only forty years old and in excellent health. How was all of this happening?

The doctor then told me I must undergo a new search to figure out exactly what was going on and how it must be dealt with.

As I drove home, I was filled with fear and anger. I might have a cancerous tumor in my thigh, and I just had back surgery and survived an accident during the surgery. I had some questions that needed answering, including how did I get into this position and where do I now turn.

The following weekend, actually during halftime of the Denver-Washington Super Bowl, I was readmitted to the hospital to begin a battery of tests. A spinal tap, which caused the most painful headache ever. Complete bloodwork. A bone scan. X-rays, CT scans, and another MRI.

Now what do I do with all this information?

We went on a national quest trying to find the best path to follow. We talked with people at Miami's Jackson Memorial Hospital, with MD Anderson in Houston, with Sloan Kettering in New York, and with the Mayo Clinic in Rochester, Minnesota. A doctor from the Mayo Clinic called me and gave me a mantra that I follow to this very day. He said that if this were happening to him, he would go to Boston because "they are doing the best bone work in the country." How many times in the thirty years since that conversation have I asked doctors, "If this were happening to you, what would you do?"

We set up an appointment with a doctor at Brigham and Women's Hospital in Boston. Two of my sisters, Kristen and Kelly, lived and worked in the Boston area. I packed up my test results and flew to Boston. I met with the doctor at Brigham on a cold Saturday morning, and after about ten minutes he said that I needed to see his good friend, a doctor at Dana-Farber, one of the top cancer centers in the U.S.

Sunday brought nothing but anxiety as I awaited my Monday meeting at Dana-Farber.

I have always lived my life by certain rules and beliefs. Be respectful, be on time, swing first, and ask questions later. Sit right behind the bus driver. You really only need a few friends.

And you don't know anything about being a patient until you are the one wearing the wrist band.

Now, I was wearing a wrist band at Dana-Farber, one of the world's renowned cancer centers. My life was going on a completely different path.

I was forty years old with a great family and a tremendous job with Don Shula, Dan Marino, and the Miami Dolphins. And now I was in Boston wearing a Dana-Farber wrist band.

One positive thing, though, had been added to my repertoire of rules and beliefs: Don't be afraid to ask doctors what would they do if this were happening to them.

In my life, fortunately and unfortunately, I have been a wristband-wearing patient at arguably the world's greatest cancer centers, from Dana-Farber to Sylvester in Miami to Simon in Indianapolis, MD Anderson in Houston, and Sloan Kettering in New York. These are wonderful but serious places. Scared, desperate people are completely dependent on the incredible health care providers in these renowned institutions.

Following a thorough physical exam and reviews of my tests, a cancer specialist at Dana-Farber told me he was very certain that the mass in my leg was indeed a malignant tumor. He believed that, due to my age, it was more likely a chondrosarcoma—a mass in the layer of cartilage surrounding the bone rather than osteogenic (primarily in the bone), which is more prevalent in those between the ages of six to twenty-six. He said that, from the tests, the cancer seemed to be contained to that area, but more tests were needed to be certain. He then added that there was a relatively new surgery to remove the tumor and the affected area. This surgery was an allograft. It would remove a section of the affected bone and replace it with a donor bone from a cadaver. The replacement bone would be screwed and plated into place.

Knowing that I lived in Florida, he told me that there was an excellent surgeon at Shands Hospital in Gainesville. He said he was a friend, and that he would call him for me. I thanked him but then asked him, well, the best question ever: "Doc, if you were me, what would you do?"

He said that was easy for him, being in Boston.

"I would go down the street to Massachusetts General Hospital and see Henry Mankin. He is the best orthopedic surgeon in the world. Dr. Mankin invented the allograft surgery that you need."

I will never forget his exact words: "The best orthopedic surgeon in the world."

I told him that I had never been to Gainesville, and two of my sisters lived in Boston, and I would be very happy to stay in Boston. He then called Dr. Mankin and somehow was able to speak directly to him. Dr. Mankin told him to send me over to Mass General.

I remember carrying all my tests through the snow while working my way to Mass General.

I came to discover that Dr. Henry Mankin was "The Man" of the medical profession. In his office, surrounded by his associates while he kept referring to me as "kid," he examined my records. On a large screen, they were looking at an X-ray of my tumor. He told one of his assistants to get "Jo Ellen's X-rays." Within moments, there was an X-ray that looked nearly identical to mine. He told me how similar her tumor was, and then in another X-ray he showed me the picture of the allograft surgery he had performed on her. It looked to me like an erector set filled with screws and plates. This was what was in store for me.

Jo Ellen Mannix was a Boston-area schoolteacher with whom I later became acquainted. I talked with her many times and would get tickets for her and her husband to the Dolphins' games against the Patriots. She shared her rehab experiences with me, and we became good friends.

Dr. Mankin told me and his "guys" that this surgery was needed immediately, and he was going to do it the next day.

Tomorrow?

He was told that was impossible. But he said to those guys: "If I need an operating room tomorrow, we will have one. Get hematology up here for some bloodwork and get over to Harvard (which has a large bone bank) and get me a big femur."

He told them that this was necessary because the tumor was osteogenic and could rapidly spread and needed to be removed. They all argued that at my age the tumor had to be chondro and not osteo. But even without the pathology, he was sure. And, by the way, he was correct.

There was no time to waste. I had not even been admitted to the hospital, and the next thing I knew, a nurse was drawing blood from me for surgery prep.

Henry Mankin was the Don Shula of the medical profession: a complete and ultimately competent professional. He was "The Boss." Before his groundbreaking surgery, an affected limb had to be removed to ensure a cure. In a lengthy and complex procedure, Dr. Mankin could save the limb and the patient.

Even Dr. Henry Mankin couldn't quite get everything ready for surgery "tomorrow." I went home with my sister to get ready to change my life. I was admitted into Mass General early on Monday morning and underwent a twelve-hour surgery that same day. Yes, twelve hours!

My entire left thigh was opened up. The incision runs from my knee up past my hip. Seven inches of my femur were removed, including the egg-sized tumor and some of the muscle that may have contacted the impacted area.

I spent nearly two weeks in the hospital and during that time developed a relationship with a doctor that will remain with me forever. I could hear him coming down the hall barking orders, giving directions, and just generally being "The Boss."

"How ya doing, kid? Let's see if you can move this a little."

The next thing you know, I would be flexing my leg muscles and trying to move a leg that basically had been cut in half.

I loved Dr. Mankin and completely believed in his expertise. To me, the toughest part of being in a hospital occurs after 10 p.m. During the day, the place is buzzing and everyone is in and out of the rooms—doctors, nurses, meals, family, friends. The phone rings all day long and time flies by. At night, the commotion ends, and you are alone. I went to sit and look out the windows and across the river to where both Harvard and MIT are located. I wondered why this had happened to me. Would I be OK? I didn't have any answers for anything, but I kept hearing, "You are going to be fine, kid. Just keep pushing it."

I believed that if I followed Dr. Mankin's instructions to the very letter, I would get back to normal. I might have to wear a full leg brace and walk with a cane, but I could get back to my family and my life that I lived in Florida. But I never for even one moment stopped believing Dr. Mankin. If he said so, I believed it was going to happen.

A number of years later, in 2003 while I was coaching with the Jets, Dr. Mankin contacted me and asked me to come up to Boston and participate in a program he referred to as "Dialogues." It took place in an amphitheater on Harvard University's campus. There were four of us. We were each former patients of Dr. Mankin's and had undergone the allograft surgery.

There were a young man and woman, both in their twenties, whom I did not know, and my good friend from New York, Sara Hobel, to whom I was introduced by Dr. Mankin. She had a similar surgery to mine, for a non-malignant type of problem in her femur. She was a brilliant young woman—a graduate of Dartmouth and Columbia—and had an extremely successful business career interrupted by her leg surgery.

As she was recovering, she was taking a walk in Central Park and watching a group of mounted policemen work with their horses. She mentioned something to one of them about what they were doing incorrectly. Now, Sara is a peanut and looks like she is in the fifth grade, but she is very strong and extremely fit. She had grown up in Westchester County, New York, and was an accomplished equestrian.

When the police officer somewhat indignantly asked her if she could do better, she got up on his horse and expertly showed him how to handle the horse.

That encounter changed her life. She gave up her prestigious Wall Street career and went to work for the New York City Police Department in the Central Park area.

I had become friends with her and her husband, and they introduced me to New York City. We had traveled to Boston together and were eager to help Dr. Mankin in any possible way.

Dr. Mankin had gathered the elite of the Boston medical community and set up a panel to question each one of us on our medical experiences. He briefed the audience on our individual stories and then the panel, comprising a hospital administrator, a nurse, a doctor, and a psychologist, would question each of us concerning our experiences.

Standing in front of that prestigious medical community and answering questions was probably the academic highlight of my life.

We were questioned on every aspect of our experiences, all the way from care to facilities to billing procedures and food. You name it and we discussed it. One could debate that this audience was the very best medical community in the world.

I will never forget one very specific question asked to me by the psychologist. He wanted to know what the most difficult time of my hospital stay was and how I got through it.

I told him that it was late at night when everyone went home. Everything got quiet, and I sat there looking out the window and asking, "Why me? I live in Miami, I am coaching for the Miami Dolphins, I have a great family, I am in great health and forty years old. Now I am by myself after undergoing a twelve-hour cancer surgery and, hell, I still have to go through chemotherapy. Shit, I was just getting warmed up. Why me?'"

He then asked me how I dealt with it. I told him that I knew that I would make it and get back to normal.

He asked why.

I pointed to Dr. Mankin and said, "Because he said so."

I believed that he was the best that had ever done this type of cancer work, and if I followed his every word I would pull through.

It is now more than thirty years later. I guess I was correct.

Over the next thirty years, I would undergo ten more surgeries, most of them major and lasting more than seven hours. I never felt sorry for myself. They greatly affected my life and career, but I accepted each one as an inconvenience. I was going to work to make my life as normal—as special—as possible and not let any of this define me.

I remember Dr. Mankin telling me to get up and go out; don't stay at home—get to work, exercise, go to dinner. You may not feel perfect, you may not look perfect, but don't let it change you. You are the same person. Fight for that person. Keep moving forward. Don't ever let this hold you back.

When Dr. Mankin mentioned "you may not look normal," I had no idea what he was really talking about: chemotherapy.

Following my surgery, all the tests showed that I was cancer free. I could now go home and start over. Not so fast, Mike.

Dr. Mankin told me that he had talked with an oncologist in Miami, and he wanted me to have a "brushing" of chemotherapy. Just enough to make sure that my system was clear. He said he had researched the doctor in Miami, and I was not to see anyone else. I was scared to death of chemo and was adamantly opposed to undergoing it. I thanked Dr. Mankin and said I would talk with him often. I had no clue how often that would be.

Dr. Bach Ardalan at Jackson Memorial Hospital and the University of Miami Medical Center was of Middle Eastern descent. He was raised in England and attended Oxford. He was a genius whose office looked like a janitor's closet. There were papers everywhere. The place was a complete mess, but he knew exactly where everything went. His work with cancer treatment was incredible. Dr. Ardalan had developed much of the treatment for colon and rectal cancer, and his work with esophageal cancer was groundbreaking. He truly was a "patient's doctor." He didn't care about paperwork or forms—he just cared about patients.

I remember him walking into an outpatient clinic with me one day for my treatment and the nurse said, "Dr. Ardalan, we don't have any paperwork or insurance forms for Mike."

He said, "Who cares? Let's get started. The NFL has money, we'll figure it out."

Sitting in his closet of an office one day, I was telling him that I did not want to undergo chemotherapy.

"All my tests are clear. Why do I need this?"

He leaned across the desk and on the desk blotter with a pencil drew a period.

"In an area the size of that dot, there could be 60,000 cells," he said. "How do we know if one of them is bad?

"I am sure of this: if you have any cancerous cells, they are at their weakest, and we are going to attack them with our strongest (medications), and you will never be back here again. I promise you."

I said, "OK, when do we start?"

For the next five months, once a month, I underwent a very strong chemotherapy regimen of two very powerful drugs: Adriamycin and cisplatin. WOW. Now I knew what being a cancer patient was really about. Most of the antidotes very common in today's drug treatments were unavailable back then, and I went through the treatment with nothing to cure the nausea and other side effects. I lost every hair on my body and I turned a new shade of green.

I can remember driving home from work one evening and pulling my hair out and releasing it out of the car window. I called Dr. Mankin on his personal phone number and asked him if this was what he meant by fucking "brushing." He told me that those two drugs were "no friend of the family." But he added that I would coach in the NFL "forever," and would be around a "long time."

That was more than thirty years ago.

Osteogenic carcinoma in 1988 had only about a 20 percent survival rate; that number is greatly improved today.

Dr. Ardalan developed a very specialized drug treatment for me. I was his only bone cancer patient—it was not his normal area—and the others, much younger than me, went to another oncologist. I was the only longtime survivor.

I talked with Dr. Ardalan recently, and he told me that he was doing some research and work with pancreatic cancer. If there is anyone in the country who can find the answer to that dreaded disease, it will be Dr. Ardalan.

Fortunately for me, I ended up with the very best surgeon in Boston, and he directed me to the very best oncologist in Miami. And that was only the beginning of my medical journey.

CHAPTER 10

Replacement Football

In 1987, the NFL players went on strike. The league canceled games in Week 3 and shortened the season to fifteen games.

But the NFL also decided that with the players walking picket lines and negotiations going nowhere, it would continue the season with what were called "Replacement Players."

Yep, replacements.

Putting the rosters together was a massive challenge and handled through a variety of sources. Most of the replacements were players who had been in a training camp and released. There were some veterans who had been out of the league for a while, and some complete long shots—guys who maybe had the physical skills but no professional experience. Players who probably never would have gotten the chance without the strike.

And 1987 became one of the benchmark years of my life. The month I spent with the replacements was one of my favorite NFL coaching experiences. More importantly, that was the beginning of my health difficulties and journey toward recovery.

Training camp and the preseason games and even the regular season started normally, but everything seemed to be in the shadow of the labor dispute and a possible strike. A blanket of turmoil covered the sport. There wasn't a day that went by that the threat of a strike was not the lead story.

The season began on time, and we went 1-1. We lost 28-21 to New England, a team I believe we should have beaten. Then we beat the Colts 23-10 in a lackluster game under the darkening cloud of a labor stoppage.

And then the players walked out. The NFL came to a halt—at least for one week.

Our third game was against the Giants, a team many people in Miami rooted for when they lived up north. So it had a little extra meaning to them. But that meeting on September 27 wasn't going to happen. All games in Week 3 were canceled by the league.

That did not mean there would be no NFL games the next week, however. The Replacement Saga was about to begin.

The NFL told us we had two weeks to put together a team and prepare to play again.

Some NFL teams were much better prepared for this than others. Some coaches and general managers seemed to look at this as a way to get some "painless" victories. The Washington Redskins, who went on to win the Super Bowl that season, probably did the best job in the NFL of putting together a replacement team.

Others, such as Buddy Ryan and the Eagles, seemed to not want to be involved at all. I believe we were somewhere in the middle. Our player selection was only average, but I knew that once we started, Coach Shula would be all-in and we would put out a very good product.

Still, putting together an NFL team in two weeks was a thankless task. Yet, it was one of my favorite times in my career.

The players knew they had this one shot, and they absorbed every word we said. Our practices went at a thousand miles per hour. Every ounce of attention was given to us in each meeting. We condensed everything and taught them only what they would need to know for each situation of each game. The team came together much quicker than anyone could imagine.

Although it was a miniature version of what the Miami Dolphins normally put into a game plan in two weeks, we were prepared to travel to Seattle and play our first game with this group of players.

One of those replacements—a very special player to me—was a defensive lineman named Al Wring. Al was a 6-1, 260-pound ball of muscle. He was a Florida prison guard at one of the state's toughest prisons. He had only played minor-league football but was tough as nails and only wanted a chance.

There was one particular day when some of the striking players came to the locker room area and were calling the replacements "scabs" and threatening them. Al walked out and said he would gladly fight any one of them, or maybe even two. Our Dolphins players were tough and not afraid of anyone. But no one was too eager to take on Big Al.

I will never forget the very first day of practice with the replacements. We were dressed in shorts and helmets and basically having a walk-through to get the players lined up in their various positions and roles. As coaches, we lined them up, moved them around, and walked through various assignments and plays. The basics—but with all these new faces from anywhere and everywhere, who knew how much they could handle?

At the end of the two hours, though, we almost looked like a football team.

The last thing we had scheduled during the practice was to kick some field goals. I meticulously lined up the offense and defense and described their assignments and techniques. We were not in pads, and the play was to be a "step through" with no contact. Big Al was on the defensive line and lined up over the center, which was allowed in those days. My long snapper, kicker, and holder, who was our punter, were players I had never seen before, so obviously I didn't know them well. They were little guys and looked somewhat like what my young grandkids Tom, Sam, and Nathan do now.

Right before the play, Big Al stood up and announced to everyone, in an extremely deep and scratchy voice: "I didn't come down here to bullshit."

I wasn't going to argue with Florida's toughest prison guard. I was just glad we were in shorts and not going full speed.

When the ball was snapped, Al smashed and ran right over the long snapper. He rushed for the kicker, blocked the kick, and knocked down the kicker into the holder. At the end of the play, all three of my "specialists"—the snapper, kicker, and holder/punter— were lying on the ground.

Coach Shula looked at me and said, "What the fuck, Mike?" Then he turned and walked off the field, something I had never seen him do before, or ever would see him do again.

Welcome to Replacement Football, Mike.

I picked up the pieces and took Al out and finished the drill. Following practice, I pulled Al aside and told him that he and I would have dinner together and that I could tell him how to practice and play in the NFL.

That night at dinner, I did pull Al aside. We went to a private table and sat down to eat and talk. I told him that the NFL was not a fistfight. It was a violent game, sure, but controlled and played in a respectful manner. There was a time for full speed and a time for walk-throughs. Al and I agreed that I would help him on the field know exactly at what tempo we were practicing.

Al was a good man. He knew he would return to his prison job, but at that time he would do anything for the opportunity to line up in the NFL.

After two weeks of some of the most intense work that I was ever a part of, it was time for these guys to line up in the NFL. We loaded the plane to fly to Seattle for our first replacement game.

While I was at Miami, the coaches sat in first class on all our plane trips. As I was getting into my seat, my hand slipped on the armrest and my leg smacked into the armrest. It hurt so badly I had to run to the bathroom to throw up. Something was wrong. That bump should not have caused that level of pain. Little did I know at the time, and would only discover following several very complex medical procedures, that the leg pain was caused by that malignant bone tumor in my left femur.

In Seattle to support the striking players, some of the unions said they would form a picket line, and if the replacements were to cross, there might be "trouble." Thankfully, that didn't happen. Maybe they didn't want any part of Big Al either.

Before the game, we were sitting in the coaches' locker room and there was a knock on the door. Al came in. He was not able to dress for the game due to an injury but would be on the sideline. He told the coaches not to worry about any trouble because he would be there to keep an eye on us. Then he turned to me, and, in his very specific voice, he said: "And no one will fuck with you because I will be right behind you."

As we stood for the national anthem, Al leaned over to me and said, "This is the greatest day in my life." I looked at him during the song and saw the tears that were running down his cheeks.

The game was played before only 19,448 fans in the Kingdome. We lost 24-20. An officiating mistake toward the end of the game—yes, they happened back then, too—helped bring about our loss. It was one of those games when I believed we'd outplayed our opponents but still lost.

The next week in Miami, we beat the Kansas City Chiefs 42-0 in front of about 25,000 fans.

In what was our last replacement game, we were to travel up to New York to play the Jets, our biggest rival. By then, the players' union was losing support for the strike and many of the players were returning to their teams—no team more so than the Jets. By the time we arrived in New York, quite a number of their regular players had returned, such as their outstanding defensive linemen Marty Lyons and Mark Gastineau and their experienced backup quarterback, Pat Ryan. They would be playing against our replacements. None of our regular players had returned; we would have to line up in what seemed a complete mismatch.

That was one of my proudest games as a coach. Our replacements played a terrific game. We were down by fourteen points late in the fourth quarter and rallied, only to lose in heartbreaking fashion in overtime, 37-31, in front of about 18,000 fans in the Meadowlands.

Coach Shula echoed my thoughts, saying, "I don't know of any other group that I've been more proud of for a short period of time. I can't be any more proud than I am right now of our football team."

Stu Weinstein, our director of security, had a bird's-eye view of the craziness of replacement football.

"At the end of the 1986 season, Coach Shula, who I jogged with, told me he was most impressed with what Mike had provided with special teams," Stu said. "In 1987, we went through a four-week players strike, with the teams bringing in replacement players. This was most difficult for all of the coaches but especially Mike. He had the most adjustments to make, but as usual, he *figured it out*, and put together an excellent special teams unit.

"We finished 1-2 in the three games with replacements, and we had almost all replacement players—one safety crossed over. Other teams had lots of veterans cross the picket lines.

"The two teams we lost to were Seattle, playing with a former NFL quarterback, and the Jets, playing with several of their players who came back before the strike ended. We lost to Seattle by four points and to the Jets in overtime.

"That 1-2 record and how these guys performed is really a tribute to our coaching staff and how they met the challenge."

The strike ended, the regulars returned, and the replacements would go home—the end of their pro football dreams at hand. Big Al had played sparingly in the other two games, as he fought through leg injuries and was very limited athletically. But he held his own and fought as hard as possible on each play.

Now he was headed back to his prison job.

He came into my office to say goodbye and to thank me for my care and understanding. Following a back-breaking hug, he told me that tomorrow he would be back at the prison, but this had been the best time of his life. He also told me that, other than his family, no one had ever asked him to dinner.

My month with those players was one of the most rewarding times of my career.

CHAPTER 11

Cancer Survivor

In 1988, I became a cancer survivor.

Every day, my health kept returning. The sickness effects of the chemotherapy faded quickly, and I got stronger and stronger. My hair grew back, and I was again walking normally. I would never be able to run again, but I could play golf, learn how to fish, and ride my bike.

I had worked through much of my ordeal—not easily, but I had struggled through it. Now that I was feeling so much better, I threw everything that I had into my role with the Miami Dolphins. NFL coaching staffs were much smaller then, and we all had various roles. I, along with Coach Shula, was the special teams coach, and I coached the tight ends and helped John Sandusky, our veteran offensive line coach. John had some health issues, and I took over and coached the O-line from time to time.

During that period, I had the privilege of being around our Hall of Fame offensive center Dwight Stephenson. He had played at Alabama and was the player who all others watched and respected. I often talked with players from other teams who told me that while preparing to play Miami, everyone just sat and watched Dwight on every play. The coach might be talking about a scheme, but the players were watching Dwight.

Dwight had incredible strength and a wrestler's balance and quickness. He was the most dominant player that I ever witnessed.

I believe that in my three-plus decades in the NFL, he played his position better than anyone else ever played theirs. If you just look at players doing their jobs, I believe he was the best player ever.

My job as a special teams coach began to develop. I had Reggie Roby as a punter—a big, powerful man who could blast the ball to the moon. I drafted Pete Stoyanovich from my old school, Indiana, who was one of the league's most accurate kickers, and, of course, O.J. McDuffie, a dynamic punt and kickoff returner.

I worked my players hard on fundamentals—the basic knowledge of rules and clock management—and I became more and more innovative. I loved trying to invent a better play. I studied everyone and wasn't afraid to borrow an idea and tweak it a little and create something special. During that time, I developed a level of flexibility that would define my career.

Chris Mattura, who would work with me in both Miami and New York, recognized what we were doing and how we were doing it.

"Mike is extremely transparent and candid," Chris said. "He doesn't put whipped cream or sprinkles on anything. I think grown men respect that. Mike is not a bullshit artist.

"The other side of him is Mike is very, very tough on the exterior, but on the interior, he is extremely compassionate and empathetic. I think a lot of these athletes—we know the socio-economic backgrounds they come from—and Mike was a mentor to these guys. He was completely open: I never saw as many people go into a coach's office to just shoot the breeze, and with him it was not Mike calling them in, they walked in on their own.

"Because he was candid, transparent, passionate and so well-prepared and was an absolutely 'whatever it takes to get it done guy'—he'd rip your ass on one play and the next day run a tape back to point out something you did well and make your head swell. He was contagious through the entire team.

"The way we practiced on special teams is second to none. The pace of a ten- to twelve-minute period of ten or fifteen reps was unlike anything I have ever been involved in—extremely detailed, organized, and exciting. Hey, the first-team quarterback would stop and watch Mike rather than throw on the sideline.

"Every drill Mike did was totally related to a situation that would happen on Sunday."

Our offense particularly was dominant, with so many weapons for Dan Marino. Many of these players were not ideally, or in some instances even remotely, suited for special teams roles, and I had to become creative. It was a necessity. How could I take a receiver with average speed who had a specific role on offense because of his excellent catching ability and find a place for him on a kickoff coverage team?

Again, Chris Mattura understood.

"We were spending a lot of time in the classroom, and Mike would have to keep people's attention," Chris noted. "He would walk around and ask guys to open a playbook to see who was taking notes, who was paying attention. He'd ask about the what-ifs in a game situation. He wanted to see the person who put the time in.

"At the same time, we might have eighty-five people with different cognitive abilities, especially in training camp. Who was a quick learner? Who was a difficult learner? How could I break down things for this person? How can I ask a person . . . to do one thing only and do it well?

"He didn't care what round you were picked in the draft. He would say, 'Just put a blindfold on the both of us, Chris, and put up the team picture of the SEC guys, and you and I will make a player out of that guy on special teams.'

"That was back when the game was very different as far as special teams go. Mike would take kids who were athletic, who had courage, and put them in positions on special teams to really excel. Give them one basic assignment and they would be very good at it. Move the alignment around but sustain the assignment.

"In addition, one of the things people have a tough time figuring out, unless you are in it directly, you might have a second- or third-round draft pick who initially will make his bones in the NFL on special teams, and most of them didn't play special teams in college. They have never been in that situation before of playing the entire field, and Mike would find some places for them to be. If they didn't want to do it, they were out. He didn't care if you were a first-rounder or a seventh-rounder.

"He is an outside-the-box guy. People were pigeonholing players, and Mike would not do that. He had his guys. Mike crafted a niche for those guys, and they probably excelled on special teams, which elevated their value."

Don Shula

One reason we were able to do all those things was the man we were working for. Don Shula was the complete coach.

In my opinion, he was not just the head coach of the Miami Dolphins, he was the head coach of the NFL. He was at the forefront of everything in the business. He was involved in decisions concerning every aspect of the NFL.

Working for him every day for ten years, I came to

appreciate the real intrinsic value of his abilities. I don't believe that there is anyone—maybe Bill Walsh or Chuck Noll or Bill Belichick—that had such a complete grasp on every aspect of the NFL game.

He could walk into any position meeting room and completely and intricately take over the discussion. He was able to call the game on offense AND defense. Coach Shula could discuss any rule, debate every situation, and explain the workings of clock management. He also understood completely the intricacies of the business aspects of the NFL.

Don Shula was very much a "routine and schedule" individual. Early each morning after having attended a Catholic Mass, he would sit at his desk and, in a spiral notebook, keep track of everything. Those notebooks should be in the Hall of Fame.

I am not sure exactly what was included. I was called into his office numerous times while he was working. I am just going to speculate that he kept track of what happened, what was going to or should happen, and his thoughts on how everything worked.

I know a bit about his thought process because I worked with him on game planning and designing plays. There was a method as to how he saw things. The approach was thorough and, in my opinion, brilliant.

Over the years that I spent with Coach Shula, he turned over more and more of the special teams planning to me. He had gained confidence in me and trusted me to handle the job. One area that he always stayed involved with was blocking punts. He loved the challenge and the methodology of attacking the opponent's punt team. His dissecting of the entire process was something that I used my entire career in every area that I coached. I believe that it helped me gain much of the success I achieved as a special teams coach.

Every Wednesday night during the season, Don Shula would walk into my office at exactly 6:30 p.m. and sit down in "his chair."

There was a big, comfortable chair in my office that only he sat in. I used to sit in the chair late at night and watch film, but I was the only person other than Coach Shula to ever sit in that chair.

He would spin around and face the board where I had several drawings, study them for a moment, and say, "OK, show me what you have."

I knew then that I had to be ready to roll because in forty-five minutes he would get up and leave. I might be in mid-sentence, but he was leaving.

When Coach Shula attacked an opponent, he broke down everything into segments. Attacking an opponent's punt, first he wanted to know their base protection scheme. He would study the drawings and then watch a few film clips. It was critical that I knew them exactly. How did they handle seven- or eight-man rushes? Which way did the center go against the various looks? Who did the personal protector block and at what depth? How did they handle the extra rusher coming from a Bandit or Banzai scheme? How well did their guards help the long snapper's block?

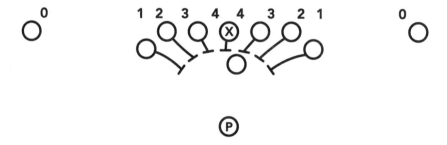

Next, he wanted to know the details of their specific techniques. Their stance, whether their feet were balanced or staggered. A balanced stance enables an individual to move laterally easily and escape more quickly and get downfield to cover the punt. But it can be more difficult to work back quickly and smoothly and form a protective cup.

NFL rules allow only the two players on the ends of the formation to release downfield on the center's snap to cover the punt. Everyone else must wait until the ball is punted before they can release. Normally, the punt team will slide back and out slightly while blocking, then release through the defender to get into position to run downfield and cover. The ball is normally punted in about two seconds from the snap, so if the technique is executed properly the punt team player can protect and be in position to cover at the same time.

Coach Shula wanted to know not only what their technique was but how each individual was executing his technique. Was his footwork correct? Did he have proper body position? Could he properly help his teammate?

I carried these procedures with me for my entire career and used them to analyze and attack my opponents. An example of this took place while I was with the Jets against New England, and after I had retired and was consulting for various colleges. Alabama was using a punt protection technique it had picked up from New England (Coach Nick Saban got it from his good friend Bill Belichick). I drew up punt blocks for Texas A&M and Clemson—two of my schools—to use versus Alabama and its New England-style punt protection. They both blocked an Alabama punt.

Another example of Coach Shula's competitiveness and ability to innovate took place on a normal Wednesday night in 1989. For me, it was a typical Wednesday special teams game plan night. My game plan scouting reports and depth charts were completed, and I was just waiting for Coach Shula's final addition of a punt block before I presented it to the team on Thursday morning.

At exactly six-thirty, he walked in, and sat in "his chair." However, in an abrupt departure from the norm, he said to me, "You know,

Mike, Ray Berry is the new coach of the Patriots. Let's see where he is. What can we give them that they have never seen before?"

He told me that Ray Berry (a Hall of Fame receiver) had played for him with the Colts and was a very hard worker and an excellent player. Coach Shula admired him and liked him, but he wanted to beat him. It didn't take much for Coach to get those competitive juices flowing. He loved a challenge and could make almost anything personal.

What had they never seen before? We were innovative and had shown many different schemes—overloads, twists, grab-and-pulls, X games. You name it, we had tried it.

He asked me, "What about a Bandit?" A rush look from a typical punt return scheme.

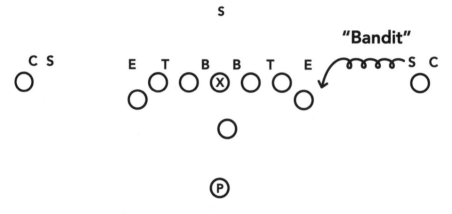

I told him that we had previously shown that, and the timing had to be perfect for it to work. I just couldn't get excited about it, and they had faced Bandits before.

Coach then asked me about "some type of Banzai?"

We had it in our notebook but had never used it, nor did I remember ever seeing anyone else doing it in a game. Maybe someone back in the early 1980s, but I didn't remember ever seeing it.

We defined Banzai as a daring, all-out punt block. It involves creating a nine-man rush—one more than the punt team's eight blockers—by rushing the cornerback, who normally covers the punt team flyer. It is risky and very rarely used.

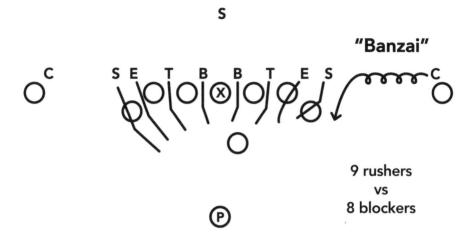

9 rushers
vs
8 blockers

I had three ways, and only three ways, to defeat a Banzai. Number one is the punt team could bring in the flyer and gain the extra blocker and therefore block the so-called extra rusher.

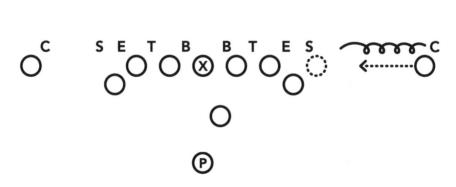

Secondly, the punt team can take a chance on punting the ball a little quicker and not count the Banzai rusher. Believe that you can punt the ball before he can get to a block position.

Thirdly, my favorite, is the punt team can call "Banzai Hot." This tells the line and wings to form a blocking cup. The ball is snapped to the punt protector (PP); I love athletic and sometimes quarterback-type players for that position: Jim Jensen, Brad Smith, Eric Smith, Tim Tebow, and Taysom Hill, for example. Those players could easily throw the ball to the uncovered flyer.

I have had several punters such as John Kidd or Tom Tupa who could also have made the throw.

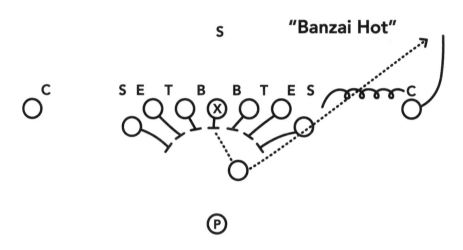

Many times in recent years this type of rush has been used, but in 1989 it was very innovative. I drew it up, presented it, and practiced it on both Thursday and Friday. We walked through it on Saturday and were prepared to use it on Sunday.

On their first punt attempt, we called it. Jeff Feagles was their punter, and we caught them off-guard. The unblocked rusher was coming clean, and Feagles tried to run. We caught him and tackled him for a big loss, giving us great field position that led to a score.

On their second punting attempt, we called it again. We had built in a way to bring a defender out from inside to aid our coverage. This time, Feagles tried to throw, and the pass was covered and fell incomplete.

The resulting field position from these plays led to fairly easy Dan Marino scores and helped us to a seven-point victory.

Following the game, Coach Shula walked by me and said, "Pretty good, Mike." He never gloated; it was just on to the next game.

Coach had asked "What can we give them that they have never seen before?" Had they ever seen it? I don't know. But it worked—twice—and helped us win the game.

The things that I learned working for Don Shula defined my career. In a quiet, special way, I loved my relationship with him.

More than anything, though, I loved knowing in no uncertain terms that I was one of "his guys."

CHAPTER 12

Working with the Greatest

Coaching on Don Shula's staff was as challenging—and rewarding—as anything you can imagine. A perfect example came after my 1986 season with the Dolphins had just ended.

I was finishing up some paperwork and preparing to go home to start what would be ten days of vacation before returning to work to begin the next year's offseason prep. Our offices were located at St. Thomas University. A tiny facility and, by far, the worst in the NFL. Nothing like the beautiful complex the Dolphins were preparing to move into.

Coach Shula stuck his head around the corner and told me to come into his office. Going into Coach Shula's office was like being summoned to the principal's office while in the tenth grade. He was all business, and after only my second year with the Dolphins I was far from being completely at ease.

Coach then said: "Mike, I just got off the phone with the Senior Bowl committee, and they would like me to coach the South team in the game next week. My son (Mike, a senior at Alabama) is going to be the quarterback. I am going to promote Dave (his oldest son and our receivers coach) to offensive coordinator. I want to give him some play-calling experience and help him prepare for a head coaching opportunity.

"Mike, John Sandusky (Coach Shula's long-time offensive line coach) is going into the hospital for a much-needed double hip replacement surgery. You are going to have to coach the offensive line—in addition to the special teams and tight ends. It is a lot, but you'll be fine. Get everything prepared tomorrow. We leave Sunday."

YOU'LL BE FINE? I felt like I was having a heart attack.

So now I am going to be the offensive line coach for Don Shula? His son, Mike, would be the QB. And his other son, Dave, would be calling the plays as the offensive coordinator. Could anyone be in more of a pressure-packed situation than that? I was a complete nervous wreck.

But I have handled pressure situations nearly the same way my entire life. I prepare. I went back into the office the next day and got every scouting report that I could find on the Senior Bowl personnel. We didn't have film of them at that time, so I just read. And read. And read.

Knowing me, I was determined to make it work. I had a good group of talented college seniors, several of them headed for NFL excellence.

Bruce Armstrong, the All-American tackle from Louisville and a future first-round draft pick of the New England Patriots, was by far the glowing star. The others were good, solid college players, but by no means a sure thing for the NFL. I had a good group to work with, but I had my work cut out for me.

I devoted every second of that week to making sure that we would be successful in every aspect. I practiced them as hard as possible and met with them for every available minute. I can remember one night I was meeting with the offensive linemen upstairs in a ballroom and holding a very unscheduled walk-through. The window of the room looked over the harbor in Mobile. There was a ship leaving the harbor heading into the Gulf of Mexico.

I stopped the meeting and said, "You see that ship? If we fuck this up, my ass is going to be on one of those sons of bitches on Sunday. We need to kick the shit out of those guys on every play."

Each morning our staff would have breakfast together and discuss any changes with Coach Shula. Dave and I were discussing the practice, and I mentioned to Dave that I did not like running our toss sweep plays from the pre-movement two-point stance. In Coach Shula's offense, the linemen started in a two-point stance with their hands on their knees, and then on the first sound of the cadence would drop a hand down to the ground in a typical three-point position.

I told him that this group of linemen was very physical, and I wanted every play to be as aggressive as possible. The two-point stance was for lateral or backward movement, but for this group we needed to be exploding off the ball on every snap.

Coach Shula had sat down with us and started his usual breakfast with a glass of orange juice and a cup of coffee. He had just started eating his cereal when Dave proposed our question. Dave had some guts—and class. It was my idea, but he presented it as ours. I wasn't out on a limb all by myself. Now I had a partner.

"Coach," Dave said, "Mike and I think that we should abandon calling our sweep plays on the first sound and run most everything from the three-point stance, being more aggressive, and let us really fire off the ball."

Coach Shula had his spoon halfway up to his mouth when he froze. He looked at both of us and then dropped the spoon into the bowl, splattering much of the milk. Coach Shula could look at you and make time stop.

"You two? You two?" he said. "Why don't you ask Lenny Moore or maybe Larry Csonka, they both only led the NFL in rushing. Maybe even Jim Kiick or Mercury Morris?"

Lenny Moore, Larry Csonka, Jim Kiick, and Mercury Morris—four of the greatest running backs in NFL history, two in the Hall of Fame, and all of them benefited greatly from the "System" to which I was now suggesting a change. I might as well have been telling a Victoria's Secret model how to dress.

Coach Shula abruptly stopped, picked up his coffee, and left.

I looked at Dave and said, "Well, Dave, that went well."

And I started considering booking a ticket on that cruise ship.

Our practices started with stretching, loosening up, and some agility drills before we had the players break into individual groups for sled work and position group skill sessions. Following that, the offensive linemen, running backs, quarterbacks, and tight ends would run plays versus the defensive line, linebackers, and two safeties. This was called 9-on-7 and is a way of executing the run for the offense and stopping it for the defense.

Mike Shula was calling the plays, and Coach Shula, Dave Shula, and I were at the huddle listening. Mike called a toss sweep play on the first sound, when the linemen would be in a two-point stance. Coach Shula stepped in and said, "No, Mike, put them down in a stance and run this on a cadence. I want to see what this looks like."

Dave and I very sheepishly looked at each other. Don Shula prepared like no other coach that I have ever known—and I have known so many of them. He never stopped learning and was always looking for something that was better.

He never acknowledged where that change came from, but he stayed with it for the rest of his career. It was a minor thing but an example of his never-ending search for excellence.

We won that game 42-38 and had a great offensive performance. Coach Shula had to be very proud. This was not the NFL, but these were his sons. Mike had done brilliantly, Dave proved he could be a coordinator and was headed toward being a head coach, and I was right in the middle of it all, helping make it work. I believe it may have been my best week of coaching—ever.

Coach Shula later congratulated me on a job well done and thanked me for all my hard work. It was the beginning of a strong relationship between us, and he helped me to become a very devoted and successful member of his staff up until the day he retired after the 1995 season.

Zach and Larry

Zach Thomas was a fifth-round draft pick from Texas Tech in his second week of his first NFL training camp. I came out to the practice field and saw that Zach was dressed in shorts, no pads, and was not going to practice that day. I was unaware of the situation and asked Zach what was wrong. He told me he had a slight hamstring pull. He put his hand out and slightly shook it, indicating it wasn't too serious.

"Just a tweak," he said, hence the hand movement.

It's important to note that the Dolphins' practice fields were located in Davie, Florida, slightly north of the flight pattern into the Fort Lauderdale Airport. As Zach tells it:

"Mike looked at me and said, 'I'm glad you told me about the tweak.' Mike then shook his hand the same way I had done. 'Because tomorrow morning when I am out here, and I look up and see that plane tweak as it flies by, I am going to know that you are on that plane flying your ass back to fucking Texas.'

"He never smiled, just turned and walked away. He scared the hell out of me. One thing for sure, I didn't miss too many practices after that.

Zach Thomas

"I came to learn later that he was only messing with me and that no one cared more about his players and their well-being."

You know, one of the favorite parts of my coaching career has been maintaining a relationship with some of the players after their playing days ended—no one more so than Zach Thomas.

Every summer, he will leave his home on the east coast of Florida and drive across the state to my place in Fort Myers to go shark fishing. On one of these trips, we got into a discussion about my book.

I've always felt that I drafted Zach. I know Jimmy Johnson was the head coach of the Miami Dolphins and actually is the guy that drafted him. George Hill was the defensive coordinator and also very fond of Zach, but I had so much to do with it that I guess I love to take credit for it. But there were many other hands just as key as mine.

Zach has clear memories of my visit to Lubbock, Texas.

"At first, man, this guy has this little cocky confidence, and I am trying to figure him out," Zach said. "He asked me what my best game was, and I tell him and then tell him my second-best game when he asked what my worst was. I tell him and he stops the film and says, 'This isn't your worst game. Let's pull out when you played Texas.'

"We got blown out in that game, and he knew it. You couldn't get that past Mike."

Zach even mentioned to me: "Coach, when you came out to Texas Tech to work me out, there had been plenty of scouts but you were the only coach; it was very different from anything that I had previously experienced. You only wanted to watch my worst game, and you asked me repeatedly, whenever I made a particular mistake, what I had done to correct it. At the end of that session, I felt like I had learned a lot about myself, and obviously you must have thought the same thing.

"Following the workout, we were getting ready to leave, and you left the room to go use the bathroom. I looked at your notes, and I read them. I was shocked you had basically lied on everything that I did. I had twenty-two bench presses, you gave me twenty-four. On every single thing. Mike, why did you do that?"

Because of the lessons I learned from Woody Hayes in 1975.

Throughout my career, I never forgot that advice, and I was not going to let a "number" keep me from getting Zach Thomas.

Zach has always been listed as 5-11 and 242 pounds. The day I was at Texas Tech, he was 5-10 1/2 and 222 pounds. So what?

He went on to play thirteen years in the NFL, twelve at Miami and one with the Dallas Cowboys. He made five All-Pro teams, which is for the entire NFL. He was in seven Pro Bowls, made the league's All-Rookie team in 1996, and to cap it all, Zach was on the NFL's 2000s All-Decade Team. Some other linebackers on that team were Ray Lewis, Derrick Brooks, and Brian Urlacher, all in the Pro Football Hall of Fame.

Zach played in 184 games and made 1,720 tackles. In my opinion, no one is more deserving—and I hope and pray it happens soon that Zach joins those guys in the Hall of Fame.

No, I wasn't going to let a "number" keep me from getting Zach Thomas.

And I wasn't going to miss on Larry Izzo, either. In fact, Larry Izzo may be the most unlikely candidate to ever have achieved such a grand level of success after having started from such a point of obscurity.

Larry Izzo

It all started with a letter from an old high school friend who was a neighbor and friend of Larry's and his family from his home in Houston. When I talked to our scouts in Miami, they assured me there was "no chance" Larry was even on their radar. Where was he going to play? One scout actually told me that the Canadian Football League didn't like him and an Arena League team also said no.

I persisted. I was headed to Texas to work out Zach, so why not stop in Houston and take a look at Larry?

I loved everything about him except his size. The day I was at Rice, he was 5-9 1/2 and weighed 215 pounds. Not exactly NFL linebacker potential, but what I saw I loved. He played at a hundred miles an hour. Watching him on film, he looked like he could make every tackle. Rice's defensive coaches used him brilliantly, playing him as a safety and moving him up to near a linebacker position. For years this role was referred to as the "Monster," a hybrid linebacker/safety. In this role, Larry excelled. He was all over the field and made play after play.

In fact, he ended up being the old Southwest Conference's leader in tackles behind the line of scrimmage—in the history of the conference. He sacked quarterbacks and blocked punts. I knew he would be a great special teams player.

I didn't care how big he was. I didn't let numbers get in the way on that scouting trip. Zach and Larry—I should have gotten a huge bonus for that scouting trip.

"Mike had such a great coaching style," Larry said. "He was hard on guys, but we always knew where he was coming from. He would get on everybody, but you knew it was coming from a good place. Obviously, with me, I had sent my tape to him coming out of college. He is the one who worked me out, got me signed. I always felt indebted to him for just helping me get my foot in the door.

"But it was also how he coached, what really fit the type of player I was. Mike was an aggressive, attack-type of special teams coach, and that really fit with how I played."

Yeah, I pushed hard in our meeting for both guys. It wasn't terribly difficult. George Hill, one of the NFL's best defensive coaches, liked Zach and was very much on board. Jimmy Johnson was a Southwest Conference player himself at Arkansas. So he had the knowledge and the interest in both players.

We drafted Zach in the fifth round and signed Larry as a free agent.

I mentioned what Zach accomplished. Larry? He went on to an incredible playing career of thirteen seasons, making the 1996 All-Rookie Team, going to three Pro Bowls, and winning three Super Bowls with the Patriots.

Yeah, Larry Izzo *figured it out.*

"He was always putting the pressure on me every practice to do something, to prove myself," Larry said. "It's a little uncomfortable to be in that mindset, sure, but it benefited me to be that way. Everything I needed to do to make the team had to come from me. I not only had to be a special teams player, I had to prove that I could also be a linebacker, as Mike would always tell me. What Mike was telling us was: 'Help me help you. I can't help you if you are not doing great things as a linebacker.'

"It was true. You could carve out a role on special teams, but if you're not adding value in other areas, you make yourself vulnerable to not making the roster. I always had to prove I belonged, be a playmaker on special teams and also as a linebacker. Always having him kind of pushing me in that way greatly helped my mentality. I think all undrafted players need to have that, and I am thankful for having Mike early in my career.

"The great thing about Mike as a special teams coach was his ability to find roles for guys. Put them in specific places where they could make plays and execute what they needed to have done. Mike had a real good feel for putting guys in those positions. Having that as a special teams coach and you are a player, knowing you are being put in the best places you are suited for, you feel gratitude for that. He is not asking you to do something you can't do.

"I have known Mike over twenty years now, and we've become very close. He is a great friend, and the relationship was player/coach and now it has grown and I think the world about him as a man.

"Having played for him and then played against him when I was in New England for eight years, every time we played a Mike Westhoff special teams unit—at that time he was with the Jets—it was the biggest challenge you would have. So many different concepts, exotic schemes you had to be ready for. He was always on the attack.

"His kickoff coverage always was the hardest to play against: motions and speed and shifts, guys playing fast. As a player playing for a coach like that, it's all you want from a coach.

"Now, as a coach (with the Seahawks), the things I have taken from him:

"1-Finding the right roles for guys and putting them in the proper places, putting the pieces of the puzzle together.

"2-Mike had the ability to put little wrinkles on different things that were challenging for your opponent; it looks the same, but it is not. Mike was able to tweak things to where you are able to attack an opponent within the same look, which made things challenging when you played against it.

"3-The mentality is the No. 1 thing he has influenced me on. That always attacking, always aggressive play style. Whether that is schemes and concepts or just in terms of how the players are playing.

"Fear was not in Mike Westhoff's DNA. Some coaches will coach the fear-based mentality of not wanting something bad to happen. His mentality was to attack with no fear, and that has carried over for me to my coaching style and how I look at the game and try to communicate with the players.

"4-His ability to connect with guys one on one and get them to play at their highest level. Mike had a great ability to push buttons, make a comment to a guy to get him to another level. That is a gift he had, that ability to connect with guys who played for him.

"One of the great things that he would do was on Saturday night before games he would always have his time in front of the team, and he would tell these incredible inspirational and motivational stories. It was unique. He always seemed to connect to where we were as a team or as a unit. The point of emphasis within the story always seemed to fit with what needed to be done the next day in the game.

"He talked about whitewater rafting and being knocked out of the boat and floating down the river, and no one is going to come in and help you. You've got to get your own ass out of the river and back into the boat. You got to find a way to get that done, not just float down the river yelling 'HELP.' No one is going to help you on the football field.

"His meetings were always entertaining and another thing I have tried to take from him: he always kept you engaged as a teacher, and I am sure his background in psychology played a role in that.

"We always enjoyed these stories. Mike was not just up there talking Xs and Os the night before the game, his meetings would lead off with a story that would lead into the Xs and Os. And really cool stories.

"He would spend hours game planning, and you go into the meeting, and he told you if you execute it the way he wanted, it would work. And if you did, it was going to lead to success. I took that as a player: do it the way he wants it done and it will work out. It did.

"Mike had a great way of finding ways to attack teams and game plan against them. Every week came a new concept he is introducing and the attention to detail with which he would present it.

"If he wasn't happy, well, he would throw the remote, or take his cane and throw it across the field. You understood why.

"Remember, we used starters on special teams, and he didn't care that they were starters. If he had a role he thought you could do well to help our unit, he was going to use you. Zach was our starting linebacker in Miami, and he had him on the punt team and kickoff return because Zach was a really good trap blocker. He would light guys up. If you could do something well for him, he would use you.

"Jason Taylor, a first-ballot Hall of Famer, was playing wing for us and covering punts in the prime of his career.

"If you could do something to help his units, not only was he was going to use you, but you looked at it as a badge of honor that he felt that way about you. He wasn't going to ask these types of players to do too many things, but maybe one thing you do really well, like with Zach. That was a real gift for him: Mike would tell a guy exactly what he wanted you to do, how it would happen. You would get excited.

"Any guy who would look at that as a demotion? You didn't want that guy on your team. When Mike asked you to do something, you felt like you didn't want to disappoint him—he selected you to do that specific role.

"We used starters all the time. On Mike's teams, we would have our core of special teams units and then add some starters you incorporate for specific roles. That is how he made up his entire unit, and he usually wound up with one of the NFL's best.

"Trace Armstrong, a starter and one of the league's best pass rushers, was really good at rushing the punter. There'd be times when Mike would leave him on the field for special teams, but not put too much on his plate. Mike would tell Trace—remember, one of the best pass rushers in the game—'Line up here and do this.' Next time, we will switch, and you will line up somewhere else.'

"All of a sudden, there are three different rush looks using a big-time rusher like Trace. He either disrupted the punter, affected the punt, or drew penalties from the opposition. That's one great example of using a starter.

"When Mike was asking, Trace was excited to do it. He was not looking at it as a demotion but rather as an opportunity to make a big play.

"From day one when we came into any Mike Westhoff meeting, he is not looking for guys who don't want to be out there. The core guys all understood their roles; that is where I fit in. Every good team needs to have value from everybody. If there are certain things one guy can do well, we are going to use him on special teams. You can have your core but have to have more than that. And Mike communicated that really well to the entire team."

Larry carried a tremendous resume into his role with Seattle, and the Seahawks will greatly benefit from having one of the NFL's greatest special teams players as their coach.

Thanksgiving

A specific aspect of coaching special teams in the National Football League that is one of my favorite experiences occurred during my years with the Dolphins.

Sure, those years contained emotions that could have been felt by most everyone, but maybe were not entirely for everyone. There was the excitement—and intimidation; try going to work for Don Shula, having never met him until I walked into his office to talk about the job.

There was the pride of becoming a part of the great teams of Coach Shula and Dan Marino.

There was the craziness of the Senior Bowl experiences and, of course, coaching the replacements.

There was an accident during a relatively simple orthopedic surgery that no one can understand—and, more in question, can figure out how I survived.

Discovering that I had bone cancer and everything involved with all those procedures while never missing work. Learning how to coach while using a cane and having the use of really only one leg.

The extreme highs of being part of such a good team and the lows of losing to Buffalo and seeing the Bills head to the Super Bowl four times while we stayed home.

Watching Don Shula retire and being part of the Jimmy Johnson era. Putting together arguably the best special teams units in the NFL, culminating with ranking first following the 2000 season, which could be debated as the best special teams year ever in the NFL—there's no debate about that in my mind.

Seeing such a great run come together in Miami but then come to such a brutal and immediate end under a coach who succeeded Jimmy Johnson and who, in my opinion, had absolutely no business being a head coach in the NFL, or anywhere else.

Part of that ending to my time in Miami was the hope of a head coaching opportunity that never came to fruition. But then, thankfully, came the opportunity to move on to the New York Jets—and the best years of my life.

During those years in Miami, my role as a special teams coach did not involve a majority of the top end of the NFL roster. My guys were not being discussed on TV—as we so much see today—as to whether or not they should be paid $160 million. We were at the other end of that discussion.

No, I had the young kids who were just trying to make an NFL team. Many were in roles they had never experienced and doing so at a particular level of excellence that they had no idea existed. These were guys who, at the time, had very few friends in the Miami area and sure as hell had very little money.

I loved molding them, demanding a level of physical play and excellence few had ever experienced, and watching them develop into a unit that everyone could be proud of and that the entire NFL would be aware of.

So, each year while at Miami, one of my favorite times was inviting these young, new guys—practice squad players and anyone else who was maybe alone—to come to my home for Thanksgiving dinner. I made sure that everyone who had no place to go had an opportunity to come together for a great meal.

I made the invitation very enticing. Everyone was invited, and if you had a friend or girlfriend in town, they were welcome too. I lived very close to the complex, and you could leave the dinner at any time. One year my parents attended, as did my sister Karen and her family, who lived close by. My brother Greg's son, Paul, and his family also were there one year.

Zach Thomas and Larry Izzo were there a number of times, especially early on when they were just getting started and had not yet gotten famous.

Each year, we had twenty or so people on hand, and it was my favorite. If you wanted to stay and watch football, of course that was fine. A few beers were OK, but there was never going to be much drinking at my home.

My wife, Marilyn, was an excellent cook, maybe the best you would have ever encountered, and the meal was outstanding. Every time.

I started an interesting tradition, also, and I am as proud of it as maybe anything I have ever done. Just before we began to eat, we would say grace. I told them that we were Catholic, and I would start it off, but then each player would say the prayer that his family would be saying in their home on Thanksgiving.

I listened to quite a variety of prayers, and I loved each and every one of them. But one will always resonate.

We had a young wide receiver from Syracuse named Qadry Ismail. He was returning some kicks for me and ended up being a very good player. Qadry was raised in a Muslim household and said the prayer of his family's faith. It was something very different for me but also very special.

That next week I received a letter from his mother thanking us for inviting her son to be part of such a special dinner.

Sometimes it is the little things that I look back on with the most reverence and appreciation. Yep, I had the best job in the world.

CHAPTER 13

J-E-T-S, JETS JETS JETS

I t was January 2001, and I was looking for a job. It had been a long time since I had done that.

I went to the Senior Bowl by myself and came home with several teams interested and two solid offers. I called Bill Parcells and asked for his advice. He had always been great to me and had some suggestions. He told me he was exploring a possibility in the league and for me to not commit to anything until I heard from him. He never told me where he was looking, but that I would love it and could "keep my boat."

You didn't have to be Sherlock Holmes to figure it out. He never did say where, but I believe I knew.

But where I was really interested was with Herman Edwards, who had just gotten the New York Jets' head coaching job.

I had competed against the Jets for years, and I knew they were a very good team. After Parcells retired from the Jets, Bill Belichick had the job for one day before bolting for New England in 2000. Al Groh was then made the head coach, but after only one season, he left for the University of Virginia, his alma mater.

As an interesting side note, before Groh left for Virginia, he had contacted me about joining him in New York.

Herman Edwards was on the job for one day, and they flew me in to talk. I was there for five minutes, and he offered me the job. I had been in New York several times before but never actually in Manhattan. This was a whole new world for me.

The Dolphins had just built a new facility, and it was beautiful—state of the art. Offices, meeting rooms, practice fields, all set in a gorgeous palm tree-surrounded environment. As for the Jets, their facility was at Hofstra University on Long Island. Hofstra? The place looked like an auto body repair shop. It was a mess. The practice field was tiny. It didn't look like you could play tennis in their bubble, let alone practice football.

The individual meeting rooms were old and tired looking. The weight room should have been Hofstra's, not the Jets'. The team meeting room? It looked perfect for a high school musical.

As I walked around their facility, quite the dynamic occurred to me: how had the New York Jets, who had been successful over the last several years, done so working out of this dump? I immediately gained a tremendous respect for the coaches and administrators who had developed a hell of a product under very difficult circumstances.

Parcells and Belichick had taken them to new heights. They had just been to the AFC championship game in 1998, and I believed this would be a good team to join. I liked the Jets' personnel, and even though I had several other opportunities, the Jets were the only team I was really interested in.

Still, I returned to Florida and waited for Bill Parcells to call. He called me on a Sunday and said that "the guy wouldn't pull the trigger." He didn't get the job.

Wherever that job was, I am not 100 percent sure, but something just didn't seem right. I don't believe Bill would talk on what was going on, but I am sure it wasn't his finest hour.

I called Herman Edwards and became a Jet.

I learned to love New York. I lived in a quintessential New York apartment in Garden City, not far from Hofstra. I loved taking the train into Manhattan and exploring the city. The restaurants are the greatest. I went to every museum and even became a patron with Carnegie Hall.

"My dad loves New York City," said my son John. "He would come into the city more and more, loved it when the team stayed in the city, and he wanted to remind everyone, 'We are a New York team.' He would walk through Penn Station and be giving high-fives to everyone. I lived in Manhattan, and he would come into the city and we would have dinner. He fit New York."

John is correct: I loved the Jets fans and will always cherish my relationship with them.

"When he got to New York, a lot more of the Jets fans knew of him than I thought would," John said. "In South Florida, people got to know him because he was there a long time and had a lot of success. And then the Jets' fan base, he coached there for the best years they have had, and they loved him. It was very much fun.

"I moved to New York and went to a bunch of games and got to know a lot of the fans. I think what the fans liked was he doesn't mind the light being on him, and he puts the pressure on himself to be the best. New Yorkers look at themselves as being in the epicenter. He's the same way. Hey, he wanted to be on national TV every week. He loved Monday night games and the chance to show everybody his group was the best.

"That's what Jets fans saw and loved."

I found out quickly that Herman was good to work with. I enjoyed his company and trusted him. In many ways, though, he was not well prepared to be an NFL head coach. He had played in the NFL and worked his way up the ladder as a scout and assistant coach. He never was a coordinator, nor was he strongly versed in game management. Clock management, situations, and coach's challenges were things he was relatively unprepared for. We practiced all of them, but we were not near as efficient as needed.

He was easy and receptive to talk with. I should have done a better job of discussing these shortcomings with him. I think I could have helped Herman more than I did.

We had a good team. Parcells knows how to assemble an NFL team. We were in the playoffs our first two years. I had an excellent group for special teams and began developing one of the league's best in that area. I developed somewhat of an all-star team but never really had a successful punter.

At first, I was really counting on Tom Tupa. An ex-quarterback and a punter from Ohio State, he had an injury in training camp, but he personally assured me he would be back for the season opener. I was patient but more than disappointed. People come back from heart and lung replacement surgery faster than he came back from his injury.

He was talented enough and did a good job when out on the field, but we were never quite on the same page. He was released, not by me but for contractual issues. He went to Tampa and did an excellent job. He publicly blasted me and was critical. I never said one word about him, but I will take my success over his any day.

And I know a little something about dealing with medical issues.

My first year in New York was one for the ages. We lost the opener to the Colts, and my debut was anything but auspicious. Tuesday morning of my second week there, I was licking my wounds and trying to prepare for a trip to Oakland.

And the world stopped.

9/11

As with most everyone else in America on the morning of September 11, 2001, my world was changed forever. And I had a close-up view of how the National Football League—and my new team, the Jets—would help America pay its respects to the victims of the massive tragedy. And how football would help America heal.

Our opener versus the Indianapolis Colts, a team that I believe we were better than, featured their young quarterback named Peyton something.

When we lost that game, it was very frustrating for me. I had just come from Miami, where for the past five years I probably had the best special teams in NFL history. My first game with the Jets was anything but memorable. We just hadn't put anything together. I didn't feel as though I'd done my best job by any means. I was trying to figure out who my real players were, and it started off very unsuccessfully. We gave up a punt return for a touchdown. I couldn't even remember the last time that had happened, or even if it ever had.

On Tuesday morning, I was sitting at my desk putting a game plan together for the Raiders. Around nine o'clock or so that morning, I received a phone call from my parents, who were retired and living in Pittsburgh. They were watching a news report that a plane—they told me they thought it was a very small plane—had run into one of the towers in New York. Initial reports had been exactly that: a small plane.

I put the television on, and like everyone else saw what was happening. The building was on fire. At first, it didn't look very major. But the more you would watch, it didn't take long to realize something very serious had happened.

Then, shockingly and all of a sudden, we all saw the second plane go into the tower. Everything seemed to freeze. We were being attacked.

America was being attacked.

My son John was a student at the University of Pennsylvania. He was playing football and was in his third year. I immediately, of course, tried to reach him. Reports were all over the television, as

I'm sure anyone who lived through 9/11 will remember, including erroneous reports that there were various attacks in other parts of the country. I heard something about some type of problem in Philadelphia near the airport. My heart stopped.

I couldn't reach my son. I kept trying, as nervous as I've ever been. Eventually I did reach him and realized it was a false alarm and that there was not a problem in Philadelphia.

But 9/11 had hit full force, and for us it was right there in our faces. From the Jets' facility on Long Island, we could go outside and see the smoke from the towers. Everything seemed to be right there in our backyard.

And we were supposed to get ready and then fly across the country to play a game in five days in Oakland.

We at first decided to try to make the week as normal as possible. Herman Edwards addressed the team, informing them that President Bush had talked with NFL Commissioner Paul Tagliabue and asked him to continue the NFL schedule to keep continuity in the country.

Practice that day was dull and listless; how could we have our minds on anything but what was happening a few miles away in Lower Manhattan? And at the Pentagon in Washington? And a field in Western Pennsylvania? NFL meetings, schedules, and practices require tremendous concentration. We had none.

Terry Bradway, our general manager, frankly was not my favorite; I thought in many ways he was barely mediocre. But on that day, he did an excellent job. He pulled the team together and explained to everyone all the options. He let the players know what he believed would be the consequences of not playing, but also made it clear to the team that he would respect their wishes—and make every effort to convey those wishes to the NFL. I thought his honesty and sensitivity were outstanding and very much needed on that given day.

That night I was in my office continuing to work on my game plan when I received a phone call from Mark Hatley, an old friend I previously worked with at TCU. He was the personnel director and assistant general manager with the Green Bay Packers. Mark called to ask about a particular player he had an interest in, but the conversation quickly turned to 9/11. He made it clear to me that the hierarchy in the NFL was preparing to play the schedule as normal, and I should be very much prepared for that. His boss, Ron Wolf, a future Hall of Famer, was very connected with the top levels of the league, so I knew Mark's information was accurate.

By Thursday morning, with so much still in flux, the players delivered a powerful message at our team meeting. They made it very clear that they did not want to fly to Oakland and play. They needed some time. I could tell by their demeanor that this was how they were feeling, and I would have been shocked to hear anything else. With the closeness of the events two days earlier, the impact it was having on each of them was deep.

Terry Bradway informed them there would be an 11 a.m. conference call among the team owners to make a decision on the week's games. He gave the players an hour, encouraging them to talk over everything and make a decision.

Herman Edwards came to my office and asked what I thought. I told him that, like him, I believed we had to fully support the players. If they were to not play and be fined a game check, then I would also give up a game check. He agreed with me.

Herman showed great leadership that day, and it was one of his finest moments as a head coach.

We met with the rest of the staff, and Herm told them what we had decided. Football absolutely is a team game—the most unselfish sport there is—and being united was essential in normal circumstances. These were anything but normal circumstances.

When everyone came together, the players, directed mainly by Vinny Testaverde, Curtis Martin, and Kevin Mawae—three great NFL players and leaders: Curtis and Kevin are in the Hall of Fame, and Vinny was as popular as any player—made it clear: the New York Jets were not going to play the game, no matter the consequences.

The decision was immediately relayed to the NFL in the conference call. I wasn't on the call, of course, and I don't know exactly what was said. But I know that in a very short time the New York Giants basically said the same thing. It was all too close and too soon.

Commissioner Tagliabue understood that his and the owners' decision would set the course for pretty much every other sport that weekend. The baseball pennant races were in midstream. College football was early in its season. Golf, tennis, auto racing—all of them would follow the NFL's lead.

And they did when the commissioner announced the NFL would not be playing that weekend, and the schedule would be pushed back a week.

Yes, everyone wanted to fight back to show our resilience and strength. But we needed a little time. We needed a timeout. It was the absolute best thing that happened at that time. It was a great move for our country.

And I'm a firm believer that it all started with the New York Jets. I will always be extremely proud of the courage that the Jets showed that day. It was the right thing to do and a great message for our country.

Zebras

When the season continued, we fought our way into the playoffs, and my group got better each week. Herman was heavily criticized by the media for his poor clock management—they said he seemed "frozen" on the sideline. In some ways, that was correct. He didn't call plays or defenses, and he left me completely alone. He wasn't a major contributor in game planning, and maybe he could have gotten better prepared for game and clock management.

But something that he did well was graphically demonstrate how turnovers and penalties affected winning and losing.

After having worked with Coach Shula for so many years, I was very aware of the rules of the game and officiating. When I arrived in New York, I told Herman that I wanted to be in charge of officiating. I wanted to hire officials for our practices and be involved with every aspect.

Bill Parcells had hired two veteran NFL officials to officiate his practices. Tony Veteri was a retired game official and supervisor, and Joe Yacovino, who ran the clock for Giants games for twenty-five years and officiated the team's practices for ten years, then did it for the Jets for twenty-three years. Those guys were the greatest. They became my close friends, knew the game exceptionally well, and worked their tails off.

With their help over the years, I was able to hire very qualified officials for our practices. Either college or really experienced high school officials. Jimmy Quirk and Wayne Mackie were hired from our practices and their college jobs into the NFL. Jimmy was still on the field in 2021, and Wayne retired from NFL games and worked in the league office.

How well did it all work? For my first eight years in New York, with both Herman and then Eric Mangini, the Jets were the least-penalized team in the NFL overall. Do you want to win some games? Be the least-penalized team.

To go a step further, with Rex Ryan, we took one of our officials, Bob Miller—a golf pro and the head of high school officials on Long Island—and put him in charge of replay challenges. He studied the rules regarding challenges and the tendencies of the various referees and their crews. He was with us for each game and helped Rex with his decisions as to whether to challenge a call. During the time that Bob Miller had this role, we led the NFL in challenge successes.

Those guys helped us win a lot of games. For a team that didn't have a quarterback that anyone would trade for, we were in the playoffs 50 percent of the time that I was in New York. Due to a lot of the little things in my twelve years in New York, we sure as hell were not the "same old Jets."

While in New York, I took full advantage of a unique opportunity. Due to our proximity to the NFL headquarters in Manhattan, I got to know the league's supervisor of officials, Mike Pereira, and was able to spend some valuable time in his office. I would take the train into the city and meet with Mike and his staff and learn everything that I could about NFL officiating. I sat in there and listened while they explained to me how the officials were taught to make calls. I then could take this knowledge and relay it to my players.

I also worked with Mike on several rule changes. These all involved special teams, and I am proud of my small role in the changes.

My first rule change involvement came after the 2002 season. Dante Hall, for whom I have great respect, was selected to the AFC Pro Bowl squad, and I was furious. I believed our returner, Chad Morton, deserved the honor. Dante had, in my opinion, taken full advantage of a terrible rule that stated that if on a punt return the returner signaled for a fair catch and the ball hit the ground, then all bets were off. In other words, the fair catch signal was nullified, and the returner could field and advance the ball.

That year, Dante had twice signaled for a fair catch and, as the coverage slowed down, he fielded the ball off the turf and returned it for a touchdown. It was a terrible rule—and I helped change it to where it now reads that if you signal for a fair catch, you cannot return the ball.

Dante Hall, for as great as he was, wouldn't have had those TDs, and Chad Morton would have gone to the Pro Bowl.

Secondly, I got involved with a rule that stated if on punt coverage a covering player was to step out of bounds, he could not make a play when he came back in on the ball. We changed that to read that a player who goes out of bounds and returns legally cannot make the first play on the ball. It was a good change—but the rule truly should be changed to read that if a player is blocked out of bounds legally and he re-enters the field legally, he should be able to make a play on the ball anytime.

I argued for this rule change, but I met stiff opposition from Bill Polian, the Hall of Fame executive who was on the NFL's Competition Committee. He stated that the rule change would encourage players to let themselves get blocked out of bounds so that they could use the cover of the sideline when running down the field.

Every official I ever talked to thought that it would be a great rule change. I had coached through that entire process a hundred times, and Polian hadn't.

I was very involved in numerous rule changes, and I very much appreciated my relationship with Mike Pereira. I cherished the opportunity to learn so much from him. On Mondays, while on the phone with him discussing what I felt were his officials' missed calls on Sunday, I wanted to kill him. But I respected him and felt he was responsible for moving NFL officiating to what I believe was its all-time highest prominence.

Roller Coaster Years

My five years in New York with Herman Edwards were like a roller coaster—dramatic, euphoric highs and gut-wrenching lows.

During that first year, we fought through 9/11, restarted the season by beating New England while watching our linebacker

Mo Lewis drill their quarterback, Drew Bledsoe—and then watched the emergence of Tom Brady.

We traveled out to Oakland and beat the Raiders in our postponed 9/11 game at the end of the schedule in what was one of my all-time favorite wins, and that propelled us into the playoffs.

We had a great special teams performance, with Chris Hayes blocking a punt for a touchdown, and a pressure-filled field goal by John Hall to seal the victory. That level of special teams play in a crucial moment set the bar for me for the remainder of my career.

One more of "my guys" who epitomized the type of special teams player anyone would want to coach was Chris Hayes.

Chris Hayes

Chris was a defensive back out of Los Angeles who went to Washington State and was drafted by the Jets in the seventh round in 1996, No. 210 overall. He played his first season with Green Bay, though, then five years with the Jets and one with New England.

Chris was the consummate special teams player. Yes, he was a defensive back, but he had virtually no interest in that. He loved special teams, he would sneak out of defensive meetings and come into my office, close the door, and sit with me and study special teams game plans. As much as I loved it, after a few minutes I would send him back to where he was supposed to be.

Regardless, Chris *figured it out.*

"I leaned on Mike more than any of those other guys who coached me. He was my guy, my coach. Not Bill Parcells or even Bill Belichick. The guy who really coached me was Mike," Chris said.

"As a player, the first thing you learn about Mike is his passion for the game from the perspective of special teams. That role played a big part for players such as myself—and so many others he was able to provide a career for. There are so many of us who owe so much to Mike for turning special teams into a NFL career."

Chris loved the various roles that I gave him. We would sit in my office and study our opponent and find a weakness that Chris could exploit. He could cover both kickoffs and punts, and block on returns, but his greatest skills were blocking punts and downing the ball on punts inside the 10-yard line.

"With Mike, it was always educational," Chris explained. "He was teaching us the game; the dude was so detailed that in practice he would teach me something like to look at how the ball was spinning so I could know where to down the ball on the one-yard line on a punt."

Without Chris' recovery of a blocked punt for a touchdown against Carolina and his blocked punt for a TD against Oakland, we frankly would not have won those games—or gotten into the playoffs.

So, it was a typical Chris Hayes moment that occurred in the final game of the 2001 season at Oakland. The Raiders had just driven for a score and taken the lead. I had huddled the kickoff return team and was getting ready to show a drawing of the upcoming play and talk about it. Chris walked into the huddle and asked me if he could say something to the players.

Normally, I completely dominated the huddle. But I said sure and stepped back.

Chris said: "Take a look at that fucking bench. You think those mothers are ready to win? We have to win this game. Not them. Us!"

We ran a good return up to near midfield and were able to punt Oakland into a hole when our offense couldn't move. Our defense kept them there and made them punt. Chris blocked the punt for a Jets touchdown and gave us a chance to win.

A short while later we were driving with that chance to win, and with just time for one last play, Herman Edwards was yelling for our offensive coordinator, Paul Hackett, to throw a "Hail Mary." I stepped in and sent John Hall on the field to attempt one of the longest field goals ever in that stadium, 53 yards.

BAM—Hall made the kick, and we made the playoffs.

Chris Hayes was correct. We had to win that game and I believe that we—special teams—did win it.

Chris is not a fan of the current NFL, where it's much more difficult for special teams to make that kind of impact.

"The way football is moving today, they are removing part of the game we all loved," he said. "We had guys who were willing to sacrifice everything for special teams, and it helped us to win. Thanks to Mike."

I loved Chris Hayes, how he studied, played, and thought. He believed that he could make the play that would win the game, and I believe that is exactly what Chris did. He will, in every possible way, always be one of "my guys."

Following that postponed 9/11 victory in Oakland, as always, I was either the first one dressed and out of the locker room, or the last one. Following this game, I was first. I was happy and proud, and as I did many times in my career, I went back into the empty stadium, sat in the stands, and reflected. Those were times I cherished and relived the game or sat and deeply reflected on a mistake or failure on my part. As I sat there in the empty stadium, I relished the creative and excellent performance that "my guys" had just given.

I can remember telling myself that I probably wasn't going to get everything I wanted as a coach in the NFL. Due to a number of reasons, a head coaching opportunity probably wasn't going to come my way. But if I did it right, I could make a real difference. Our coverage was superb and hard to block. Bud Carson's defensive blitzing concepts were working nearly exactly as he had described. My kickoff return scheme looked as though we might score every time. I didn't have a punter who could kick the ball out of his bedroom, but what we were doing with the protection, formation, and coverage was innovative and effective.

Our punt block and return team were different on every play and could scare opponents to death. Moving players to different spots nearly every snap was giving our opponents headaches and creating big plays for us.

Aa I sat in that crummy Oakland stadium, at night and by myself, I told myself that I could change the game. I know this might be thought to be arrogant, but yes, I believe I actually did that. And at least most everyone will acknowledge that I greatly aided in changing the kicking game in the National Football League.

Just recently I was rewatching a movie I had seen several times and very much enjoyed. *Moneyball*, starring Brad Pitt in what I believe was one of his best acting performances, portraying Billy Beane, the general manager of baseball's Oakland Athletics. He was coaching a major league team with the lowest budget and absolute worst facilities, and—through a very creative method of analytics—put together a championship team.

Following one of their games, which Beane would personally never attend—instead sitting in the locker room or weight room and listening to the radio—he did go into that empty, completely rundown stadium. He sat there, at night, with his assistant GM/analytics guy, and talked about the season. The A's had moved from last place and were starting to climb up the ladder. Beane said if they could win a championship—his only goal, by the way, with MLB's worst budget and facility—and get this motley group of players to have success by following their creative but unusual pattern, they could change the game.

He could change Major League Baseball.

Believe it or not, following our great win in Oakland, I sat by myself in that crummy empty stadium and knew that I could change the game.

By getting into the playoffs with that great win, it earned us a return trip to Oakland. After leading at the half in that playoff game, we lost to the Raiders in a hard-fought contest.

Special Jets

The special teams units I was able to develop with Herman Edwards were unquestionably some of the league's best. Our 2002 group helped the Jets win the AFC East. Players such as John Hall, Santana Moss, Chad Morton, Jamie Henderson, Chris Hayes, Jason Glenn, and James Dearth were exceptional.

In our opening game in Buffalo, we excelled in every aspect of special teams, included two kickoff return touchdowns by Chad Morton—a 98-yarder, and then a 96-yarder to start and end the overtime. It was arguably the best special teams game ever played.

We were a very good team, with two Hall of Famers, running back Curtis Martin and center Kevin Mawae. We had three top wide receivers in Santana Moss, Wayne Chrebet, and Laveranues Coles. Our offensive line was very solid, and Vinny Testaverde and Chad Pennington were the quarterbacks.

Vinny was the saddest case for me. It was nearing the end of his career, and he just didn't move as well. But he could throw the ball like few others. Paul Hackett was the offensive coordinator, a West Coast offense guy. He was a good coach, but he did not believe in the shotgun formation. Vinny was up under center and had to drop back each time.

From the shotgun, Vinny would have been unstoppable. Dan Marino, who was doing the CBS studio show at the time, called me one day and said, "Mike, if that stupid ass will play Vinny in the shotgun, you will go to the Super Bowl."

Coaching is about adjusting to people. Not putting Vinny in the shotgun was the stupidest coaching non-move I have ever witnessed. Yeah, we were good—but could have been so much better.

Chad Pennington took us further, but after his shoulder injury in 2004, he couldn't throw across the street, and we were headed downward.

The first game of my second year in New York was that overtime win up in Buffalo. Pennington emerged as the quarterback and helped lead us back into the playoffs. A 41-0 win over Peyton Manning and the Colts was, in my opinion—and next to Joe Namath's guaranteed Super Bowl victory over the Baltimore Colts—the most dominant playoff victory in Jets history. Everything we did that day was outstanding. We ran up and down the field and threw and caught everything. On our only kickoff return, Chad Morton went 70 yards. And our defense totally stymied Peyton Manning.

In a side note to that game: that year, I got the Jets to hire Chris Mattura, the former high school and local college coach who grew up in and lived in New York City. Chris worked for us at Miami doing advanced pregame scouting. Chris is a brilliant football guy. He watched film twenty-four hours a day and worked like a demon. Chris helped both our offense and defense as an intern and adviser; his contributions were outstanding.

Chris came up with an idea to time Peyton Manning at the line of scrimmage. We would line up in a particular defense and then quickly shift to another look. Peyton would see this shift and begin to adjust. Then, after a prescribed amount of time, we would shift again. This threw Peyton for a loop. They had to call some timeouts and got numerous delay-of-game penalties.

It was a brilliant plan and kept Peyton off the board. And it was set up by a guy Herman Edwards said "would never coach in this league."

Sometimes we shouldn't judge a book solely by its cover.

"Beginning in the summer of 1989 through the summer of 1995, I visited the Miami Dolphins training camp to assist in developing my craft as a college football coach," Chris recalled. "Don Shula was the head coach, and no stone was left unturned. The practices were crisp and abnormally short. There was no standing around. The completion time was less than two hours on a daily basis.

"Besides the pace of practice, one thing stood out to me. Miami's special teams coordinator, Mike Westhoff, conducted one of the fastest and most aggressive practices I had ever witnessed. But why was he always squeezing a blue racquetball during practice? I had read that Mike had overcome osteogenic sarcoma in one of his legs, but nothing was ever written about some type of hand/wrist injury.

"It was about seven to ten years later when I found out one of the reasons Mike was strengthening his hands and wrists. He needed to work on circulation. Squeezing the ball in both hands would do that. Squeezing the ball certainly did not only improve his circulation, but it served another purpose. Now I know why Mike continues to this day to squeeze a blue racquetball. He has unbelievable hand strength to deal with the sharks he fishes for.

"Meeting Mike in 1996 has been an invaluable benefit for me as a person and football lifer. Mike pursued getting me hired with the New York Jets the same way his special teams units attacked returners. He mapped out a plan, walked me through it, and executed it to perfection. I also believe I did my part by watching film relentlessly and with purpose.

"I started out as a training camp intern, then was promoted to a part-time special projects coach, and then eventually to a full-time, on-the-field coaching position as a paid defensive assistant.

"Mike and I talked football, education, politics, authors, and the best restaurants in New York City. Mike took tremendous advantage of New York City. He lived on Long Island [and] worked at the Jets' complex at Hofstra, but all his other waking hours were in New York City, specifically Manhattan.

"I was with Mike at Elio's having dinner as Tom Selleck, along with his agent, sat at their normal corner table when the New Orleans Saints called Mike [in 2017]. Mike and the Saints had a great run, only to be upended on their trip to the Super Bowl by a great catch and a non-call.

"Mike Westhoff has been a mentor, big brother, and unwavering supporter of me as a person and football mind. Who could ask for more?

"Just ask, and Mike will be there for you."

Herman's Demise

In 2004, we were back in the playoffs for the third time in four years—something the Jets had never done before and haven't done since. But we lost in Pittsburgh in one of my most frustrating games as a coach.

We won a crazy playoff game in San Diego and then headed to Pittsburgh. In a restaurant in Point Lookout, New York, I was celebrating New Year's Eve at dinner with my girlfriend, Patti. Point Lookout is a cool little town on the south shore of Long Island. The town resembles a New England fishing village and was the perfect place for a hopefully romantic New Year's Eve dinner.

Patti is a big sports fan, and we were talking about the upcoming game. I told her that I felt great about a punt return and believed I could hurt Pittsburgh with it.

The table had a paper tablecloth, and I asked the waitress for a pen. I drew the entire punt return I was planning to use: "Double Vise-Bandit Blue."

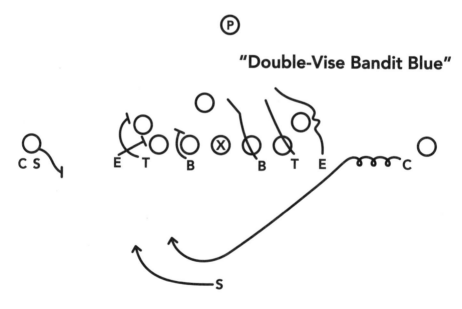

"Double-Vise Bandit Blue"

I would fake a rush, which is Bandit; pressure from my right and force the punt to our left. Blue was a left return, and we would turn a rush look into a return.

It worked perfectly. Santana Moss ran it for a 75-yard touchdown. I think Patti still has the drawing.

That game was cold and wet, typical for Pittsburgh in January, and the field was sloppy. A terrible place to kick anytime, and this particular day was no exception.

With two minutes left and the scored tied 17-17, our kicker Doug Brien missed a 47-yard field goal—47 yards for him on this field on that day was Herculean. He hit the crossbar, and that is about as far as he could kick it. Heinz Field had one of the lowest field goal success percentages in the NFL, and that day showed exactly why.

On the next play, we got a break and got the ball back when David Barrett intercepted Ben Roethlisberger and returned it 24 yards to the Steelers 37. We had two timeouts and the ball.

We got it to the Steelers 25-yard line with :56 remaining in regulation. I made it clear we needed to get inside the 20-yard line to attempt a more realistic field goal under these conditions.

We ran two plays and gained only two yards and called a timeout. Don't forget that we had an excellent offensive line and Curtis Martin. But with six seconds left, we took a knee, losing a yard, and called timeout.

Possibly the worst play calling and clock management anywhere. Ever!

I know a field goal from the 24-yard line should be made in the NFL, but it would take all of Doug's strength to make that kick, on that field, on that day. He muscled it, hooked it, and kicked the ball into the Steelers' locker room, I think.

My bubble had completely burst. We lost in overtime and went home.

The next year we really struggled and kind of fell apart. Herman departed for Kansas City following the season, and an entire new era was beginning for the New York Jets.

Herman Edwards did a lot of good things for the Jets and then went on to coach the Chiefs. But the part that I will never understand was his firing of so many assistant coaches.

I read an article about business philosophy prevalent in Japan during the 1990s in which they pretty much dominated the modern business world. It was believed that you solved problems by discovering solutions, not affixing blame. Herman affixed blame.

I should have done a better job and intervened. I will take some of the blame, but not much because this has been a consistent occurrence in his entire coaching career. It could possibly be argued that he has fired more coaches per time as a head coach than anyone in football. He fired our defensive coordinator, Teddy Cottrell, who in my opinion was an excellent coach, and replaced him with a guy who probably has been fired more than anyone ever in football history, Donnie Henderson. He had been fired by the Mighty Mites, the Junior Varsity, and maybe the Little Sisters of the Poor.

This guy has been fired by everyone and he replaced Teddy Cottrell? Affixing blame and consistently firing coaches is not the solution for long-term success.

Man-Genius

Following his departure from the Jets, Herman Edwards didn't have much success with the Kansas City Chiefs, and he moved on to work for ESPN before going back to coaching at Arizona State.

I'd had four good years with the Jets. My units had ranked near the top every year and had become explosive and innovative. But it was a different NFL from today for special teams.

Players in the league now would have absolutely no idea what to do in all the variables that we presented on every play. On kickoff coverage today, the players are neatly lined up, with five on each side of the kick. They basically run straight down the field.

We lined up everywhere and anywhere and ran downfield a million different ways. It would be like the defense lining up in one look and blitzing from all over the place. I was proud of the creativity and success that we had generated with the Jets.

I was the assistant head coach, and with the notable exception of not preventing nearly all our coaches from getting fired, I was proud of how I handled that role, too. I helped with clock management, coach's challenges, and penalties. I hired and worked closely with our practice officials; together, we made the Jets the least-penalized team in the league.

So, I asked for an opportunity to interview for the head-coaching position. I believed that I was prepared. Being a special teams coordinator, especially in the multifaceted time I held that role, I believed that the complexity of the job was excellent preparation for head coaching.

The special teams coach deals with the entire team. Each week, the number of active players affects the special teams more than any other. Reacting to situations is a special teams necessity and a head coaching necessity. The next time an offensive or defensive coordinator looks at the scoreboard to check the time will be his first time.

Offensive coordinators and game management? Please! They would complete a pass and then think they had won the Super Bowl. Ask Atlanta fans about the second-half play calling with a 28-3 lead versus New England in the 2017 Super Bowl, and you will get some idea of offensive game management.

I worked with Don Shula and Jimmy Johnson. Coach Shula called plays; Jimmy certainly did not. But both were very good at managing the game. I learned a lot from everyone I worked with and believed I was well prepared to be a head coach. I sure would have *figured it out*.

You know, I figured everything else out pretty damn well—and Terry Bradway, the Jets general manager in 2006, sure wasn't going to tell me differently. It didn't really matter that I had zero chance of getting the job.

Several candidates were interviewed, which really didn't matter. The Jets were going to follow in the footsteps of the New England Patriots, a team they often followed in the standings.

Mike Tannenbaum, the personnel director, was locked into Eric Mangini. They had spent time together in Cleveland and were well acquainted. Mangini was a young New England assistant and was preparing to execute a move worthy of Harry Houdini.

Bradway conducted my interview. I said that I would only interview if the owner, Woody Johnson, would be in attendance. I had done well in my job, was under contract, and they didn't want to lose me. But they were only doing me a favor, and no way was I being considered.

Bradway didn't interview me; he interviewed himself, as it looked as though his job also might be in jeopardy. (He was correct in that assessment).

I know that I could've been a successful head coach. Everything I did in the NFL I excelled at. But it didn't matter what I said that day, the die was cast.

Several weeks later, after Eric had been hired and I had agreed to stay with the Jets—and Bradway's and Tannenbaum's roles had miraculously been reversed—I thanked Terry for the opportunity. I also told him that his interview had been horseshit. He countered by telling me that I hadn't even ranked in the top whatever.

He was somewhat correct in the ranking, but it was notably reversed. I ended up ranked at the top of my profession and, as a general manager, he was not even on anyone's fucking list. When he was the GM, he worked in New York and lived in a house in south New Jersey. The rest of us in the building marveled at his lack of attendance. We were sure if Woody Johnson was fully aware of it, Bradway would have been fired.

Almost every one of the players who talked to us for this book said they thought I would have been a good head coach. Did any of them say that about Terry Bradway as a general manager? I must have missed those comments if they did.

So, Mike Tannenbaum was the general manager, and his old friend Eric Mangini became the head coach. How did that happen? You will probably need to consult Albert Einstein to figure it out.

I had never met Eric, didn't know him at all, and at first I couldn't have been more unimpressed. I thought that he was a complete know-it-all pain in the ass. But as time progressed, I saw a good coach. He had a good vision of how to build an NFL team.

There's an interesting dynamic concerning Bill Belichick's assistant coaches. Other than Nick Saban, who has dominated college football at Alabama—but failed miserably in the NFL—none of Belichick's coaches has accomplished very much. I am currently holding out on Joe Judge with the New York Giants. I am impressed with him and believe that he will be successful.

Bill Belichick is an excellent coach, but trying to become him may not be the smartest approach.

Eric Mangini had learned a lot from Bill and did a strong job of incorporating many of his ideas. His attention to detail evaluating personnel and managing game situations was off the charts. His dealing with people was also off the charts—in the opposite direction.

Mangini's drafting and signing of free agents, and even tryout guys, was very good. Darrelle Revis, D'Brickashaw Ferguson, and Nick Mangold were draft examples. James Ihedigbo, Eric Smith, and Blake Costanzo were less notable but valuable NFL contributors.

I signed Blake, a linebacker from Lafayette, as a free agent. We had him on our practice squad, and I didn't want to lose him.

I received a call from Buffalo, one of our main competitors and a division rival. I didn't want to see him elsewhere, but I wanted to help him. I told their coach he would be their best special teams player. I was absolutely correct, and he eventually led Buffalo, San Francisco, and Chicago as their best special teams guy. For a period of about five years, it could be argued he was the NFL's top special teamer.

Eric did a hell of a job assembling personnel. His detail in addressing game and clock situations was outstanding. From studying film of situations to very diligently practicing them, he was exceptional.

But, in my opinion, he failed in two areas.

We practiced crazily, way too much and far too long. We lost more players in practice than ever should have happened. He eventually backed off some, probably to avoid a rebellion.

He also was poor at talking to the players. He always seemed to be talking somewhat down to them, in a condescending manner. Eric had a way of being irritating. Coaches need to be forthright, but communication skills are critical. Corrections are a constant and integral part of coaching, but there is a fine line between corrections and criticism. Coaches must know the difference.

I kept a sign in my office reminding me of this: "Put some space between your anger and your intellect." Mistakes can make you angry. Know how to correct, not criticize. I am not sure that Eric ever saw that line very well.

In a team meeting, he would ask the kickers to tell the team about the opponent's defensive line. I know it was all about attention to detail, but it came across as intimidation—no one appreciates being intimidated.

In regards to Eric, I believe it was purely a lack of maturity. As I got to know him, I began to see through all that bullshit. I saw an intelligent, hard-working, and very caring person. He just couldn't get out of his own way. He wanted to be Bill Belichick and just couldn't pull it off.

I believe if I had been with him longer, I could have helped smooth him out. He is a good man and a good coach.

Eric let me do anything that I wanted with my area. He never questioned or criticized me in any fashion—except once.

I was doing a punt team drill that I had run a million times. We were working on the protection and, as a team, punting and releasing and covering five yards in the punt's direction. I was very intently coaching the interior of the punt team, and one my assistants was checking the release of our flyers and gunners in the opposition's double-vise.

In watching the film, Eric complimented me on how hard the punt team was practicing, but with the notable exception of the flyers, whose work he described as a "glorified walk-through." I was furious. No one had ever been critical of anything that I was coaching in that manner. I was fuming.

But he was correct. They were, for the most part, just going through the motions. I changed that. I made it clear in a film session that the interior of the punt team was working their asses off, and the flyers basically weren't doing shit, and it was completely my fault.

"One thing he has never done is shy away from responsibility," my son John noted. "If something went right, he deserved the credit. But when things went wrong, which wasn't too often, he took the blame. I know players respect a coach who does that."

Yep. In my career, I am sure that my critics would say that I had absolutely no trouble accepting praise, but what they will never fully understand is that I was so much more adept at accepting criticism and blame. When it was my fault, I completely accepted that. I was harder on myself than I ever was on my players and assistants. When I was wrong, I was wrong—and I only strived to improve.

I then demanded that the players must now release and run eight yards full speed, and the defense must do everything to stop them on every punt. After three punts, I would stop the interior guys and only the flyers would have to release and cover all the way to the ball. Full speed versus the defense and everyone had better be going full speed.

I also instructed our film crew to zoom in on each guy and film a "candid camera" shot. During the film session, the entire screen was taken up by only one player, and the entire special teams group would be watching him in what looked like a drive-in movie. That got their attention. And mine.

I did it for the rest of my career.

I wanted to kill Eric, but what he said was absolutely correct and made me a better coach.

Eric's first year in New York, 2006, was outstanding. We finished 10-6 and earned a playoff spot. He was praised by the media as Eric Man-Genius.

After that season, I lost Sam Gash as my assistant coach.

"That one year I was with Mike I was hoping we'd get into the playoffs, and we did with Mangini—and basically riding on our special teams is how," Sam said. "After that year, Mangini called me into his office and told me what I was doing with Mike wasn't worth the money they were paying me. I kind of had told Mike 'I don't think I will be here,' and Mike said, 'No you will be here,' so I was expecting to be there.

"But then Mangini and Tannenbaum came in and said they would cut my salary and 'will pay you $50,000.' I said no. I had a couple kids and living in New York is expensive.

"Mike helped me get to Detroit, and I ended up getting a running backs coach position. But I should have stayed with special teams. I should have fought harder to stay in New York with Mike. I would have been Mike's assistant for the rest of my career, but I would not have cared."

In 2007, it all fell apart. We had a number of injuries, our quarterback play was terrible, and we finished 4-12. From 10-6 to 4-12 is as rough as it can get, but it was like a drop in the bucket compared to what was ahead for me in my personal life.

More Health Issues

For years following my allograft surgery in 1988, I had battled problems with my leg. I broke the graft and had two major surgeries to repair it. After moving to New York in 2001, I was introduced to Dr. John Healey at Memorial Sloan Kettering. He had been an assistant to Dr. Henry Mankin at Mass General Hospital in Boston, but he had moved to New York to head up the oncological orthopedics program. Sloan Kettering is at the head of the class in that area. Dr. Healey is the absolute best in his profession.

I was most unfortunate with some of my health issues, yet I was also the luckiest guy in the world to be under the very best possible care. Dr. Healey had done everything to aid in the very complex healing process of my surgery. I wore a bone stem device attached to a battery pack that I carried in my pocket. It emitted an electrical impulse to my leg to help with bone healing. The only time I removed it was to shower.

It helped some but not enough. So Dr. Healey performed a lengthy and complicated surgery to redo some of the previous surgery and insert bone chips from my hip into my femur to stimulate growth. But even though there was improvement, it was just not enough to completely strengthen and heal. A full leg brace and cane were always needed.

"Coach Mike Westhoff was my new commander, whose leadership, guidance, and mentorship would prove invaluable not only to myself but, more importantly, to one of the league's best special teams units," said Ben Kotwica, a West Point graduate who had become my top assistant. "His ability to command a room and impart instruction in such a tone and manner inspired our players with an intense desire to obey and succeed. Whether it be in a unit meeting in the auditorium or on the field for a walk-through or practice, Coach led the way.

"His cane, which aided his movement during the early part of our tenure, served in part as his staff: pointing out his troops' direction on the battlefield. In addition, this 'staff' also served as an instrument of frustration when things did not go a certain way—it would be thrust onto the field in disgust.

"As the aide-de-camp, part of my duties was to retrieve this staff 10 to 20 yards downfield and return it to its rightful owner."

As you surely can tell, Ben has a strong military background, more of which I will describe later.

"All the players were aware of his health issues," added Leon Washington. "We understand. We are football players and deal with injuries all the time. This man had to have hip or knee replacements, and he's standing on sidelines with some pain and coaching his ass off. That is how we thought about him. Another reason you want to play hard for Mike Westhoff."

Following X-rays and meeting with Dr. Healey in the fall of 2007, he told me, my son, John—who had graduated from the University of Pennsylvania and was living and working in Manhattan and always accompanied me on my doctor visits—that a "radical" surgery was needed to maybe save my leg. He showed me a drawing of a very large metal prosthetic that would replace most of my femur. It looked like something that belonged in a car, not my leg.

I reminded him I was going to be sixty years old, and this seemed like a lot to undertake. He assured me that he could do it and that I would handle the surgery. I remember leaving his office and going down Second Avenue to Elio's to have a late dinner. Yes, Elio's is my favorite restaurant in New York, but that night we just pretty much just sat there and worried about the future.

John is the greatest. He told me, "Dad, I don't think that you have a choice. Dr. Healey is the best, and he is worried about your leg. This will work. I will be there every second."

As always, he was.

"I was lucky to be too young when his first more serious battles with cancer occurred," John said. "There wasn't an obstacle that he was afraid of. He didn't have excuses. If he had to coach with a cane, he did it. When he was with the Saints, people didn't know … he was coaching with a fractured hip. He's never been one to make excuses.

"I was there every week for the meetings in New York and the doctor appointments. He had to learn the hard way you really have to be your own advocate.

"He was fortunate to find the right doctors. And he has never settled. He's never been intimidated by them either; he would ask questions, all the important questions. Of course, he was respectful of them. His case is so unique, and he knew everything about it, as much as anybody."

John has been with me for all my New York and Indianapolis surgeries. Patti, my girlfriend, was also with John for the surgeries, and the two of them waited for hours in the hospital waiting rooms. They were always the first people I saw when coming to. Hearing "Dad, Dad, wake up"—it doesn't get much better than that.

The surgery was set for January 2007—and now my world was really going to change.

Following discussions with Dr. Healey and Troy Hershberger of Biomet, I began to prepare for a very complex surgery. Installing the new implant, even though it was a first of its kind, wasn't the hardest part. Removing all of my previous "orthopedic train wreck" was going to be demanding of anyone, including the industry's very best, Dr. Healey. It was tedious and time-consuming work and would result in substantial blood loss.

This was going to probably result in at least a stop to my coaching career, or even possibly the end of it. There also were some changes of direction.

"During a New York appointment with Dr. Healey, he was talking about building a new piece for dad's leg. My father is weighing it out and says to me, 'I don't like this idea.' Sure enough we're at the next appointment and Dr. Healey said, 'This is not the right move.' My dad is one to ask the questions. He's not afraid to speak up for himself."

I had one year remaining on my contract, and the Jets could not have been more gracious. They were greatly concerned with my well-being and made everything easy as possible for me. I would take a yearlong medical leave of absence. I would stay on my NFL medical insurance and be paid normally.

The Jets had always been great to me, and I will be eternally grateful to the owner, Woody Johnson, and the entire organization.

I spent part of January finishing up the season and helping them find a replacement coach. My assistant, Ben Kotwica, who frankly should have been promoted, was going to stay and helped with the interviews. Kevin O'Dea, a longtime NFL assistant, did a good job in the interview and was hired to take my place.

I now began preparing myself for a life without football. I contacted Susan Bratten, who works for AON, a company that manages pensions and did so for the NFL. There is not an NFL coach who doesn't know Susan. She knows every rule and situation and will walk you through every option and scenario. She is the best.

Because of my long NFL service, I had qualified for an early retirement. The "Rule of Seventy-Five" basically required one to have at least fifteen years of NFL service, and if that plus your age (minimum of fifty-nine) added up to seventy-five, you would be eligible for early retirement. The last NFL team you were with paid 80 percent of your insurance, and you were paid an annuity based on the average of your highest five years of salary. When you reached age sixty-five, you became eligible for Medicare, and you were able to accept your full pension.

So the "Rule of Seventy-Five" is a bridge retirement plan to help you get to age sixty-five and full retirement benefits.

Susan directed me through all this, and I was prepared after one year to move on to a completely new life.

As a young coach with the Miami Dolphins, I was part of an organization called the NFL Coaches Association. It resembled a union and informally worked to enhance our salaries and pensions. Little did I know that those efforts might now dramatically affect my life.

The surgery, as complicated and tough as it gets, lasted twelve hours. Plain and simple, it beat the hell out of me. About a month after the surgery, I was back at Memorial Sloan Kettering for an X-ray and follow-up visit with Dr. Healey. As I was sitting in an X-ray room, a technician walked in and asked if I remembered him. I told him I was sorry, but I did not. He said he had been on duty for my surgery, and he had never seen anything like it before in his career. He told me he would take an X-ray, Dr. Healey would examine it, and then go back into my leg and remove a piece of metal or fragmented bone.

Over and over, he did this until the entire area was cleaned out and prepared for the metal femur. This took so long that the X-ray technician had to be relieved. He told me that Dr. Healey was like no other surgeon he had ever observed.

He told me, "I don't know how he could do what he did for so long. The guy is incredible."

John and Patti were there when I woke up after the surgery, and I was again assured that everything would be fine. I was released from the hospital, went back to my apartment in Garden City, and began my rehab ordeal.

I am a hard worker and very disciplined. I spent twenty-four hours a day getting better. I went to rehab, walked, exercised, and ate—all to fight and get back to normal. I can remember walking in my apartment building down to the elevator and back. That, at first, was a big day. The next thing you know, I am walking all over town. I believe I was able to push myself as hard as anyone, and I just kept getting better and better.

After a few months, I was walking normally and riding my bike all over Long Island. Dr. Healey agreed to let me return to my home in Florida, and now I was walking or riding my bike every day and swimming and exercising in the pool. I was even going out on my boat and back for shark fishing. One thing I knew for sure, though, was that my football career was not over by any means.

The Shit Hits the Fan

As the summer approached, I hired an agent. I didn't need his help to get me a job, but rather which one I would take. With the approach of NFL training camps, I contacted the Tampa Bay Buccaneers, my good friend Joe "Joe D" DeCamillis at Jacksonville, and Bill Parcells with the Miami Dolphins.

I asked each of them if I could visit and observe their practices. I wanted to get back into the feeling of the NFL and also let the media see that I was fine and wanted to return to coaching.

My Tampa visit was canceled due to a terrible storm, but I spent two great days with Joe D in Jacksonville and watched the Jaguars' preseason game with Miami after spending some quality time with Joe discussing Xs and Os. It felt great; I loved being back in that environment.

I was eager to drive from my home in Fort Myers to Miami and to visit with Bill Parcells. I had known Bill from my playing and his coaching days at Wichita State, and I had talked with him many times during my career. He talked with me about joining his coaching staff on two occasions. One was in 2001, which didn't materialize, and then also with him in Dallas. I was under contract with the Jets, and he said that he could hire someone for one year and then I could join him.

I said "thank you," but I just couldn't do that. It didn't feel right to me, and knowing what I do now, it was for the best.

I had always admired Bill and appreciated my relationship with him. We talked many times, and I really looked up to him. He was a great help to me on many subjects. I saw him as something of a big brother, if you will. No, not in a familial manner, but just someone for advice and direction.

But then the shit hit the fan.

My best friend in Fort Myers is a retired policeman named Frank Mikaska. He accompanied me over to Miami to watch the Dolphins practice and visit with Coach Parcells. We ate lunch with Bill and then went out to watch practice. I rode with Bill in his golf cart, and Frank sat in the family section of the stands.

Bill and I spent the entire practice observing and discussing training camp practice in general. Following the practice, Tony Sparano, the newly appointed head coach, came over to talk with Coach Parcells and was introduced to me. After a few minutes of talking, Tony asked me an interesting question. He wanted to know if there was anything special about the practice that I had noticed.

I was very honest with him. It was a typical terribly hot and humid South Florida August afternoon, and his team had been out, in my opinion, way too long. I had coached there for fifteen years, so I was very familiar with the Florida sun and heat. I told him that most of his practice looked sharp and well organized, but the last forty-five minutes were terrible.

Before the practice started, they had conducted a walk-through outside. The "big guys" were out too long; it is too humid and hot for those guys. At the end of practice, they could hardly move.

I told him that Coach Shula, who conducted very hard practices, never had a training camp practice that lasted more than one hour, twenty minutes. Including the walk-through, this group had been out for nearly three hours. Too damn long!

Tony told me that made a lot of sense and thanked me.

The media approached Coach Parcells to conduct his post-practice interview. Many of them recognized me and asked how I was doing. I told them that I was feeling great and that someday I would return to coaching.

Frank and I thanked everyone, especially Bill for his kindness and generosity. It was a great day and made me more eager than ever to return to the NFL.

Then it got crazy.

A little while after I left Miami, the Jets traded for Brett Favre. A week later I got a call from Mike Tannenbaum, now the general manager, and Eric Mangini. They told me that Brett looked great and had turned the entire team around. All of a sudden, they looked pretty damn good.

But they thought their special teams were awful, and they wanted me to return. Eric had no confidence in Kevin O'Dea and wanted to replace him as soon as possible. I believe that if Eric had some patience, things would have been fine with Kevin, but the damage was done and there was no turning it around.

I said no, I was gone from the Jets and could not go back.

Eric and Mike didn't give up. They offered me a new contract and a lot of money. I still said no.

After about a week of calls, I told them I was returning to New York for a visit with Dr. Healey and I would see what he had to say.

Dr. Healey examined me and looked at X-rays at Memorial Sloan Kettering and was extremely pleased. He said he wanted to talk with me, and asked everyone, including Patti, to leave the room, and then he closed the door.

He told me had been reading the papers and knew that the Jets were trying to get me to return. He said that if I didn't want to return, he could easily say no, and that would be the end of it all. He preferred that I not return to the constant wear and tear of being back in coaching, but if I wanted to return, the leg was healed and strong enough.

I thanked him for his kindness and thoughtfulness, but I only wanted to know if I would be able to go back. He said that he preferred I not, but I was completely medically able to return—proving he is the very best in a hundred different ways.

I called Eric and Mike and told them I would be in to talk that night. We met, and I agreed to return. I turned down the new contract and the money, but we agreed that following the season I would be offered a contract to cover me for the next several years and pay me at the very top wage.

I also told them they could not fire anyone. If they fired Kevin, I would not come back. I would make it work, and no one needed to be released.

So, six days before we opened the season with the Dolphins in Miami, I returned to work with the Jets, who had moved into their state-of-the-art training facility in Florham Park, New Jersey.

It took me about two seconds, and I fell right back into the rhythm. I am sure it was tough for Kevin, but it was not my fault the rift had developed between Kevin and Eric. I would never embarrass Kevin and would work to make the situation as easy as possible for all of us. I didn't have time for pleasantries; we had less than one week to prepare.

To make it all worse, I received a phone call and an email copy of a letter from Bill Parcells. Why was Bill Parcells calling me?

He was upset that I had rejoined the Jets, and his letter to the NFL office clearly stated so. I was wrong when I visited the Dolphins. I was still under contract with the Jets, and it is illegal and improper to be at another NFL team's training camp while under contract. I didn't know this. I obviously had never visited a training camp as I had always been in one. I did not know the rule, but I was wrong, not Bill Parcells. He did not know I was under contract, and if he had he would have not permitted me to visit.

But in his letter, he had insinuated that I was scouting the Dolphins—and was cheating. I made a mistake, but I sure as hell didn't travel to Miami to cheat, and I was sure he knew that.

He wanted me to not coach the game against his team, as I would have an advantage. That is the stupidest thing that I have ever heard and a completely chickenshit thing to do.

I was furious. I completely apologized for my mistake, but what real harm had I caused? One thing was for sure—I was not cheating.

The NFL security department investigated me, my friend Frank, and Joe DeCamillis in Jacksonville. I had to give a sworn disposition—yes, "Do you swear to tell the whole truth, etc.?" It was ridiculous. Sure, I made a mistake, but I sure as hell didn't go over there to cheat.

NFL security recognized my mistake, but they thought Bill was completely off base and I could coach the game. With five days of preparation, I coached the game in Miami—and I never spoke to Bill Parcells again. I have an email copy of his letter, and I debated publishing it, but then I would be the one who was wrong.

With a miserable, chickenshit letter, he destroyed what I believed was a great relationship.

Here Comes Rex

The 2008 season was filled with excitement. The trade for Brett Favre during training camp was a heck of a risk, and it nearly paid off brilliantly.

The Jets played some great football and were fighting for a playoff spot when Brett suffered a shoulder injury and the season collapsed. We finished a disappointing 9-7 after starting 8-3. Eric Mangini was released.

To this day, I don't believe that Eric deserved to be fired. Maybe he stepped on too many toes and couldn't get out of his own way. But I believe that he would have matured and become a good coach.

I don't know what happened to Eric in Cleveland, where he went after the Jets, probably more of the same. I think it's a shame he hasn't gotten back in the NFL. He is knowledgeable and loyal and got a very bad rap. But Eric Mangini would be a very good addition to anyone's coaching staff.

For me, that season will always be marred by one distasteful incident, a miserable letter than never should have been written.

Following Eric's dismissal, I again expressed my interest in the head coaching position. The Jets did not want me to leave, but Mike Tannenbaum didn't exactly have me in mind as the head coach. Mike, as the pro personnel director, I liked him. When he became the general manager, not so much. An interesting aspect of any job is it can come down to the question of knowing how to do the job as opposed to knowing what to do. Mike was at the helm of two ships, the Jets and Dolphins, as they sank to nearly unparalleled depths.

Mike agreed to have me talk with him and Woody Johnson about my ideas on some of the paths necessary to get the Jets headed in the correct direction. Mike made it very clear this was a discussion, not an interview. He told me this a hundred times. After ten times, I pretty much had *figured it out*.

In a very short time, Rex Ryan, the very successful defensive coordinator of the Baltimore Ravens, was hired as the new head coach. I honestly don't know if they talked to anyone else. I am sure that they did, but I don't know who and could not have cared less.

I had never met Rex, but I was familiar with his dominating defensive teams. Rex's father, Buddy, was one of the NFL's all-time great defensive coaches, and I was sure that Rex had followed in his footsteps. I met with Rex on his first night in New York. I liked him and immediately agreed to stay. Rex was great to talk with. He had a vision of NFL success, and I couldn't have agreed with it any more.

Rex believed in a multiple attacking style of defense, running the ball (our quarterback was Mark Sanchez), and controlling the clock on offense—and making big plays and winning every week on special teams. He wanted me to completely handle my area, and we would work together on any special calls or plays. Rex openly communicated with all of us and did, in my opinion, an excellent job of having us as coaches all contribute in our own areas but also be on the same page as everyone else.

Rex walked into a good, solid team of both players and coaching staff. In fact, a bit later, in 2011 during the NFL's labor dispute and lockout of the players, we brought in then-retired NFL and college coaches to conduct clinics. Jon Gruden was working as the analyst on *Monday Night Football*, and he spent six days with us.

Jon is a personal friend, and later he told me that the 2011 New York Jets coaching staff was the best he had ever seen in his experiences.

Rex inherited on offense Brian Schottenheimer as coordinator; he did a damn good job with the Seattle Seahawks after that. Bill Callahan always has been one of the league's top offensive line coaches. Anthony Lynn, who I believe is an absolutely excellent coach, coached the running backs and soon became the head coach of the Los Angeles Chargers.

I had the special teams, and Ben Kotwica, my assistant, went on to be a coordinator with the Jets, Washington, and Atlanta. Rex, Bob Sutton, and Mike Pettine headed up an excellent defensive staff.

It didn't take too long before we added some key free agents and draft choices to a very good group of veteran players. All of a sudden, on offense we had center Nick Mangold, left tackle D'Brickashaw Ferguson, guard Alan Faneca (a Hall of Famer), and Damien Woody, who could play tackle or guard. We had such skill position players as LaDainian Tomlinson, a Hall of Famer; Thomas Jones; Santonio Holmes; Braylon Edwards; and Dustin Keller.

On defense we were led by Darrelle Revis, maybe the best cornerback in the league. We had such key players as Bart Scott, David Harris, Calvin Pace, Jim Leonhard, Bryan Thomas, and Antonio Cromartie.

I had an all-star team, with the obvious exclusion of a punter. Leon Washington, Jay Feely, James Ihedigbo, Larry Izzo, Justin Miller, Brad Smith, Eric Smith, Jason Trusnik, Robert Turner, Danny Woodhead, Wallace Wright, Nick Bellore. And the NFL's best long snapper, James Dearth.

We had a good team, and Rex did a very solid job. He was fun to work with and was experienced and knowledgeable. I loved when he would come into my office at night and discuss everything. He would get on the board and draw a defensive scheme that he had prepared for the week. I would watch it come to life on Sunday and could only stand there and smile.

We were a tough, physical team; we exemplified that type of football, and Rex loved it. Teams just didn't want to play the New York Jets.

In 2009 and 2010, we fought many battles and ended up in two AFC championship games. We lost to two great teams, the Colts with Peyton Manning and the Steelers with Ben Roethlisberger. But we made the New York Jets a team for its fans to be very proud of.

Hell, we were a team knocking on the door of the Super Bowl.

Rex kept things stirred up with the media. I would read something he said and just shake my head and laugh. Never did any of his craziness show itself around the team. We had an organized, disciplined program that showed no signs of Rex's sometimes crazy media antics. Everyone was on time and carried out all parts of the day in a first-class manner.

Our team was made up of quality individuals who were extremely competitive and conducted themselves at the highest of NFL standards. We didn't have "off the field" problems, and every day at work was a pleasure to be a part of.

Rex sometimes seemed to be off the wall, but don't ever believe that even for a minute we weren't a disciplined and extremely hard-working team of coaches and players.

Rex helped make a tough, demanding business fun. He attended every one of my Saturday night meetings. Then when the entire team was present, he would be warmed up and ready to go. He would discuss various aspects of the upcoming game but quickly reverted to a common theme: "We are going to be the most physical team."

Before long, he made it clear that we were going to "beat the shit" out of our opponent. Before long, the opponent was not given any credit or credence. We just were going to "beat the hell" out of them.

All of a sudden, Rex would explode with, "We are going to kick their asses. Now let's go and eat a fucking snack!"

So, fifty people would get up at once and head into the team meal room to eat a snack—and kick the shit out of anyone who got in the way.

There was always something exciting about Rex, but one of my favorite memories came on Thanksgiving Day in 2009. We had our meetings and practices all in the morning in order to free everyone up in the afternoon to celebrate Thanksgiving with their families.

It was a typical cold, damp November day in New Jersey, and we were in the team part of the practices. For the past several weeks, our offense had committed an abnormal number of penalties, and Brian Schottenheimer was raising a little hell. If anyone got a penalty, he immediately made them run a lap.

Frankly, I think that's ridiculous. Running a lap while the rest of the team is practicing important plays? I would rather that they would be disciplined for their penalty by running after practice. No one left one of my practices to run a lap. If someone was penalized and I was angry, I might keep them after practice and run them until I got tired.

We were moving along with our offensive team period when Wayne Hunter, one of our tackles, jumped offside. A flag was thrown, and Brian made him run. Justin Miller, one of our defensive backs and my league-leading kickoff returner, was playing on defense against our offense. Justin talked a lot and couldn't help himself, and he was teasing Wayne as he ran.

First of all, Wayne is a 6-5, 300-pounder and the one guy in the NFL you would not want to fight. In my NFL career, I believe the two absolute toughest players I ever met were Ron Heller and Wayne. Although Ron could be reasoned with, Wayne—maybe not. As he ran by, Wayne told Justin to "Shut the fuck up."

When he returned from his lap and resumed practicing, about five plays later he was flagged for a false start. So off again he went on his penalty lap. To be expected, Justin had something else to say. That was all Wayne needed to hear, and he went after Justin.

Now Justin was a strong, tough guy, but he was not a match for Wayne. Fortunately, plenty of players were there and quickly broke up what would have been ugly. Things calmed down, and Wayne resumed his lap.

But when he returned, the shit hit the fan. He stood in front of the entire team and told Justin that when practice was over, he was going to beat the hell out of him in the locker room, and that no one could stop him. Those guys are tough, and Justin would fight, but Wayne was right: he would have beaten the shit out of him, and no one could stop him.

Rex was standing next to me and asked what I thought. I said I wasn't really sure, but knowing how tough Wayne was, Rex better somehow get out ahead of what was coming.

Rex called over Justin and told him in no uncertain terms to leave the field immediately. Go into the locker room, do not change your clothes, and go home. Justin was no coward, but he did what he was told to do. I will never forget, on a Thanksgiving morning, watching Justin Miller in his uniform, with the helmet still on, driving his truck off the facility and heading for home.

No one ever criticized Justin; everyone knew he did the right thing.

The next morning Wayne—we were very close—came into my office and apologized for his actions. He told me he had talked with his wife and calmed down. His wife and my girlfriend Patti were good friends, and I am sure this aided in his wanting to talk to me.

I told him not to worry, it was over and forgotten. And Justin Miller was alive and well.

I look back now and laugh. I can still see Justin in his uniform with his helmet still on, driving out of the facility on Thanksgiving morning. Only in the NFL.

The Lockout

The good, the bad, and the ugly. That pretty much sums up my last two years with the Jets.

We finished the 2010 season in freezing Pittsburgh with a hard-fought loss to the Steelers in the AFC championship game. We were a good team with high hopes for the future. But what the hell happened?

The offseason was greatly disrupted by contract complications between the players and NFL management. When the negotiations stalled, the owners initiated a lockout and closed all NFL facilities to the players. Everything came to a halt.

We were trying to conduct business as normally as possible but without seeing the players on an almost daily basis either in our offices or the weight room. The organized team activities (OTAs) and minicamps were canceled, and we seemed to be stuck in a whole other universe. It was awkward, uncomfortable.

As I mentioned, during the lockout we did an outside-the-box type thing by bringing in ex-coaches for clinics. Jon Gruden came in to work with our offense and enjoyed it so much he stayed for five days. Dan Reeves, one of the most successful NFL coaches ever, shared ideas with each of us on his beliefs for what specifically makes the NFL work.

George Hill, an NFL defensive veteran with Philadelphia and Miami, was an expert in coaching the 3-4 defense and had led Miami to several years of No. 1 rankings. He talked specifically with our defensive coaches about the many variations of the 3-4, especially involving the secondary.

Tom Moore and Jim McNally, both very successful coaches, spent valuable time with our offensive coaches, so much so that they stayed on with us through much of the upcoming year.

Ben Kotwica and I went on a slightly different path. We brought in Steve Crosby, a veteran NFL coach and special teams coordinator who had recently retired from the San Diego Chargers. I had competed against Steve several times and always thought he did a good, solid job. I wasn't interested in what he was specifically doing, but rather how he as an opponent viewed us, exactly what we were doing, and how to defend and attack me. I asked him to bring his scouting reports and game plans to explain and show what he saw and how he specifically would try to beat us.

It was an excellent exercise. Steve was gracious and completely transparent and honest. It is extremely interesting to see how an opponent sees you and, more importantly, how he plans to attack you. I liked his ideas and thought they were sound and very thorough.

One thing, though, that he really didn't account for was our constant and subtle adjusting and changing. He wasn't quite prepared for this, and I knew that we could edge him. And we had. Actually, one game in San Diego in 2002, we killed them and drastically affected the 44-13 win.

I was extremely appreciative of our time spent with Steve and his valuable honesty.

Another thing that Ben and I did was to bring in Jeff Feagles, a twenty-two-year veteran punter who'd recently retired from the Giants. Jeff played for New England, Philadelphia, Arizona, and Seattle, and had a superb career. Jeff was arguably the best directional punter ever in the NFL. He had many great ideas both mentally and physically he shared with us.

We went out for a session and demonstration. He walked us through every aspect of how to directional punt. Where to stand, body angle, and weight distribution. Exactly how to hold the ball, and what to focus on as a target. He explained steps and the precise leg swing.

It was invaluable information and being right there as he explained and then punted couldn't have been any better. We filmed and recorded the entire session and kept it as a valuable learning tool for every punter who wanted to learn the intricacies of directional punting, especially in windy conditions.

I thought that during this disturbing lockout time the Jets fully took advantage and benefited greatly. I believe that Ben and I did more than maybe anyone else. We hit a home run in benefiting from this unusual set of circumstances.

If these things went so positively, what the hell happened?

Beginning of the End

In 2011, after starting so incredibly strong with two good wins, it quickly leveled off, with us realizing that we were really only an average 8-8 team. Of our eight losses, only in the 19-17 defeat in the last game of the year at Miami did I feel that we could have won. We were soundly defeated in our other losses and hardly at all resembled the championship-game team we had once been.

Still, 2011 was a solid year for me. We had a number of personnel changes, and it was somewhat like starting over. NFL teams have numerous roster changes in the middle or at the bottom end of the roster. So it is very normal to have to incorporate young, new players into starting roles. If you are going to be successful in the NFL as a special teams coach, you had better have a system in place that can be quickly learned, fully understood, and properly executed.

Ben and I took a relatively new team and transformed it into a very competitive unit. We were solid at everything, made very few mistakes, and pretty much edged our opponents each week. But where we were really special was as a kickoff return team. We had a great group of blockers and a dynamic return specialist in Joe McKnight, a running back from USC. Joe had a lot to learn as a kickoff return specialist, but his speed and burst, combined with excellent blocking, landed him at the top of the NFL.

One of my all-time favorite returns was Joe's 107-yard TD against Baltimore. John Harbaugh, a former special teams coordinator with Philadelphia, had been given a chance at a head coaching position with the Ravens and was doing a very good job. Several years earlier at a kicking clinic conducted by a man named Ray Pelfrey in Reno, Nevada—and annually attended by nearly every NFL special teams coach—I presented our yearly Special Teams Coach of the Year trophy to John.

I had previously won the award and am very proud to have been honored by my peers. I gave a speech in which I encouraged John to be prepared for someday hopefully being in a position to accept a head coaching role. Special teams coaches basically had been bypassed for this job, myself very much included, and I was encouraging John to be prepared. He must have paid attention, as he got the opportunity, landed the job, won a Super Bowl, and to this day is doing a damn good job.

Any time, though, when I played John Harbaugh, he was going to get my "A" game. I was never envious or jealous in any way as to his getting an opportunity that I desired. I respect and admire what he has accomplished, but I always wanted him to know, though I believe he was a good special teams coach, that compared to me he wasn't even close.

Did he change the game? No, he rode the change. Go back to 2003 and ask any special teams coach if you want to face Westhoff or Harbaugh. I will bet a lot of money on that outcome.

I admire what he had done, but I couldn't wait to play him.

That 107-yard return was one of my favorite designs. We trapped or doubled their best players and basically just beat the hell out of them. We got one TD and were a step away from another.

I believe that I always played well against John, and that continued in 2018 when I was with the Saints.

One thing for sure that John Harbaugh has dramatically proved is that a special teams coach can be very successful as a head coach. I would like to see Dave Toub of Kansas City or my buddy Joe DeCamillis of the Rams be given a head coaching opportunity. They have been very successful with their various teams and have shown durability, resilience, creativity, and a thorough knowledge and flexibility. All those are characteristics that a successful head coach must have.

"I'd been an NFL assistant coach for thirty-two years (the same as Mike) going into the 2020 season," Joe D said. "During that time, I had worked with seven NFL head coaches and ten assistants that have either become NFL or college head coaches. The knowledge that I have been exposed to during that time is really immeasurable.

"During my career, there are four coaches that I would say have influenced and shaped me into the coach that I am today. I was on the same staff with three of them. The exception is Mike Westhoff.

"NFL coaches who read that are going to say 'not possible.' The NFL is not a league known for professional courtesy, or one that shares knowledge between assistant coaches from other teams because of the intense level of competitiveness. Many coaches are so insecure and protective of their 'knowledge' that they would never divulge any secrets or tricks of their trade.

"That did not apply to Mike. He decided to help a young assistant that he did not owe the time of day to. When our relationship first started, it was completely one way—only benefiting my young career. Mike really got nothing from it other than passing on a craft that he respected greatly. In fact, I would imagine there were times he probably thought 'Can this guy quit bothering me?'

"Mike worked for the Miami Dolphins, and I worked with the Denver Broncos and then the New York Giants at the time. It was way before cell phones, so the long-distance phone calls to the Dolphins facility were probably troubling to both clubs. I would call Mike constantly and ask him about techniques, schemes, scheduling—every facet a first-time NFL special teams coach needs to know. What is truly amazing now that I look back on those days is that he not only answered the questions but spent the time to explain the answers to me.

"Over the years, we became great friends and spent many Tuesday nights—game-plan night in the NFL—drawing each other's schemes and ideas. The conversation would always be lively and was usually based on something one of us had seen on film. The guys that know Mike will remember the phrase 'That guy stole that KOR from me. Hell, I ran that for a TD.' Mike was never shy about telling you he had come up with an idea that worked.

"Now that I don't get those Tuesday nights anymore, I wish I would have saved every drawing, every note, every idea that was talked about, and put it in the 'Westhoff File.' I'll always be grateful to Mike for the knowledge that I gained from him. However, the thing that I will be most grateful for is him showing me how to respect our craft. And, of course, becoming one of my life-long friends.

"Mike showed me that a special teams coordinator could not only affect NFL games but win NFL games."

We had ended the 2011 season at 8-8 and with plenty of bumps and bruises but nothing even close to what was ahead in the upcoming offseason.

If 2011 was the beginning of the end, then 2012 was the icing on the cake. We had salary-cap issues in 2011 that only seemed to get worse as time progressed.

We offered Mark Sanchez a new contract. To me, that got the ball rolling. I can remember standing in my office and asking Mike Tannenbaum why he had given Mark a new contract? He told me that is what a championship-game QB must be paid.

I told him that I would agree with that if he had anything to do with us getting into that game. Mark is a great kid, but he was only a manageable quarterback at best. We led the league in rushing and had an excellent defense and a very good special teams unit. Now we were going to be Tom Brady and the New England Patriots?

All of a sudden, we were losing Alan Faneca and LaDainian Tomlinson, and we were replacing them with Plaxico Burress and Derrick Mason? This was one of the stupidest things I had ever seen in three decades in the NFL. We signed receivers who never practiced. I was standing on the practice field with Joe Yacovino, one of our officials, during a Thursday practice. We were practicing an end-of-game or end-of-half two-minute drill. Joe asked me, "Who are these guys?"

Sanchez was running a drill without any of the receivers who would be dressed for Sunday's game. It was a joke and a disgrace.

I am going to blame Mike Tannenbaum for this mess, but Rex needs to accept some of the responsibility. Maybe he didn't fight hard enough, but this football team didn't ever come close to looking like the one we had in 2009 or 2010.

Tebow

To add to this chaos, in 2012 we signed Tim Tebow. Another good kid, but not an NFL quarterback. It took him all day to deliver the ball. Ask New England if you don't believe me; the Patriots tried him also.

I was asked if I would use Tim on special teams. I said yes, but only as a personal protector on the punt team, where he would be a fake threat. I did exactly that, and it worked well. We ran several fakes and had some great success. Tim would come into my office at night, and we would draw them up. I enjoyed these meetings. I also believed if we used him in a particular fashion, he could be a big help to our offense.

We ran a great fake on the Colts. We showed an unbalanced line to our left, and following a direct snap to Tim and his running to the unbalanced side, he pulled up and threw back to our right tackle, Nick Bellore (#54), a linebacker who was eligible as the end man on the line of scrimmage.

It was a good fake that went for about 25 yards and an easy first down.

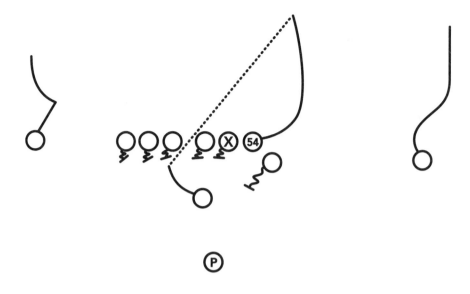

I never used Tim on any other special teams. It just wasn't him. He was not a tackler or blocker. People have asked me to compare him to Taysom Hill of the Saints. They are not even in the same league. Taysom Hill is a much better football player, and, as a quarterback, Taysom can throw.

Taysom blocked punts, covered kickoffs, and was a great blocker for me. I believe he was and is one of the NFL's best special teams players. Tim Tebow? No chance. Taysom Hill could snap for kicks and return kickoffs and punts.

Don't get me started.

I liked Tim Tebow, and I felt badly about what happened to him. He believed he would be used as a "wildcat" QB and multi-purpose offensive player. That didn't happen at all.

I was told that we would have special plays on offense for him. That was all bullshit—we did nothing. The whole thing was a disgrace and a mess. I am the only one who kept my end of the bargain. I wanted him as a fullback on my punt team to run fakes and make our opposition play a soft/safe look versus us.

That is exactly what happened—except on one occasion, when our starting personal protector, Eric Smith, was injured, and Tim had to fill in. We were playing Miami, and they ran a block look at us that we had practiced a hundred times. Tim, of course, wouldn't step up and block anyone, and I suffered one of what I believe was three or four punt blocks in my entire career.

Thanks, Tim—and whoever else was involved in this complete fiasco.

Everyone Was There

So, we had finished 8-8 in 2011. We were out of the playoffs and just didn't feel like the tough, hard-nosed 2009-2010 teams that had gone to the AFC championship games. The 8-8 season was a disappointment, but one game will always resonate with me.

We opened the season with a Sunday prime-time game versus the Dallas Cowboys. It was the tenth-year anniversary of 9/11, and it couldn't have been handled more perfectly. It was one of the best examples of what the NFL is all about.

The stadium was overflowing with energy and nostalgia. It was the most patriotic event that I was ever part of. Everyone—and I mean EVERYONE—was at the game. President George W. Bush was in attendance and so was everyone else who could get a ticket or sideline pass. Members of the New York Police Department and New York Fire Department who were involved in the 9/11 rescue efforts were there to be recognized and honored. The pregame was my personal second all-time favorite; the first I will talk about a little later.

There was a flyover that set the stage. For the playing of the national anthem, the largest American flag I have ever seen was unfurled. It covered the entire playing surface and took every available military member, police officer, and fireman to help unfurl and support. The flag was so heavy that we as members of the coaching staffs, and the players, joined in to help.

I felt proud, honored, and humbled.

As I mentioned earlier in this book, the national anthem holds a special place in my heart. While listening in a Miami hospital room to the national anthem being played during a Fourth of July fireworks celebration on July 3, 1988, I made that pledge of appreciation that traveled with me to more than 600 games. The song led me to a special place in my mind to remind me how fortunate I was to live in such a great country.

We don't do everything and haven't done everything perfectly, but I don't want to be anyone else, and sure as hell I don't want to live anywhere else. I have been fortunate enough to have traveled much of the world, and each time when I return, someone will ask: What was your favorite place?

Each time, I give the same answer: When I landed back in the U.S.

That Sunday night at the Meadowlands made me especially proud to be an American and doubly proud to be part of the NFL. The night was perfect and the atmosphere electric. The ceremony was beautiful and emotional. President Bush conducted the coin toss. The Secret Service is so impressive, and it was a great honor to be on the same field. It was a great tribute to the values and principles that make America such a special place.

The game was an example of what makes the NFL the world's greatest sporting event. It was a hard-fought and well-played game. For me, it was one of my all-time favorites.

We were down 24-10 in the fourth quarter but fought back.

Guess who was the special teams coach of the Cowboys? Yep, Joe DeCamillis, my good friend. During Joe's first stop at Jacksonville, in the summer of 2008, I was at my house in Florida while on medical leave from the Jets. My leg surgery had gone much better than expected, and I was thinking about returning to coaching in 2009.

I called Joe and asked if I could come up to Jacksonville to visit with him and attend the Jaguars' second preseason game. They played on a Friday night, and I arrived on Thursday afternoon. While in his office at the stadium, we fell right back into our routine of talking about special teams.

Joe was experimenting with an innovative punt formation. It was an unbalanced line promoting directional kicking and helping with the protection of turning and punting to the side.

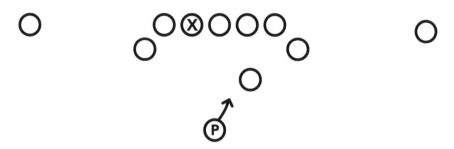

I thought that it could be a weapon. It could be quirky and had some blocking questions, but I was intrigued.

Joe said he had a meeting to attend and asked if I could spend some time drawing a way to defeat the protection. I spent the next hour exploring methods to attack this type of formation and protection.

When Joe returned, I told him that I liked the idea but had come up with a way to possibly attack this type of protection by creating a moment of confusion for the PP, and possibly getting a free runner at the punter.

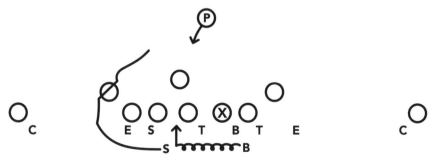

Technically, it shouldn't be that difficult to block, but I felt that by aligning my best rusher as the stacked Number 1, and right before the snap shifting him to the play-side Number 1 position—followed closely by the motioning of the back-side Number 3 to a play-side position—I might be able to draw the PP's vision to his far-right side—and also to my best rusher. Maybe that would free up the motioning Number 3 or a play-side Number 4. Creating doubt within the protection is one of the key components in blocking a punt.

I wasn't sure that this was a perfect block for this type of punt protection, but I believed it might have merit.

When Joe returned, I told him my thoughts on attacking this protection, and we studied my drawings. Joe acknowledged the possible problem but felt that he would be able to handle it.

I returned to coaching that next year and used that punt formation for the remainder of my career.

I had an exceptional group of players that performed at a very high level. Eric Smith (#33) was one of the best punt blockers in the NFL and my key ingredient. I was going to shift him right before the snap to a spot where I believed he would be hard to block for their wing, and he'd be rushing right in the face of the punt.

Following his shift, I would bring Joe McKnight (#25)—a running back and league-leading kickoff returner—in motion behind the shift, and then run him through between their kick-side guard and tackle. I believed the PP would block McKnight, but he might hesitate with the shift and motion and make the wrong decision.

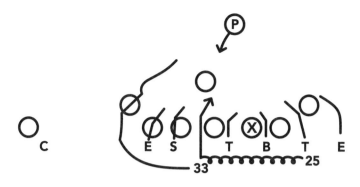

I also thought that Smith versus their wing was an advantage. I thought their PP would either pick up McKnight or the kick-side Number 4.

Remember, four years ago I believed that this block might cause a problem. I was right. It did.

McKnight, who had never before and never again would block a punt, did it in that very special moment. Isaiah Trufant (#35), brought up from the practice squad the day before, picked up the blocked punt and ran it into the end zone for the tying score.

The place went crazy, and our guys on the sideline went nuts. There are many other coaches in football I'd have rather done it against than Joe. Joe didn't get beaten. He practiced against that possibility many times, but someone hesitated and the play worked. We executed it perfectly.

The Jets intercepted Romo's pass a few minutes later, and Nick Folk kicked a 50-yard field goal to win the game. What a game—and a four-year-old idea played a major role. I was ecstatic. For me, it was very special.

Aside from playing a great game, the Jets finished the night with no penalties.

It was the perfect ending to a perfect night. How could we not surge forward? How could we screw this up?

Happy Returns

My final two years with the Jets were filled with ups and downs. My first ten years had been incredible: we were an exciting, explosive team. We were in the playoffs six times—three under Herman Edwards, once under Eric Mangini, and twice under Rex. We'd advanced to two AFC championship games. One thing was for damn sure, we weren't the same old Jets.

As I watch the Jets today, I am not sure if five players on their roster could have made any of those teams.

In my time with the Jets, we were in direct competition with Bill Belichick, Tom Brady, and the New England Patriots in the AFC East. And yes, they were Super Bowl champs and had a distinct advantage. We had beaten New England several times, including a playoff game in New England following the 2010 season. I firmly believed that we were in a position to compete with the Patriots each year.

Our multifaceted defense looked as though it would be a tough match for Brady each and every time. On offense, we could run the ball and had an excellent short, controlled passing game. Those aspects enabled us to control the clock and keep Brady on the sideline.

I had a damn good special teams unit. We were ranked near the top of the NFL each year. We could cover and block kicks. We made field goals and had some of the best starting field position numbers each season. Where we dominated each year was in the return game.

Our punt return—with Santana Moss, Chad Morton, and Jeremy Kerley—was very good. But our kickoff return was great. Chad Morton, Justin Miller, Leon Washington, Brad Smith, and Joe McKnight all led the NFL. In my twelve years in New York, we had nine returners who led the league. Try and beat that record—especially today, when there are virtually no returns and 95 percent of the ones that are tried look like no one is blocked.

"You talk about special teams guys," said Hank Bauer, one of the NFL's all-time greatest special teams players. "They are the only guys that have to play and use the skills of almost every position set. A punt protection guy has got to know how to protect like an offensive lineman. If you rush the punter or kicker or have to get off a block, you've got to know the swim moves or rip-and-under like a defensive lineman. A gunner or someone on the outside trying to block you is using the skills of a receiver or a cornerback. If you line up as a linebacker on kick teams, you have to be a linebacker. You find all the skill sets of every player.

"You've always got to know what you are looking for. Nobody knows for sure until you get into the live fire. Great special teams players come in all sizes, and Mike always has understood.

"Steve Tasker was a mighty mite. Then you might have big guys with great instincts even if they are slow. The only way to find out is to show it in a game, but you have got to get them to that point. First you have to identify it—there's, like, an IDing gene, and Mike is the professor who knows how to do that. Mike is able to see what other people can't see."

An interesting aspect concerning ball control occurred during Rex's first year in New York, which was 2009. During the offseason, I was studying kicks and punts in various situations in our games. We played in windy, cold, and relatively tough kicking environments. The more I looked, the more unhappy I was. My field goal percentage wasn't great, and my punting successes, which for me had to be inside the opponent's 10-yard line, were also not what I deemed satisfactory.

I sought the help of our IT guys. A young man fresh out of college, somewhat of a computer whiz, was working as an intern for the Jets. I asked him to tally everything that occurred on fourth down for the offense when driving from the 50-yard line to the

40, and from the 40 to the 30. What happened when a team went for it on fourth down, punted, or attempted a field goal.

We played in the Northeast, and I only wanted those specific teams, and only at home: the Jets and Giants, Pittsburgh, Buffalo, Philadelphia, Baltimore, Cleveland, Washington, and New England.

He broke it down over a five-year period and basically discovered that nothing good happened. The success of going for it on fourth down was minimal. The field goal percentage was poor. And punts inside the minus-10 were nothing to get excited about.

My goal became how to improve our chances of success in each of those areas. I discussed these findings, and with our type of running team, we turned this area of the field into "four-down territory."

No, that didn't mean we would go for it on fourth down. We would let our coordinator know on first down he had four opportunities and to call plays accordingly. If something negative happened, then the fourth-down call would revert to me, and I would decide whether to punt or attempt a field goal.

I can recall looking at Rex and holding up four fingers (usually not needed, though) and then him turning to Brian Schottenheimer and telling him he was in "four-down territory." Knowing for sure that you, as a play caller, are in that territory on first down is a hell of a lot better than being told on fourth down to go for it.

We made this a key part of our game plans. Rex was very much on board because it fit right into his philosophy of conducting a game. Brian did an excellent job of calling plays with the four downs at hand. I worked specifically on makeable field goals and punts inside the minus-10. We improved in all areas, and it became one more step in leading us to two championship game appearances.

"Special teams in the NFL is the only group or phase of the three phases that on every play you are dealing with, by average, the biggest exchange of yardage and/or points being scored," Hank Bauer said. "That is why they call it special. If you look at how many plays are run, [fewer] than half the number of offense or defense in a game, everything is so magnified as to the importance of each play.

"Special teams hold the keys to the game; the last thing I always say is they are the great equalizer in the NFL, and I don't care if you have the worst team versus the best team—turnovers or big plays given up or made in the kicking game are so important. In 90 percent of the game, if you win in the kicking game, you win the game.

"Look at all the so-called dynasties. They all have been solid if not great in the kicking game."

So how in the hell did this good football team fall apart?

Teamwork

I coached with Rex for four years. The first two were incredible. Each week was an exciting challenge. We battled every step of the way, got into the playoffs, and ended up playing those two AFC championship games. We were a tough, hard-nosed, and balanced team.

On offense, we led the league in rushing and had a solid passing game. Mark Sanchez was our quarterback, and there was nothing really special about him, but he managed the game and, with our running attack, the play-action and underneath passing game, it was efficient enough.

On defense, cornerback Darrelle Revis was the key. He could do anything. It seemed like Rex would put him on one side of the field and everyone else on the other. Antonio Cromartie also was very good for us on the other corner, and with Rex's creativity, we gave every offense a tough time.

I always thought Rex's real strength as a coach was in his complexity and yet his simplicity. Rex would move people all over the place, presenting seemingly many complex problems, but from that complex look he would drop into a very simple, solid scheme. When it looked as though we would have to be playing man-to-man, Rex would end up in a simple two-deep, five-under zone. Or even with six underneath zone defenders.

But then, from that very same look, he would bring the house and the offense would be completely outnumbered and get blown up. When you were an opponent preparing for the New York Jets and Rex Ryan, you were going to get absolutely no sleep.

Rex's defensive philosophy really was simple. He wasn't going to KISS (Keep It Simple Stupid). He wanted KILL (Keep It Likeable and Learnable). Rex wanted his defenders to be able to understand and learn what appeared to be a very complex scheme but in reality had a somewhat simple premise.

The key to the complexities of NFL football is for the players to completely understand every aspect of what they are being asked to do. When you have complete knowledge and confidence, you can play a very physically challenging game with the speed and certainty necessary to excel.

During my four years with Rex, I had for the most part a great time. I developed a great relationship with my assistant, Ben Kotwica, a West Point graduate and former Army football player. Following his graduation, he was deployed to Iraq as an attack helicopter pilot. Ben was a platoon leader and combat veteran. He handled Iraq, and he could sure as hell handle the New England Patriots.

"The National Football League is a demanding, results-driven business where no one is immune to the lack of results," Ben said. "And that includes a former attack helicopter pilot who commanded over forty soldiers in combat.

"After serving eight years in the world's greatest army under some of our nation's best leaders, it had been time to transition to one of our country's most competitive industries. The margin of error in professional football is so small that over 75 percent of the outcomes are determined by one score or less. This slight margin puts a premium on structure, organization, and leadership. This leadership must transfer down to the player in the form of instruction and performance."

Ben Kotwica (right)

We worked great together, had a lot of fun, and we were damn good. It was easy to see Ben developing as a coach, and it is no surprise that he went on to be special teams coordinator with the Jets, Washington, and Atlanta.

During those years that we were together, following practice on Wednesday and Thursday, Ben would hold extra meetings in his office and specifically work with players on an individual or small group basis. Ben was the perfect antidote for me. I would throw a million things at the players, and Ben could break everything down, smoothing out some of the bumps that I had created.

"Where do the great ideas come from?" Ben asked. "Some come from hours and hours of planning on the Monday or Tuesday before the practice week begins and the battle commences on a Sunday afternoon. Others are more spontaneous.

"As I settle into my seat for a two-hour plane ride, I replay the game just concluded in my head over and over again. Visualizing more of the plays we left out on the field than the ones that we had made. As the engines spin up and the doors in the belly of the aircraft close shut, a tap comes on my shoulder.

" 'Ben, Ben, put this in for next week. We are gonna get 'em with this one,' Mike would say. 'This one' is the latest punt block design for the week, handed to me on the United Airlines 5x5-inch napkin that begins the process for next week's opponent. That napkin will turn into a computer design, and that computer design will manifest the next game plan, which will be played out in front of millions of people six days later."

Find Me a Punter

We were a damn good special teams unit and were successful nearly every week. We had an excellent group of core players that could do pretty much everything well—except punt.

I believe that my twelve years in New York were as productive as anyone had ever experienced anywhere. But I failed miserably in finding a punter.

Remember, with the Colts, I had Rohn Stark, one of the NFL's all-time best. Miami's Reggie Roby would be on everyone's all-time top five. And later with the Saints, I had Thomas Morstead, my personal pick as the NFL's best punter. Ever.

I can pick punters, and I can coach them and coach a punt team. But at New York, my punting brain went to visit another planet.

With the Jets, we had some great punt team personnel; I just couldn't get the punting position figured out. It started badly and got worse. Because we had that great supporting cast, our numbers were never terrible, but compared to my two previous stops and my time in New Orleans, the Jets' punting results were not even in the same discussion.

All my struggling punters were great guys except one: Steve Weatherford. I couldn't stand him. He had been released by both New Orleans and Jacksonville—two damn good places to punt, by the way. We brought him in for a workout, and, based on the results, he absolutely deserved to make the team. But I just didn't feel good about him.

Weatherford was athletic, a hard enough worker, and could basically blast the ball. His hang time was mediocre, and he punted nearly everything in the middle of the field. In New York and the AFC East, we always had wind, and I believed in directional punting to a side. I protected the punting kick side and basically asked him to kick to a particular number. We would funnel the coverage to a small area of the field. He was not adept at this, but to his credit he worked his tail off and greatly improved.

Also, when we got him, he was a terrible holder—a role most punters also have. We did not use him at first, but again he persisted and greatly improved. Work ethic was not his problem. I just didn't believe in him. I felt that under pressure he would freeze. I was right. Because I didn't like or believe in him, I am sure I greatly contributed to the problem.

We were playing at New England, and with the score 0-0, we lined up for our first punt. I had asked him where he wanted to punt, and he told me to our right. I called "Red Slam." There was no wind, the snap was perfect, and we executed the protection correctly. And he hit an 18-yard shank out of bounds.

I was furious and clearly voiced it as he came off the field. He got all shook up and told me that I wasn't helping anything. Well, maybe not, but after that sorry-ass punt, at least I felt a little better.

We were in Chicago while fighting for a playoff spot, and again I asked him where he wanted to punt. The wind was blowing like hell, and he again said to the right. I called it again, and what did we receive? A line drive to our left, right to Devin Hester. Thanks a lot, Steve.

Somehow, we miraculously covered one of the NFL's all-time worst punts and held Hester to a minimal gain. I don't imagine that our sideline was too pleasant after that bullshit punt. Thanks again, Steve.

In my dealing with Steve Weatherford, one thing needs to be straightened out. Several times he had taken the snap and taken off running on a fake. He was athletic and could run. These happened in Oakland, Miami, and Green Bay. He had some success in the first instances but failed miserably in Green Bay—and I believe that aided greatly in our defeat.

Each time afterward at our Monday press conferences, I stood in front of the media and lied. Yes, absolutely lied. I called many fakes in my career but not those. He ran each one on his own. We had fakes in which he ran, but I never called any of those. I stood there and covered for him by saying that we had that particular fake in the game plan, and he saw the right look and took off. I never sold him out. I protected him. I wanted to kill him, but I never publicly criticized him.

I was the one who released him. Not Rex, me. Not even Mike Tannenbaum. Me. I cut him. I didn't believe in him or like him, and I released him. He was quoted later as saying that he and I "didn't see eye to eye." No, that had nothing to do with it. I couldn't stand him, and I cut him. That's it.

He was picked up by the Giants, had a great year and very much helped them win the Super Bowl. I helped start him in the correct direction of learning to hold and being able to punt to a side. He worked his tail off and is solely responsible for his success. I'm sure the Giants did a much better job coaching him than I did. The Little Sisters of the Poor could have handled him better than I did.

While at the Giants, he and his buddy, their kicker—whose name I honestly don't know and refuse to look up—criticized me publicly. I never said a word about him. I never criticized him publicly when he failed, and I covered for his complete stupidity.

I loved my time with the Jets, and we were greatly successful, but this was one area that was a failure in many aspects.

Shark Fishing

I entered the offseason in 2012 on a wave of emotion. Happy, sad, nervous, anxious, excited, and sometimes maybe even a little scared.

It was going to be my last year in the NFL. I had turned sixty-five in January, and after coaching in the NFL for thirty years, I was going to retire.

I owned a beautiful home on a golf course in Fort Myers, Florida, and I was ready to live there full-time, resume playing golf, and get back out on my boat and continue my favorite hobby: shark fishing.

I own a twenty-two-foot center console typical Florida fishing boat. It has a Yamaha engine, and I have had it for more than twenty years. It looks and runs great. I call it "Playmakers" and keep it in a barn at the Port Sanibel Marina, just before the causeway leading to Sanibel Island. I contact the marina via email, and they put it in the water. I load up and off I go.

I love to boat in the beautiful waters around the Sanibel barrier islands, in the Gulf of Mexico, and the Pine Island Sound. I boat and fish around the most gorgeous islands in the U.S.: Sanibel, Captiva, North Captiva, Cayo Costa, Cabbage Key, and Boca Grande. The islands are bordered on the east by Pine Island Sound and the west by the Gulf of Mexico.

This area has some of the best fishing in the world. A number of my friends travel out into the Gulf for twenty or thirty or fifty miles in search of grouper and snapper. But I prefer to stay close to the islands. I am often alone or with my girlfriend or one or two other of my friends or former NFL coaches. At least once per year, I go out with Zach Thomas, Larry Izzo, Wes Welker, and any one of several other NFL players. I don't want to be out in the Gulf alone in my twenty-two-foot boat when one of the Gulf's frequent storms comes up out of nowhere. You don't have to travel too far to be in the middle of America's greatest fishing. Snook, redfish, and trout are abundant—and make good dinners.

I fortunately have learned a great deal about fishing from my good friend Rob Wells. Rob and his wife Phyllis own Cabbage Key, a hundred-acre island just south of Boca Grande. The island consists of a marina, several homes and cottages, and, in my opinion, America's best restaurant and bar. You can only get there by boat, but when you do you will be treated to what Jimmy Buffett referred to as the "Cheeseburger in Paradise."

The bar and restaurant are packed all day long, doing normally around 600 lunches. But in the evening, when it is much less crowded and quieter, a dinner is served that would rival most of New York City's great restaurants. It is my favorite place in the world, and you might just run into your favorite celebrity.

Rob Wells, aside from being a gracious restaurant host, is maybe Florida's best fisherman. He is a real pro. He nets his own bait and knows every inch of the area's backwaters. He is a true sport fisherman and has won numerous tournaments. He has been honored as the Florida Sportsman of the Year.

I have gone with Rob many times, and I have always done incredibly well. I landed a gigantic tarpon (over six feet) with him, as well as a forty-five-inch snook. When I am with Rob, I act like an NFL rookie did with me. I listen to every word and do exactly as he says.

Much like me, he is not for everyone. He is tough and very demanding, but he knows what the hell he is doing. If you pay attention and follow exactly, you will have the fishing day of your life.

Maybe fishing can be a little like the NFL. Pay attention and learn what to do, follow instructions, bust your ass, and *figure it out*.

This entire area is home to a year-round migration of numerous varieties of fish, headed up by the tarpon, who flood the waters by the thousands in the spring. Those beautiful silver monsters running all over and exploding out of the water are any fisherman's dream. Tarpon are a great game fish and have bodies as solid as a rock. They are for catching and releasing, not for eating—except by one predator: the shark.

Sharks eat anything and everything, and to catch one is a great fight. You don't have to be an expert fisherman, you just have to love the fight.

"He pursues, faces, or attacks everything in his life, and he will do it any way he can to succeed," my son John said of my fishing. "It went from catching two-foot sharks with $14 spinner rods to a few years later he has all the top gear and catches ten-foot bull sharks. He has schooled me in fishing now. It is fun, but he is also dead serious. If you miss one, it is like you missed a tackle. Sometimes I have to remind him I am here to have fun."

"When everybody on the boat can fish, he is dead serious. When I have my kids on the boat, he is more like a guide and helps you set up and get hooked up and wants to see you make the catch. My boys have caught sharks from when they were eight and five years old."

I first caught a shark completely by accident, and I loved the fight. I was able to fight the two- or three-foot shark to the boat, pull it out of the water, and with a pair of pliers release the hook, then dump the unharmed shark back in the water.

As time progressed, we got more and more efficient. I learned the proper bait: bonita, mackerel, and lady fish—all bloody, oily, and great for sharks.

I fish the passes between the islands from the Gulf to the Pine Island Sound. I look on my depth finder for twelve-foot water and then anchor. I have excellent rods and reels, and I make my own wire leaders; sharks' teeth will bite through normal fishing line. We use what is referred to as "J" hooks, and we flatten the barb, the sharp inside part of the hook designed to hold the hook in the fish's mouth.

Remember, we are releasing everything, and there is no need to tear up the shark's mouth. I like to let a shark "explode" and run with the bait and then pull hard back at a forty-five-degree angle to set the hook. Now, the fight is on.

As we have learned more about how to shark-fish, our goal has increased. Now I am really only trying to catch sharks six-foot or more. Black tips, spinners, reef sharks, bulls, and, for me the hardest ever to catch, the hammerheads.

We have caught twelve-foot bull sharks and ten-foot hammerheads and dozens of six-foot black tips. I have caught sharks that you couldn't wrap your arms around—not that you would want to—and have fought several for up to an hour. It is not for everyone; that is why I love it.

If they are four-foot or under, I can carefully grab the shark by its gills and remove the hook. With the long guys, we lift the shark up—sometimes a real challenge—and cut the leader with wire cutters. We use saltwater hooks that, when left in the shark, will break down after a short time and disintegrate. We are trying to be as harmless as possible.

We never bring a shark into the boat. Everything is done to release the shark outside the boat. It is dangerous, but, if done correctly, both exciting and exhilarating.

One of my best friends, John Gamble, the former strength coach of the Miami Dolphins, is my fishing buddy. He lives in Fort Lauderdale and travels over to my home, and we spend all day on the water. John is the strongest man I have ever known—and I coached thirty-two years in the NFL. He is the perfect partner as a shark fisherman. We have made some catches that are incredible, and we have released everything.

I know I can be a little bit cocky about many things, but John and I are about the best at what we do in all of the Southwest Florida fishing area.

If you want a great fishing experience, get ahold of me. John and I will take you out. You will never be more than a half-mile from land, and usually in about ten feet of water. You will not get "seasick," and you will eat—you have to pay, by the way—the best lunch ever. You will get nervous, but if you can land a six-foot shark, you will remember it for a lifetime.

Drafting—and Push-Ups

The 2012 offseason was going to be my last. What I wasn't aware of, though, was that it would also be one of my worst.

Knowing this was going to be my last year, I was determined to finish really strong. Ben Kotwica and I worked doubly hard to excel in both free agency and the draft.

Free agency for us was a waste of time. The Jets didn't have any salary-cap room, so there went my hope for finding a real punter. Well, in the punter role I had pretty much struck out for eleven years, why not make it twelve?

So, free agency? Forget about it. But the NFL draft had always been a special yearly occurrence for me.

I really enjoyed preparing for the draft. I had followed a similar procedure for my entire career. I would look at our area scouts' general information on each player on my list. Remember, I didn't care about numbers: height, weight, etc. I wanted football players—athletes, overachievers, guys who make plays, and gym rats. They might not have a top draft grade, but they were all over the field as a college player.

I personally would talk with each of our scouts and get their take on the types of players in their areas. I talked to various agents and accepted letters and calls from anyone. Several times, I would talk with my good friend Joe DeCamillis and compare ideas and notes. We were always very general and would not venture into each other's team's specific information.

I used a specific form and method that I had developed from Jimmy Johnson and had kept my entire career. It was both concise and precise. All the information I needed, plus a very simple method to grade the film that was right in front of me.

I categorized all my players into groups. Kickers, punters, long snappers, return specialists—both punt and kickoff. I then graded separately running backs, tight ends, wide receivers, defensive backs, linebackers, and some specific defensive linemen. We were grading them as special teams players. I didn't care, other than the specialists of course, what special teams they were on. I wanted to watch them play their offensive and defensive positions and look for my specific criteria while they were playing their normal offensive or defensive roles.

I wanted to see aggressiveness, athleticism, quickness, burst, instincts, mental awareness, the ability to play in space, tackling and blocking in the open field, the ability to play according to the rules, and second effort. I believed that I could transfer their specific position talents to the skills and abilities that I was looking for in an NFL special teams player.

Ben and I graded each player on a minimum of three of their films. Our "all-star" guys from five films. I would look only briefly at the "highlight" films many agents sent out on their various players. I might watch a few minutes, but then I reverted to the game film.

By being very specific and having my precise grade form on which to record, I could work through a film very quickly. We noted exceptional or very poor plays and would share those plays with each other. I would spend hours watching film and writing up the player. I was not affixing a grade; that was for the scouts. I was ranking the player by position as special teams players. I didn't care what draft grade they had received. My ranking was how I saw them helping our team. I didn't care how we got them. I just knew about them according to my and Ben's ranking that this is who we wanted.

We would then talk with each position coach to see how they would feel about particular players and maybe generate some additional interest in one of our top prospects.

The general manager and the head coach put the "team" first during the draft. Everyone else? Their own particular areas to cover their asses is what is out in front. It is human nature and don't tell me any differently. One thing for sure, special teams are not at the top of the list. With the greatly reduced number of special teams plays today, special teams are even further down the list.

But in 2012, I believe that Ben and I did our very best job of draft preparation. We wrote up and put into the computer full reports on 105 players. I don't know how many teams are that thorough with special teams rankings.

Just before the draft and after all the other coaches and scouts had made their presentations, I would have my day in front of the entire organization. We presented our rankings and specifically discussed each player. We made it clear who we wanted and precisely who the hell we didn't want.

When I left the four-hour presentation, I felt proud. Ben and I were very thorough and had covered a broad spectrum. As always, I called Jimmy Johnson. No, he is not in any way a good friend or buddy of mine, but I always very much respected what I had learned from him in preparing for the draft. And I wanted him to know how efficient the procedure was and how appreciative I was for his direction.

Now came the time for a few last-minute adjustments, and then the draft weekend.

For my previous years in the NFL, I had spent much of the draft in the board room. I loved the procedure and the excitement. Much of the time I sat back and watched and listened, but I was always prepared for a question or opinion. The last day of the draft, I believed it was my turn. I was prepared to stand on the table for anyone who I really wanted. Over the years I was involved in drafting players or offering opinions on players in every round.

At Miami, John Offerdahl, O.J. McDuffie, Pete Stoyanovich, Bryan Cox, Jason Taylor, Zach Thomas, Louis Oliver, Troy Vincent, and Richmond Webb were all excellent players with whom I helped.

In New York, I was involved in every level of the draft to some extent. My first year, Santana Moss was our first-round pick, and my Miami connection was a very big help for us there. Jonathan Vilma, Leon Washington, Eric Smith, Joe McKnight, and Mike Nugent are among numerous others I lent a helping hand in getting.

This draft, though, was going to be a little different. Yes, I had my time in front of everyone, and our rankings were present during the draft. But Mike Tannenbaum had invited only specific individuals into the draft room—and I wasn't on the list. Ben and I were to watch the draft on TV and would be called upon if our opinions were needed.

Total Bullshit!

We had gone from a championship-level team to a bullshit operation, and this was another example.

Ben and I devised a little game we played during the draft. Following each pick, we would drop to the floor and do the same number of push-ups as the pick number. I spent the entire draft in my office watching on TV and doing push-ups. No one ever asked my opinion on anyone. We wrote up 105 players, then watched TV and did push-ups.

I was now the angriest—and strongest—fucking coach in the league. I was sure it was time to go.

Following the season, Woody Johnson, the team's owner, met with me in his office in downtown New York, and he asked me to stay. I told him that after what had taken place, and including the draft bullshit, I was going to end up in one of two locations. Either my home in Florida or Riker's Island, the New York prison, as I was going to kill Mike Tannenbaum.

I wisely decided on Florida, and my great time in New York was coming to a sad end.

More Health Challenges

So far, my last year was a mess. Still no punter. Free agency was a joke, and the draft had been highlighted by watching TV and doing push-ups. At least I looked pretty good.

There was one positive aspect of that draft. Both Bob Sutton, a very good coach, and I liked a linebacker named Demario Davis. He came out of nowhere and took a long time to develop, but he turned out to be a very good player. He moved on to New Orleans and has done an outstanding job leading the greatly improved Saints defense and was an All-Pro in 2019.

The offseason had been nothing like I had hoped, but now we had our team and I could prepare for training camp and the start of the 2012 season. Ben and I would use our minicamp and OTAs to get our units organized, drill fundamentals and techniques, and see if we could complete our checklist of special teams situations.

I had created a checklist of about sixty areas that I wanted to address each year in practices. It consisted of things like punt protection versus every possible block, taking a safety under difficult time scenarios, kicking off and receiving after a safety, how to execute and receive a squib quick, and kicking off and receiving a kickoff from the 50-yard line after a penalty.

Also covered was how to play a free kick following a fair catch with no time remaining at the end of a half or the end of the game—and many, many more scenarios. Each had to be addressed and practiced before I could check it off my list.

I loved this challenge and looked forward to working on this each and every year.

We were also eager to incorporate Tim Tebow into our punt team and get prepared for the "nine million" fakes I believed we could run. I couldn't wait for the OTAs and a strong finish to the 2012 offseason.

Not so fast, Mike.

Before the start of our OTAs, I decided to take a trip to Indianapolis to visit John, his wife Elise, and my grandson Tom. John, who had graduated from Penn, was in law school at Indiana University, and this would be a great opportunity for a long weekend visit. I flew to Indianapolis, had a great dinner with them on Friday night, and on a Saturday morning we were taking a walk on Butler University's campus. It was a beautiful day, my grandson was in the stroller, and I could not have been happier or more proud.

(Elise was a fundraiser at the Indiana University Medical Center, one of the great surgical and cancer centers in the country. They currently live in Washington, D.C., where she has maybe the top fundraiser job in the country as executive director and CEO of the Philanthropy Roundtable. John has his degree and passed the bar exam and works as the senior vice president of mergers and acquisitions for Alarm Funding Associates. They are both extremely bright and very accomplished. By the way, I now have three grandsons: Tom, Sam, and Nathan. My best buddies!!!)

As we returned from our walk and were at John's house, something very unusual occurred. I noticed a clicking noise coming from my leg. This had never happened before, and it startled me. I went outside with John, and he could also hear the sound. I called Dr. Healey and told him what I was experiencing, and he instructed me to get to a hospital for an X-ray.

Elise was friends with the Indiana University Medical Center's executive director and called him for some help. He told us to come in, and he would get everything prepared for an X-ray. John and I stopped at a Walgreen's and bought a cane. I hadn't walked with one for three years, after having used one for over ten years, and it felt strange having to rely on one again.

While in the X-ray waiting room, I got up to use the restroom. As I walked in, my leg snapped in half and I fell pretty much headfirst into the toilet. I curled up in a ball and called to John. He hadn't heard me fall, and he came running into the bathroom. My leg resembled a pretzel, and he helped me straighten it out and sat me up on the floor.

John ran for help, and two orderlies came in and somehow got me onto a stretcher and over to the X-ray room. One of the joints in my prosthetics had broken. They are made out of titanium. How in the hell could this happen?

This will give you an idea, as explained by Troy Hershberger, director of Patient Matched Products for Biomet, Inc: "After the original surgery, I was able to meet Mike when he gave a motivational speech at a national meeting for Biomet team members. He had taken the time to tell everyone how important their jobs were to the patients they serve and how much it means to have his mobility restored. It was an incredible talk. At that meeting, he exchanged phone numbers, apparently, with the CEO of Biomet Inc., Jeff Binder."

That's correct. The previous summer I had given a speech in Orlando, Florida, to about 600 Biomet employees, dealing with motivation and appreciation. I had been given the cell phone numbers of Jeff Binder and of Troy. I had immediately called both of them about what I was experiencing that was never supposed to occur.

Jeff was in London and could not believe what had happened. He promised me they would stop at nothing to resolve the problem. I talked with Troy a number of times, and he said that they basically shut down the company to completely concentrate on solving the problem.

"Mike fractured the implant at one of the taper joint connections used to couple together the modular components," Troy explained. "This is an incredibly rare and disappointing occurrence, as the tapers are all made of titanium and are an incredibly strong and proven connection.

"This landed Mike in the care of another orthopedic surgeon, Dr. Dan Wurtz, to whom we had also provided multiple custom implants in the past. He was also known as a go-to surgeon to fix orthopedic disasters in the Indianapolis area.

"Upon arrival at the hospital and seeing the X-ray of his leg showing the implant had broken, Mike immediately called the Biomet CEO directly from his hospital bed. Moments after that my phone rang and I was told to call Mr. Westhoff, as there was a problem with his implant. I recall having this sick feeling and was sure that one of the bone ends had come loose from the implant.

"I talked with Mike and reassured him that we would engineer a solution immediately and get it to Dr. Wurtz. Dr. Wurtz then called me and said something like, 'The implant appears to have broken through the taper connection, but the bone segments look secure. Hurry, because this guy is going nowhere until we can fix him.'

"Immediately, we designed a new middle segment for the implant with increased taper diameters for this apparently high-demand patient who was more than a little hard on implants. The team worked twenty-four hours a day to design and manufacture the new implant in a matter of days.

"The new implant was installed between the two custom ends of the previous implant that were now fully grown in and anchored to the hip and knee ends of the femur, and apparently stronger than the titanium implant in between, just like Dr. Healey had hoped.

"I recall having numerous phone conversations with Mike throughout this process and telling him how surprised we were at the failure—and incredibly sorry that it had occurred, because we take these cases so personally. It's much more than just a job in the Biomet PMI (patient matched implant) department.

"He had every reason to be angry or disappointed, but instead he took the opportunity to coach. I recall the conversations to be encouraging and sometimes a bit animated, much like I would imagine his halftime or pregame talks to his players might be.

"I've come to realize that Mike is truly one of a kind and looks to the opportunity to motivate and coach wherever he is."

Yep, 2012 just kept getting better and better.

So now I am in an X-ray room looking at a picture of my titanium, unbreakable prosthesis, and it's snapped in half. How could this happen?

I called two of my best friends, Rick and Dan Galbraith, who I went to high school with and played football with. They owned a fencing company about twenty miles north of Indianapolis. About an hour later, they were sitting in the X-ray room with me.

There is one very definite thing that I have learned when it comes to dealing with medical issues—and I have had a hell of a lot of medical issues. I have been associated with the very best physicians in the country, and in some instances (Dr. Mankin and Dr. Healey), maybe the world. But no matter what, YOU are the most important doctor that you will ever deal with.

You must stay on top of every single aspect of your care. Be aware, ask questions, ask the doctor what he would do if it were happening to him, and always ask the nurses for help and opinions. Stay involved.

As I looked at the X-ray of the break, something didn't look right. The graft comes in sections, not just a long bar. I had my natural hip and knee joints, and all the bone in between was removed. My original tumor was in the middle of the femur, and now I basically had no bone, only metal. I had four sections and, counting from the top down, it was the second section that had broken.

Something about this section really bothered me. When it is your leg that has snapped in half, and you are just sitting there looking at it for hours, you pay attention.

I asked my friend Dan, who makes a living building fences. He welds his own gates. I know this sounds silly, but I asked him to look at the X-ray. The second section of the prosthesis that had broken was a five-inch area that was configured with two two-and-a-half-inch pieces to allow the rod some give and take.

Dan studied the picture and said very simply that the broken area experienced too much stress. The two-and-a-half inch pieces needed to be just one five-inch piece to handle the stress of the area.

Yeah, I know, a football coach and two fence guys, and we can see a problem? Well, maybe.

But I do know this: when the graft was repaired, the two-and-a-half-inches pieces were replaced with a five-inch piece.

Maybe football coaches and fence guys actually are kind of smart.

So, be your own doctor. I am not in the least bit critical of Dr. Healey or Biomet. They are geniuses, and what they developed is incredible. But there is always room for improvement.

The IU Medical Center is a great hospital. I had a private room and the very best care. I was in traction, as there was nothing holding my leg together, and moving around could be very dangerous.

Dr. Wurtz, the Dr. Healey of the Midwest, was familiar with the type of procedure and assured me that this was basically a "hardware" repair, and he was very capable and willing to proceed. I next talked with Dr. Healey, who was in Italy, and he very much wanted me to return to New York. Everyone was concerned about the dangers of traveling, and then the two doctors agreed on the procedure.

Now, I just had to wait on the new piece. You can't go to Home Depot and pick one of them off the shelf. These are completely hand-tooled out of blocks of titanium and configured to the finest of specifications. This is medical science at its very best. The guys are the real deal and at the very top of their profession.

I really liked Dr. Wurtz and completely trusted him. He just looks like someone who knows what he is doing, and you can trust that I was a little scared to not be with Dr. Healey, who I know so well. But I felt I was in very good hands.

One interesting thing about Dr. Healey (and Memorial Sloan Kettering)—and something he reiterated to me in February 2018 before my last and most complex nine-and-a-half-hour surgery—he assured me that for this "complex" surgery, he would have his entire "A" team.

Dr. Wurtz is a talented and brilliant surgeon, and the IU Medical Center is a great hospital, but they didn't exactly have the "A" team. Frankly, they had a dipshit anesthesiologist.

Before my surgery, and during my twelve-day wait while in traction, an anesthesiologist came in to talk about my upcoming surgery. I believe that I am good at judging people, and I instantly didn't like him. He seemed to be bored and disinterested. I had at least ten major surgeries and several very lengthy ones, so I was accustomed to being out for a long time.

I told him that each time when I woke up, I experienced severe nausea. He told me it was somewhat common and not to worry.

Yeah, you don't have to worry when you are not the one throwing up everything you have ever consumed.

I also told him that I experienced some trouble with a catheter if it was removed too soon. I told him I wanted to keep it in for a while to let my system calm down and start to return to normal. He looked at me like, "What the hell are you talking about?"

He actually said to me, believe this or not, "Orthopedic procedures are the easiest. Sometimes during them I do crossword puzzles."

Yeah, he actually said that to me. I was furious and let him know in no uncertain terms.

Well, I was right. The doctor was the best, the hospital was the greatest, but this guy was a complete dipshit.

The surgery took about five hours. Dr. Wurtz explained to me that removing the broken pieces was very difficult and time consuming. The surgery was difficult. The incision runs basically from my hip to my knee. They pretty much cut your leg in half.

While I was in intensive care's recovery room, Dr. Wurtz told me that everything had gone well, and the new piece fit perfectly. Just a short time now and I would be back to normal.

Unfortunately, this was the 2012 offseason—not so fast, Mike.

While still in the intensive care unit and slowly starting to awaken, I was feeling slightly nauseous but not terrible when a nurse told me to try and urinate, as my bladder was beginning to fill. I asked her why, as I was still catheterized.

She said no, the anesthesiologist had removed my catheter right after the surgery while in the intensive care unit.

Through an IV, I was receiving lots of fluids to keep everything moving through my system. During the surgery, my lower body had basically been numbed to aid in the pain reduction. That was now wearing off, but I really didn't have much feeling to enable me to urinate.

When I got to my room, I felt good and was again greeted by John and Patti. Soon after, I became very sick and began to vomit. It usually only lasted a short while, and I had experienced it before. The nausea ended, but then the next problem began.

An ultrasound test had revealed that my bladder was filling, and I needed to urinate, but there was no way that was going to happen at that time. They had no choice; I had to be catheterized. Try that when you are wide awake. Not at all pleasant.

Hopefully, things would return to normal. But they did not. The problem got worse.

Throughout the night, I had to be catheterized several more times, and it became very painful and I began to bleed. I spent the entire next day standing in front of the toilet, and nothing was working. I could have killed that anesthesiologist. If he had just left me alone and given me some time, everything would have returned to normal and the catheter would have been successfully removed. Instead, I was a mess.

Thankfully, in the middle of the second night, a nurse said, "The hell with this," and she told me that this would hurt some, but she was going to catheterize me and leave it in. I felt total relief and finally slept.

I kept the catheter and was forced to keep it for the next several weeks after I had returned to New Jersey. Woody Johnson sent his private plane for me, and Patti and I returned in style.

Dr. Wurtz's surgery was great, and I had healed quickly. I spent several weeks at my home resting and rehabbing. The tough part was returning to the NFL and being involved in practice while being catheterized and wearing a refuse bag attached to your leg.

Wearing a catheter was not the end of the world, and I learned to live with it. You just have to *figure it out*.

The fucked-up free agency, having no punter, and the half-assed draft procedure suddenly didn't seem so terrible. I had bigger problems to solve.

I also discovered that our offense wanted nothing to do with Tim Tebow, and he was basically getting no offensive work. Now, I was the only one playing him, and he could do only one thing for me.

By the way, I talked to the hospital administration, and they completely apologized and talked with their anesthesiologist. For what he put me through, I would rather have beat the shit out of him.

Well, the 2012 preseason and start of the regular season were right around the bend. What the hell could be next for 2012?

Training Camp

The NFL season was getting underway. For me, it was my thirtieth year in the league and my last. I was determined to make it my very best.

Good luck, Mike.

The offseason could not have been worse. Free agency was a miss. I still didn't have a punter—somewhat my fault, by the way. Sometimes personnel problems were my fault also. I could let my confidence, and maybe even arrogance, get in the way of good, solid decision-making. If a player had good basic skills and was a hard-working guy, I believed that I could turn him into a successful NFL player. I firmly believed in my ability to teach and motivate to a particular level of success.

You know, "I will make it work. I will *figure it out*."

Maybe not always.

The draft was highlighted by push-ups. I broke my "unbreakable" prosthesis and spent nearly three weeks in the hospital. I learned how to coach on the field while wearing a catheter with a bag attached to my leg.

Oh, also, I had Tim Tebow, who our offensive coaches could not stand and really did not want in any fashion. He was not my idea, but I had signed off on him, liked him a great deal, and was determined to find a role for him.

Well, here we go.

Training camp was, for me, something very special. It had evolved from a six-week torture chamber, with constant two-a-day padded practices, to basically a "football country club." Double-session days were never consecutive, and a pad-wearing practice had to be followed by one without pads. Walk-throughs had now become the new theme.

There had been a great number of changes, but it was still a grind of meetings, weight room work, and nearly daily practices.

For me, I loved it. Putting a special teams unit together was an exercise in creativity. So many new faces. Where to line them up? What are their best roles? Each day was a new challenge and an evolving process.

Every practice, I would experiment with an altered roster. Putting the pieces together was a gigantic chess match. I loved the challenge and was always trying to think outside of the box to come up with something special and maybe even different.

My favorite part of training camp was my night meeting, which included so many new, young guys hoping to find a way to make the team. At the level that they would be asked to play, most of them really didn't have a clue about special teams. They were nervous and scared.

Don't get me wrong, they were tough as hell, but they were scared. They had a lot to learn. With me, that meant learning every rule, assignment, and technique. I demanded an exactness that had to be executed perfectly. If we were going to set a double-team on the 24-yard line, your ass better be on the 24-yard line.

I would pass out part of a game plan with a play drawn exactly. I would then show film clips of various points of that play being practiced in a manner to get it perfectly correct. Then we would watch game film of the play—both good and bad—and learn from the entire process. When it was done correctly, I don't believe that anyone ever did it better than my guys. It wasn't just about Devin Hester running past everyone. This was the perfectly executed play that any number of players would have benefited from.

In my opinion, if you want to be considered a really good coach, find a way to make the average player special. Make everything about *what* and *how* you are doing something, not just *who* is doing it.

I know that Drew Brees is a first-ballot Hall of Fame quarterback, but Sean Payton taught that offense in such a way that the Saints could win a hell of a lot of games without Drew. They did.

In my twelve years with the Jets, we had nine players that led the NFL in either punt or kickoff returns. Try and beat that!

I loved walking into that meeting room at night and looking at the nervous, unsure faces. My goal each night was to find a way to turn them into special teams experts. I had to get them up and fight their discouragement. I often tried to supplement my presentations with stories relating to specific areas. I wanted their complete attention and would try numerous methods to achieve this.

"What I observed during my time with Mike was the way he related with the players and got them to play at a high level," said Bill Callahan, the outstanding offensive line coach who led the 2002 Raiders to the AFC title as head coach. "To me, coaching special teams is about developing an esprit de corps, and Westy brought that concept to life. He had a unique way about himself and in the manner with which he instilled confidence within the unit and its players.

"The thing is, players respect coaches who can elevate their game, and Mike did that. He could inspire the players through his storytelling and the personal experiences in his own life. He showed true leadership at all levels of coaching, whether it was in the classroom, on the grass, or off the field. It just wasn't enough for his units to be good, he wanted them to be the best in the NFL, and they were.

"He evoked a standard of performance from the first day of training camp that was rock solid all the way through the playoffs. True to form, when his players hit the practice field, it was all business. He had great belief in himself and what he was teaching because his production and results spoke for themselves. He did not tolerate mental mistakes or lack of concentration in a practice. He would blow a gasket if a player didn't know his assignment or wasn't in the position he wanted him to be in. God help you if you were that guy because you didn't want Mike's wrath laid upon you.

"I really admired his command and style on the practice field because that is where true coaching and results take place. It was really fun to watch him teach, motivate, and demand excellence from his players."

I remember in this particular camp in 2012 relating a story to them that I had read somewhere during that summer. It was about an American journalist who had traveled to Australia to do a story on a very large, successful sheep ranch in the Outback. As he traveled to the ranch, he was amazed at the miles and miles of vast, open range. How could anything this size be managed?

When he arrived at the ranch, he had a very long conversation with the owner. The rancher pointed out that there was a severe labor problem due to the short number of "ranch hands" that all basically had to live there nearly all year due to travel problems. He then told the writer that his most valuable tool was their sheep dogs. It was these very skilled dogs that herded the sheep and enabled them to move the herd from one pasture to another. Without the many skilled dogs, his ranch would not operate.

He then told the writer how they obtained the dogs. Once every two years, they would travel to a breeder to inspect a new litter of pups. After examining the newborn pups, they would identify two with strings of yarn in different colors that they would tie around the pups' necks. One would be the strongest, best-looking pup, and the other would be basically the "runt of the litter."

After about two months, they would return to see how the pups had progressed. They knew that the stronger one would have developed, but what they had hoped to see was if the runt had survived and flourished. Because if it had, then they knew they had found something special.

You see, if the runt survived, then it had severely persevered. It had overcome its obstacles and had grown. It had to be smarter, more aware, more instinctive, more aggressive, and more competitive just to be able to compete against the rest of the more capable litter. If it were to have accomplished these goals, then by now it would be grown to an equal size and have the special attributes that set it apart from the rest of the litter. It was now a leader with special, learned skills.

This is now the dog they wanted to work their ranch. It had acquired special skills both mentally and physically.

They would take this particular dog back to the ranch and then, in a most cruel manner, they would place the remaining pups into a sack and drown them in a lake. I told the players that we were not going to do that to them, but with several it had been discussed.

Those particular skills that were so very necessary for a successful sheep ranch were the same skills that a young player needed to make it against the more adept and more experienced NFL veterans. The hardest working, most relentless, most aggressive, smartest—and the player that will never give up and just keep coming back, over and over again—this is the guy who is going to make it in the NFL.

I didn't care what they looked like, a "number" wasn't going to make up my mind as to who would succeed. We were going to be the best unit in the NFL; that was the only goal, every year. Anything less was my failure, and I wasn't real good at that.

I loved the entire process, and each year I couldn't wait for it to begin. It is one of the things that I miss the very most since retiring from the NFL.

This last training camp was in Cortland, New York, at SUNY-Cortland, a state university school located about a three-hour drive northwest of Manhattan in the Finger Lakes area of the state.

The area is beautiful, surrounded by mountains and with great, slightly cooler weather. The campus also was beautiful and the facilities very accommodating. Our practice field looked like a golf course, and their stadium was more than adequate for our needs.

The university president, Dr. Erik Bitterbaum, could not have been more hospitable. The town completely welcomed us, and fans flocked in for every practice. We brought in a lot of business and money into a somewhat depressed area, and everyone seemed to benefit from our three weeks in Cortland. I loved every minute of having training camp there.

The arrival of Tim Tebow dominated the news. Every day it was nonstop: "What is Tim Tebow doing?"

ESPN brought in a set and covered us all day every day. Sal Paolantonio and Hannah Storm were full-time covering every minute of Tim Tebow.

I had expressed an interest in doing some media work following my retirement and was eager and appreciative to be interviewed by Sal and Hannah many times. They are great media professionals and helped me in many ways. Sal showed me how to sit and place my hands correctly while being on the air, and where to focus and how to answer questions. Throughout my five-year media career, I remembered and utilized many of the tips those two pros taught me.

So the Tim Tebow media blitz wasn't a complete mess. I benefited greatly.

The football side? Not so great.

We just didn't have an identity. Who were we? What kind of team were we going to become? I couldn't see anything we really looked good at. I was told we would have "special" plays for Tim. Our offensive coaches must not have heard that because we never did have them. The entire Tim Tebow thing was becoming a fiasco.

An awkward incident occurred before one of our practices. I was standing on the sideline talking with our scouts and one of our doctors. He was new, in his first NFL year. Mike Tannenbaum came over and scolded him for standing around talking and not doing his job of checking on our injured players' rehab work. It was unnecessary and humiliating.

I covered for him by saying that I had asked him about one of my players on the injury report. (I had not asked, by the way.)

Just an example of acting like a complete ass. Good luck with this camp.

It was becoming clear that my last season with the Jets was not going to be my most memorable—except in one very, very special way.

My Last Season in New York

Training camp was over, and we were now back in Florham Park. Our preseason games were behind us, and we were preparing for our home opener versus the Buffalo Bills. For the first time in my thirty years, we lost all four preseason games. You didn't have to win them all, but you sure as hell don't want to lose them all either. Just one year ago, I felt like we could beat anyone, and now I am questioning whether or not we will be able to beat anyone.

The NFL is a "short trip," either up or down. We had moved away from back-to-back championship games, and now the championship game seemed as far away as the other side of that sheep ranch.

But the 2012 season for me and our special teams started off very well. We beat Buffalo in the opener, and our punt returner, Jeremy Kerley, ran a "Giant White" (seven in the box, middle) for a touchdown, again putting us at the top of the class as a kick return unit.

We next lost to a very good Pittsburgh team, then traveled down to Miami and won a hard-fought game. Our special teams continued to play well, highlighted by a Tim Tebow fake for a first down that led to a Jets score.

We returned home to face the 49ers, who were headed to the Super Bowl. Our administration should have come down to the field before the game and taken a good look at that team. They looked like an NFL team. We looked like the junior varsity compared to their guys. The athleticism of their skilled players compared to ours, and the size of their defensive line and line-backers—we didn't even look like a high school team compared to them.

They completely kicked our asses. I was embarrassed and angry. I was going to retire, but our entire front office should have come with me. This was the beginning of the end. In 2020, Jets had still not *figured it out*. We ruined a damn good football team.

We lost at home the next week to a very good Houston team. I had a good special teams day with two really long plays. Joe McKnight ran for a 100-yard TD, and Tim Tebow executed another successful fake punt against Houston's top-ranked defense. The fake was a "Shark" check-with-me call, and when Houston did not adjust to our unbalanced line, we successfully ran the fake.

We played well on special teams, but overall, the Jets were terrible. We were now 2-3 and headed nowhere. The next week we got back into the win column against the Colts and had another excellent Tim Tebow fake: a sprint out to an unbalanced line and a throwback pass to Nick Bellore.

Next, we were headed up to New England to face Tom Brady and Bill Belichick. I was having an excellent year and was determined to make something great happen and maybe give us some type of edge. Joe McKnight was leading the league in kickoff returns, and I was sure that New England would be scoring often and therefore kicking off a number of times. I was going to make them pay something on every kickoff.

I had competed against them many times and knew their kicker, Stephen Gostkowski, very well and could tell exactly by his alignment where he was going to kick the ball. I was going to run all our returns with a check-with-me call that I would signal each time from the sideline. Many teams do this, but usually with someone from their front line of blockers giving the signal. I did it my entire career and studied the entire procedure very diligently—and never got one wrong.

"What made Mike really great is the fact he had a sophisticated scheme for the way he coached," Leon Washington said. "And yet he made it seem simple. Terms like 'Check With Me,' which would mean Mike would look at the kicker and his walk-off and see where and how he would kick it. And then we would look over right before the ball was kicked off and Mike would give us a play.

"That type of coaching is unheard of, pretty much. Coming up with things on the sideline and making adjustments during a game and knowing personnel—you're talking about one of the best people in identifying players on special teams. Then knowing where to put players to help them succeed."

I also changed our front line, which normally lined up 13 yards from the ball and had very specific techniques for retreating into a blocking position. We lined up in a balanced stance like a baseball shortstop, and on the kicker's approach, while focusing on the ball, we would shuffle back for two steps before turning and sprinting back to our designated blocking area.

If you want to give an opponent an onside kick, cross over and turn your shoulders. That is what you look for if you are going to try an onside kick. But that week in New England, I instructed our front line back an extra five yards to enable us to set up properly. I know, 18 yards? Mike, you are giving them the onside kick.

I was sure, though, that Bill Belichick wasn't going to try to beat the New York Jets with an onside kick.

I was correct; he did not. And we had several good returns and helped our offense with their field position. We fought hard but lost to an extremely talented New England team.

The next week we played Miami at home in what was the worst NFL game in my career. I moved our front line back to our normal 13 yards but cautioned that Miami had seen the 18 yards and would be prepared to onside kick. I practiced it during the week, and in the huddle before a Miami kickoff, I reminded our guys that this would be a good time for them to try the kick.

They did, hitting the ball right in the chest of my left guard. It bounced off of him, and they recovered. I will give them credit for kicking the ball to the correct guy, but we should have made the play.

They also ran a double-wrap punt block. We practiced it a hundred times, but our personal protector, Eric Smith, had gotten injured, and Tim Tebow now had to fill in and block. No, not run a fake. BLOCK.

If he just stepped up into the line, there would be no room for the two defenders. But not Tim, and they blocked our punt for a TD. I had one or two punts tipped, but very few damn blocks.

We had only one great return, and if we had Joe McKnight, we surely would have scored, but he was also out, so we only came close. It was a terrible day for me, my worst ever. I lost the game. No one else. Just me.

I never went home after that game, only to my office to study the film. Everything was exactly as I thought. We got out-executed, not tricked or out-coached, but that didn't help much. I was in charge, and I got beat. I don't like losing, and I got beat.

I remember Rex Ryan coming into my office saying he and his wife had stopped by on his way to pick up something, and asking what the hell was I doing here. I told him that the game was completely on me. No one else should get any of the blame.

He just smiled and said there was plenty of blame to go around. Rex knew, though, that I firmly believed what I was telling him. He knew the level of ownership that I accepted.

What the fuck had happened to 2010? This was my last year, and it was a total fucking fiasco.

After losing to Miami, we won three of our next five games and maybe could continue on to a winning season. We beat St. Louis, Arizona, and Jacksonville—all relatively poor teams who two years before we would have beaten with our eyes closed, and now we were just happy to have sneaked by.

The two losses during that stretch were at a complete opposite end of the scale. We lost in Seattle to a good team in a well-played and extremely hard-fought game. But then, after the victory over the Rams, we came home to play New England on Thanksgiving night. I am sure that when the network and the NFL were picking that prime-time Thanksgiving matchup, they saw a championship game team that had beaten the Patriots at their home in the playoffs.

What they got, though, was a dinner-ruining mess that upset stomachs all over the country.

I had been involved in two Thanksgiving Day games and was undefeated. The Miami versus Dallas snow game in which Leon Lett mistakenly touched a blocked field goal, giving us another shot at Pete Stoyanovich's field goal and a chance to win the game, which we did. Also, three years earlier than this meeting with New England, on Thanksgiving night against Cincinnati, Brad Smith ran a kickoff return for a TD while losing his shoe at the 50-yard line and finishing the run in one shoe.

"There were a number of games, especially on kickoffs, where things just clicked—when we got a return for a touchdown, and it went down the way Mike would always draw it up," Eric Smith said. "There was one guy we would have to account for, and then every time it worked.

"I remember that Thanksgiving night playing Cincinnati and Brad Smith loses his shoe and still returns it for a touchdown. We were in Pittsburgh, we needed something to happen, and Brad runs it back for a touchdown on the opening kickoff. It got to the point every time we went out there, if everyone gets to the block the way Mike has it drawn it up, it will be a touchdown.

"Not to take anything away from any returners we had, who were amazing—the entire crew we put out there—but we had a heck of a group of blockers, so good you could almost put anybody back there and get a big return.

"Joe McKnight was one of the guys Mike got mad at. He should have had five or six touchdowns on returns, and Mike would freak out because the kicker would get him, or Joe would run out of gas.

"Joe probably could have set records for kickoff returns, but he would always get tired or let the kicker tackle him. If there is the one guy Mike couldn't account for somehow, that was the guy who would get Joe down.

"He could point guys out—by body size and ability and know what role they could play—and then rep after rep he would work on it. He designed the returns where you might line up in a different spot but would be doing the same technique and you could be successful that way."

I loved playing on Thanksgiving and was excited for this rematch. Oops—we got killed.

New England beat us on seemingly every play. This was the famous "Butt Fumble Game"—when Mark Sanchez ran into the rear end of one of our offensive linemen and fumbled the ball, which was scooped up by a Patriots player and returned for a touchdown—and a complete embarrassment.

Standing on the sideline, for the first time in my career I felt embarrassed to be there. I had gone from feeling such pride to one of humiliation. When is this shit going to end?

I wanted to blame Mike Tannenbaum, and I believe he got the ball rolling downhill, completely by himself. But I was helping coach this heap of crap, and I have to accept my share of the blame.

We had three games left to play after beating the Jaguars and still had that chance for a winning season. We lost to Tennessee in a fairly well-played game. I was proud that we were fighting back and going down swinging.

Next, we returned home. Our last home game—and my last game in front of the Jets fans. I loved New York and the Jets fans. I felt as though I had in some ways become one of them. My first ten years with the Jets, we had been in the playoffs six times and had gone to two AFC Championship games. We all had a lot to be proud of.

I believe that one could argue during that time we were the best overall special teams unit in the NFL. Chicago might try to make that claim, but overall, top to bottom, I believe we were the best.

We had those nine league-leading return specialists. Every year, we were near the top of starting field position rankings. We had blocked numerous kicks and had received very few. We created turnovers and had experienced very few. We were one of the least-penalized teams and showed the ability to make strategically aware plays. Our kickers were very good, and even though we didn't really have a punter of any notoriety, our punting numbers didn't kill us.

The Jets fans were good to me and showed it in many instances. I would travel into New York City for dinner and was often greeted with encouragement and thank yous. I loved New York and only wished we could have turned one of those AFC Championship games into a Super Bowl.

"I think 'Hard Knocks' was really how Jets fans got to know him," John said. "I remember he called my house one time when it was on (HBO), and he asked about the show, 'What did you think?' Then he asked to talk to my wife, Elise, and said, 'I don't really curse like that.' I told him, 'Sometimes you do, I just saw you doing it.'

"He's not like that at dinner in any way with the family, with his grandkids. He's a teddy bear. The person he was on the practice field is not who he is as a dad or a grandfather."

Bidding Adieu

The Jets were going to do a wonderful and unique thing for me at my last home game. Before the start of the game and after our starting lineup was introduced, I would also be introduced and could run—for me, limp—down the ramp and out onto the field with the remainder of the team. I don't know how many times in the NFL that a coach was introduced with the team. I was over-whelmed and very emotional.

I received a standing ovation and the team swarmed all around me. I could not have been more proud or more grateful to Woody Johnson, Mike Tannenbaum, and Rex Ryan: THANK YOU FOR A WONDERFUL MOMENT!

It should have been an incredible way to end a home appearance before the Jets crowd.

Seven years later, also at MetLife Stadium, I received a similar honor. I was given the Lifetime Achievement Award by the Professional Football Writers of America for accomplishments as an NFL assistant coach. The very small number of recipients of this highly prestigious award made it special. And that very special night I shared with my son, John; my two grandsons at the time,

Tom and Sam; and my girlfriend, Patti—that was one of the highlights of my coaching career.

My last home game in New York began against San Diego, and I was standing on the sideline filled with pride and emotion. It couldn't get any better.

But this was 2012. And we have to punt. My twelve-year punting curse comes back to smack me right in the face.

The Chargers don't have anyone special over there, and I am expecting to move them back and keep any return to a very minimum. Does it look like a punt? NO—more like a Dan Marino perfect pass. Right to their guy on the wrong side of the field, and he runs 63 yards for a touchdown.

My heart was somewhere down near my shoes. I actually felt like calling a timeout and walking out to around the 20-yard line, turning to the crowd, waving good-bye, and running my ass back up that fucking ramp, out of the stadium and right the hell home. That would have been a fitting way to end the 2012 season.

But there was one more game.

My NFL career, at least I believed so, was coming to an end. It was my 625th NFL game; I count everything. Yes, regular season, preseason, playoffs, and the Pro Bowl. If they keep score, I count the game.

We were traveling to Buffalo, and I might have been setting a record as an opposing coach. This was going to be my thirty-fifth trip to Buffalo, combining playoff and regular-season games. I should receive some sort of presidential award to have gone to Buffalo that many times as an opponent.

Actually, I loved it. I had some great personal games in Buffalo, and I always admired and respected their great fans.

The Jets were doing another very special thing for me. They were inviting my son John to travel with us and be on the sideline with me for my final game. Maybe they were being so nice to make sure that I was actually going to retire and leave. I am sure there were a number of people in the building that felt that way. I am not always for everyone.

John was living in Indianapolis, having recently graduated from the law school at Indiana University. John grew up in Fort Lauderdale while I was coaching with the Miami Dolphins. He spent much of his youth in our locker room, on the Dolphins' sideline and their practice fields. He went to St. Thomas Aquinas, America's top football high school and an excellent academic school, where he lettered three years as a long snapper and offensive guard. He received his first championship ring from St. Thomas when it won its first state title when he was a junior.

We lived very close to the Dolphins complex, and he would often receive calls from our kicker, Olindo Mare, to come down and snap for him to help him practice his kicking. Our holder at the time was Doug Pederson, Dan Marino's backup quarterback who won a Super Bowl as head coach of the Philadelphia Eagles.

Not a bad way to grow up.

"He didn't let me play right away, and I had to beg to play tackle in the eighth grade," John recalled. "He thought there was no need to rush it, and the coaching is so poor technically for kids. It was the complete opposite of what people thought: he never pressured me to play. Whatever my pursuit, he encouraged me.

"I always saw the warm and caring side instead of the intimidating side. He could flip the switch. It could be five minutes before practice, and he turned to me and he asked me about my team and practice. And the second he walked onto the field, he was in coaching mode, and it all changed. When he would come home, we saw nothing of that.

"I was a freshman at Penn when he joined the Jets. I may have been the only coach's kid who went K through 12 in the same school. I didn't realize how many offers he had that he turned down. I had a good situation, and he wanted to keep me where I was. It was much later in life before I thanked him for doing that.

"His going to the Jets, it made the NFL more of a business to me. Dan Marino and Don Shula I idolized, and this made me realize it is a business. I grew up a Dolphins fan, and I hated the Jets; there was no team I hated more. Then I woke up and my dad was coaching in New York and I was a Jets fan.

John Westhoff (left)

"Some friends couldn't understand. I told them, 'Am I supposed to root against my father's team?' I became a big Jets fan."

John lettered three times at Penn and won two Ivy League championships. He has three rings; I have none. Way to go, Dad.

It was a very special time for me, and I will always be very appreciative. Every trip for me was an exact procedure. On the bus I always sat in the same seat, right behind the driver on the first bus. Coach Shula sat right across the aisle from me and started the tradition, as that is where he told me to sit so he could talk to me during the ride. No one had ever sat in the seat next to me, but now here was John, and I couldn't have been happier.

He had shared my first-class plane seat and even had a ginger ale just like me. Sometimes parents can be a pain in the neck. We just can't help ourselves.

The team got John his own hotel room, and he was able to eat with our coaching staff and myself. He went to Mass with me and attended my last Saturday night pregame players meeting.

My last meeting was very special and emotional for me. Most of our coaches attended, and, of course, John was there. I gave my normal game plan and scouting report rehash and explained specifically how we could make a difference in the game. I had a short film I was going to show the team. It was a beautiful collection of the greatest moments in sports, all set to *Dream On*, by Aerosmith. Short clips of everyone from Babe Ruth to Muhammad Ali, Michael Jordan, Tiger Woods, Mickey Mantle, Larry Bird, Jim Brown, and many, many more. It was really cool and conveyed a great message:

Dream on. Sports are about dreaming, and even as an NFL player, it is OK to dream.

I didn't know it, but in the middle of the film, our media guys had inserted clips of our special teams over the last several years. They had included several TV videos in which announcers had been very kind to me. There were some excellent clips of some of the great things that we had accomplished. It was an honor and a thrill. I couldn't have been more proud.

I finished the meeting by telling them that I had always dreamed of what I could do in the NFL, and I lived that dream every single day. Some things just can't get any better, and this was one of them.

My last game with the Jets was very much a reflection of what we had become. We got beat 28-9, and that is exactly who we were. Our defense was mediocre; my group had some bright spots but just as many not-so-bright sports. And our offense was the worst I had ever been associated with in my thirty-year NFL career.

Yes, the worst—and it wasn't even close.

The game day was special but not memorable. It was a typically cold December day in Buffalo. John rode on the bus with me, and our equipment guys outfitted him in the proper winter clothing. He had a sideline pass and was free to walk around the stadium and enjoy just being a part of game day.

Once I got off the bus, I immediately fell into my game-day ritual. I always dressed up a little for a game. I never wore a tie, but I often wore a sport coat or suit. I wore a black cashmere topcoat and a sporty Irish cap that I bought in Ireland. I respected the NFL and believed the proper dress was a part of that respect.

Upon arriving at the stadium, I would go to my locker and retrieve my sideline pass. Because I had been in the league for so long, most of the stadium security guards recognized me, and I would not need my pass, but I always made sure that I had it, just in case.

Then in my dress clothes I would walk into the stadium and walk all over the field. I would check the wind and the field conditions at every possible spot where we might have to kick.

I often would say hello to opposing players and coaches and sometimes media personnel. I only talked for a few minutes, as I really wasn't in the mood to see any of them anyway. I only had a few real friends in the business. I respected most everyone but cared for only a few.

I then would go back into the locker room and get dressed to come back out for the pregame. In many stadiums, Buffalo included, there are areas where the fans are very close, and I was often greeted with not-so-friendly reminders of who I was and where I was.

"We will kick your ass today, Westhoff."

Of which I would remind them, "Every time I am here, I beat the shit out of you."

I am not shy, and I fight back. It happens in nearly every stadium, even New England. The worst place, absolutely, was Oakland. Nowhere else was even close. I had been there for several playoff games, and our special teams had always played exceptionally well. One time, as I walked into the stadium with my cane, I was greeted with "Westhoff, you crippled mother, we are going to kill you today."

My answer wasn't as gross, but somewhat in line. Most of the fans are great, but sometimes well . . .

The absolute best part of my last game with the Jets was standing on the sideline next to John during the playing of the national anthem. The song will always have a very special meaning for me in several fashions.

It was always an emotional moment for me, but standing next to my son, in my last game, was a moment that I will never forget and will always cherish.

The game began, we kicked off, and I was back to reality. Following the game, and a few words with each of my players in the locker room, I took John and went back out to the field. We sat on the bench, and I reflected on what a great run I had experienced. More than 600 games in the best job in the world. The ending was sad, but after all I had been through, I was the luckiest guy in the world!

Yes, the luckiest guy.

CHAPTER 14

Retirement? Not Quite

Following my retirement from the NFL in 2012, I left my apartment in New Jersey and moved full-time into my home in Fort Myers, Florida. I spent months preparing my home and life for retirement. I traveled back and forth between Florida and New York, where my girlfriend Patti lived, and Philadelphia, the home of my son John, his wife Elise, and my three grandsons: Tom, Sam, and Nathan.

I live on a golf course and got back into playing again. I had not played as much golf in recent years due to my many leg surgeries, but I was feeling stronger and now was trying to regain some form. Most of my leisure time, though, was spent on my boat, fishing for sharks in the Gulf of Mexico.

During this retirement period, I also went to work for ESPN Radio in New York. I would frequently guest with Michael Kay, the station's main talk show host, his co-host Don La Greca, and with Stephen A. Smith. I also did a NFL football show on Sunday mornings from ten to noon with Anita Marks, and in later years with Chris Canty.

Anita Marks did an excellent job and was as well-prepared as anyone I have ever been in contact with. I felt that she, Chris, and I had an exciting and informative NFL show.

So did Anita, whom I had known when I was with the Dolphins and she worked for a local TV station.

"When I came up here to New York to work, Mike was with the Jets," Anita said. "So, I knew him, but we had not had any long conversations. I was told he was going to be doing the New York Jets Game Day Show with me on ESPN radio, and he called and left a message for me saying, 'Before I take this job, I want to talk to you first.'

"He was very honest. He said, 'I am out of coaching, and this is all new to me. So, I want to get a feel for you, and do you want to work with me?' That's the type of decency and the kind touch you don't see much in this business. When I hung up with him, I was more than ecstatic to do the show with him.

"When the show kicked off, there was a lot of feeling each other out. The one thing Mike brings that is so fantastic is the way he was able to explain and give us visualization on what one would have to do on a play. The Xs and Os and schemes on defense, and what the Mike linebacker has to do; the way he was able to explain it and what the defense needed to do versus opponents is something most people can't do. Especially on radio. I think it was a gift."

It wasn't all smooth sailing for Anita and me on the program. She has a certain area of expertise that I don't.

"What was challenging was my specialty was fantasy football and gambling, and he wanted nothing to do with it," Anita said, still chuckling at those memories. "Mike didn't quite understand how somebody's analysis like his, an expert, helps us with our fantasy football decisions. Like which wide receiver do you think will have a better day so you can have him active? Mike couldn't get that connection.

"That was fun and funny, and we had this back and forth quite a few times.

"The sports conversation has changed immensely. Not only was it impressive to watch Mike grow and develop and mature as a broadcaster, but also it is a new day in what drives the conversation. What people want to talk about and what matters, it is the gambling and fantasy that are driving the needle. Mike got that, and said, 'OK, I understand we have to talk about it.'"

While I brought my coaching perspective to the program, Anita was able to look at the game from a playing aspect. She played football for five years. She knows football.

"My terminology and way I see a game and analyze the game," Anita said, "what you can tell is I have played football. I've had a lot of really great ex-pro football players and coaches say, 'You know your stuff.'

"That is the thing Mike would do all the time, give me the credibility. When Mike Westhoff says, 'Well, Anita, you know your stuff,' it gives me so much more credibility. The amount of respect he provided me was immense."

I really was just trying to be myself on the air. You know, no bullshit, the same way I had coached. I believe the listeners or viewers deserve that.

So does Anita.

"I think it is refreshing when you have an ex-coach or ex-player that is totally honest and doesn't hold back his opinion and doesn't shy away on his opinion regardless of how it might be received or who it might piss off," Anita said. "How many listeners or readers understand there are guys who are afraid of what they say because of the negative feedback they can get? It was a treat to work with somebody who was in the business and very successful, and he was very honest and forthcoming about his take. I think that made the program great.

"There's a lot of transparency there with Mike, and when that happens, listeners know it. Viewers see it. No BSing anyone, and you get even much more respect, and I think they appreciate that.

"I still have listeners who see me at an appearance who will say, 'I really loved when you and Mike did the shows together.' That speaks volumes."

I also worked at SNY-TV hosting the Jets' postgame show and, in 2017, the pregame show. I worked with Jonas Schwartz; Ray Lucas, who had been a Jets quarterback; Jeane Coakley; Chad Cascadden, a former Jets linebacker; and Willie Colon, who was an NFL offensive lineman for a decade and won a Super Bowl with the Steelers. Curt Gowdy Jr. was the executive producer of the regional network and did an excellent job of presenting sports to the New York area.

I loved the show and the interaction with my co-hosts—especially our Thursday night pregame shows with Jeane and Ray. I think that it was the best show on the network.

My fall weeks were extremely busy. I would spend hours preparing, mostly for my radio shows. I would study the same statistical comparisons that I used as a coach. I was able to accurately determine the strengths and weaknesses of the teams and then present thoughts of what each must do to win.

Much of my week's preparation also went toward my SNY Jets pregame shows. Each week, I would explain how the Jets compared to their opponent. My favorite segment was the "Coach's Chalk Talk." I would pick a particular area in which I would show that if the Jets executed properly, they would gain a specific advantage. I loved doing this; I actually got to draw up a play or two—much like I had done my entire coaching career. I was now getting to do that on TV.

I worked hard with one of the station's employees who taught me the intricacies of the Telestrator. I became more and more comfortable with the procedure and improved each week.

Every week, I would fly to New York and stay for a few days to work on the TV show. I was able to see Patti and enjoy the restaurants of New York, then drive down to Philadelphia and visit my son and his family (his three boys, my buddies).

One such weekend, out of nowhere, my life changed . . . again.

New Orleans Calling

It was Saturday, November 11, 2017. I was in New York to do my shows. My girlfriend was having a shower for her daughter at her home in Long Island, so I was staying in the city. I had dinner with my good friend and former Jets coach Chris Mattura at my favorite restaurant in the city, Elio's, located on Second Avenue and 84th Street on the Upper East Side. It is, in my opinion, New York's very best—and that is saying something for New York. I would eat there every night, if possible.

Following dinner, I was in the hotel watching the Notre Dame-Miami game when I received a phone call.

It was from Mike Ornstein, who I have never received a phone call from in my life. I knew Mike from his work with the Oakland Raiders as an assistant to Al Davis, the Hall of Fame owner, and his work with NFL Properties in the league office. He asked me if I wanted to go back to work. I told him no, that I was happy with my retirement and my TV job.

He said the New Orleans Saints wanted me to come to work for them and would be very generous with their offer. I told him I didn't know anyone with the Saints and no thanks. They were halfway through the season. I had never met the coach, Sean Payton, and I had zero interest.

He told me that they were in Buffalo to play the Bills. Would I talk with Sean on Monday? I told him I would be driving to Philadelphia on Monday, and I would talk to him, but I wasn't going anywhere.

A few minutes later, I received another call, this time from Doug Miller, the Saints' sports information director. I knew Doug from his days with the Jets when he had a similar job before leaving for New Orleans. I liked Doug and felt he was very good at his profession. He told me that the Saints were a very good team but had lost confidence in their special teams and needed me to implement a change. The relationship between the head coach and Brad Banta, the special teams coordinator, had deteriorated and some change was needed.

I knew Brad from his playing days, and he had also worked for the Washington Redskins and my longtime assistant, Ben Kotwica, who was the Redskins' special teams coordinator.

I listened to Doug and basically told him the same as I had said to Mike Ornstein: I had no interest in moving to New Orleans, but I respected the Saints and Sean Payton, and I would be willing to talk with them on Monday.

What the hell was I doing? I knew who Sean Payton was and thought he was an excellent coach; I later found out I was exactly right in that regard. But I had never said hello to him. He never knew this, but if I had taken Bill Parcells' job offer years earlier in Dallas we would have worked together.

I finished my SNY shows in New York, the Jets had played Tampa, and I was proud of how my TV work was progressing.

The next day, however, as I drove to Philadelphia, I could only think of one thing: the New Orleans Saints.

I was driving across the RFK Bridge from Long Island to cross Manhattan and head south to Philadelphia when Sean Payton called. I put him on my speaker, and for nearly forty-five minutes, I listened and talked.

They had beaten Buffalo the previous day and were at the time one of the best teams in the NFL. He loved his team and thought it could win it all, but he had indeed lost confidence in special teams. Sometimes coaches just drift apart. Sean is a very knowledgeable coach. He knows all parts of the game and can involve himself in any and all aspects. He just needed and wanted a change. I was recommended to him, and he was reaching out.

He discussed some of the problems and how he believed that they could be solved. I told him that I didn't care about any of that. If I were to become involved, I would handle everything in my own fashion. He said he would sign me to a contract for the rest of the year and for the next as well. I said no thanks. I wasn't the slightest bit interested in the next year.

I told him that if we worked a financial deal, I had to have two things. First, I was going to control the entire special teams. I was going to do everything my way. Within the constraints of his philosophy and schedule, and in conjunction with him, but I was running the show.

Secondly, he could not fire anyone. I don't know if he would have done that or not, but I would not come if he fired anyone. It wouldn't be the easiest thing, but I would make it work. I am sure that Brad Banta would feel like he got punched in the stomach, but I was not the problem. I was going to be there to work together and solve the problem—and build an exceptional special teams unit.

I only wanted to be No. 1. I sure as hell didn't reach that goal every time, but I had reached it a number of times, and it was my only destination.

The next day I received a call from Saints general manager Mickey Loomis, a thirty-two-year veteran of the league who had been with the Saints now for more than fifteen seasons. We discussed a one-year contract, a car, and a place to live. It was a very fair contract, not only for me but also for them. Considering what they have done lately, I could have done much, much better, but it was very fair for everyone, and I will always feel good about my dealings with the Saints. Mickey Loomis might be the best GM in the NFL, and in my opinion one of the very best executives in professional sports. He understands all aspects of the business and is innovative and exceptionally bright.

In some ways, the New Orleans Saints are the "best-kept secret in the NFL." They are a small-market town that doesn't get the notoriety or credit they deserve.

Sean called me back, and we discussed how it would all take place. He knows a hell of a lot of football, which was obvious from our first phone conversation.

I returned to Long Island, phoned a friend in Florida, and asked him to look after my home and to forward the mail. I packed one small bag and headed to New Orleans on a Wednesday morning, preparing to coach a practice that afternoon with not one person I had even met.

Actually, I was wrong. Kevin O'Dea had been hired as their kicking coach. We had worked together with the Jets, with Kevin as one of my assistants. I had always liked him and thought him to be a good coach, so I was taking some comfort in a familiar face.

I met with Sean, and we discussed the situation and what he was hoping for. I told him that I only knew one way to do things, and I was going to start that afternoon. I went to the coaches' locker room and was given something to wear to practice. Then I went upstairs for the toughest meeting of the day.

I sat down with Brad Banta, Kevin, and Deuce Schwartz, the quality control and computer coach. Now they have me—what the hell must they be thinking?

I made it clear that I did not seek the role but now was determined to *figure it out*.

Brad was the most hurt; I was stepping into his shoes. I had to assure him, encourage him to take a deep breath and believe that we—not me—would straighten this out and move forward. I asked about his family and if I could meet with his wife on Saturday. I actually did meet with her, and I assured her I was not there to take her husband's job but to work with him and maybe save his job and accomplish a lot while doing so.

Brad is a big, powerful man at 6-5, 270 pounds, but he can be quiet and somewhat soft-spoken. He is not loud or demonstrative, but don't mistake that in any way for weakness. I know Brad very well, and if under provocation he might grab you and pull a body part off and put it in his pocket. I was taking over, and he was going to do things my way, but an unusually drastic change was not needed. Just some tinkering and adjusting, and everything would get back on track.

"Imagine being a twelfth man on the Chicago Bulls in 1995 and finding out Michael Jordan was returning from retirement," said Deuce Schwartz, one of my assistants in New Orleans. "Well, that's how I felt when I got wind Mike Westhoff was about to walk up the stairs and start working with our staff. I have the utmost respect for Bradford Banta and Kevin O'Dea, the other special teams coaches I worked with prior to Mike's addition, and they taught me more than I ever thought I'd learn about special teams. This comparison is by no means a knock to them but a tribute to Mike's excellence.

"As an aspiring football coach and avid New York Jets fan, I revered Mike Westhoff. Needless to say, when I first received the news that Mike would be joining our Saints' special teams unit, I was ecstatic."

That afternoon I attended my first Saints team meeting. I thought Sean Payton handled dealing with the change in a very professional manner. He said that he wanted to add some changes and adjustments, and that I could provide that avenue. He was making a major change but did not demean any of the special teams coaches in doing so. He told the team he knew of my reputation but had never met me.

Then Sean said: "If I brought the top NFL writers into this room and told them to write down the two best special teams coaches in NFL history, I would receive a number of names. But every one of them would have written down Mike Westhoff."

It was a great compliment, and I was exceptionally proud. I later learned that the level in which he presented me was one at which he saw nearly everything associated with his team.

He gave me some big shoes to fill, and for the first two weeks I was there, not only did I not fill the shoes, I couldn't even find the fucking laces. Based on the level of play I was used to, we were terrible. What the hell was I going to do?

CHAPTER 15

Back in the Game in the Big Easy

My first game back on the sideline after having been out for five years was an overtime victory against the Redskins. Drew Brees and Kirk Cousins were the stars; it didn't seem as though they could throw an incomplete pass.

I was trying to learn who my players were. I was directing and calling the game as always. But I felt very awkward. I was aggressive but without much success.

Ben Kotwica, my assistant for six years, was also in his new job—across the field—thanks to his old boss. I was in Florida following my "retirement" when I received a phone call from Jon Gruden. He told me his brother Jay had accepted the head coaching job in Washington and asked if I would go with him as the special teams coordinator. I told him I was not interested, but he should hire my old assistant, Ben Kotwica. Jay Gruden did hire Ben, and it was a smart move.

A very key play occurred late in the game. Our defense finally stopped Washington and made it punt. The ball was backed up in Washington territory—not the best circumstances—but Ben ordered a fake punt. Against his old boss!

They executed it well and were successful. Way to go, Mike: this was not a good start in New Orleans.

How could that have worked? I had called a look with seven people in the box, playing fake first and then running a return. In this situation, I had used that call a thousand times. How could it not work?

If you play this type of look the correct way, you can do a million things from it, including rush the punter as well as build a return. All the while, you are defending any possible type of fake. The key is utilizing the correct personnel.

Good luck, Mike.

Drew Brees was the greatest, and we won in overtime. I smiled but felt like shit and limped home thinking: "Don't worry, next week will improve."

I knew then my biggest job was to figure out who I had. What were their strengths and weaknesses, and where to line them up? I had to figure out the roster—now.

There were no weeks of training camp available for me. I had two days. What did I actually have? I had to find out.

The long snapper, Zach Wood, was efficient. Working with Brad Banta, who had long snapped in the league for eleven years, I knew he would end up being very solid. I got Brad to spend extra time with him and that area shored up.

Wil Lutz was our kicker and clearly one of the NFL's very best on field goals. He could score from anywhere and could blast his kickoffs. He just needed to work on his kickoff placement and figuring out what he did best.

Tom Morstead was the punter and, in my opinion, the best in the NFL. I wouldn't trade him for anyone. I have never seen anyone work harder at their craft. He could do it all: direction, hang time, and get-off. You name it, he is the best; also, he's a great individual and teammate. I set his bar incredibly high, and I made him meet that level every day. It was not easy—I can be relentless—and often can be the hardest and the most critical of my best players.

"He would always talk [the same way] you speak to children if, say, they are horrible at math," Tom said about me. "He would tell them they could do it. He would reinforce qualities that they have. He would emphasize the positive, not the negative.

"Sure, sometimes there was friction with players when Mike would be so hard on guys, but the way he spoke to them—you are going to be whatever quality he wanted you to be."

Here's an example of that: after a relatively poor punting session one day during my second year with the Saints, I told Tom as he walked by me that my six-year-old grandson could fucking punt better than that. He was mad as hell at me but knew that I was correct that he had performed poorly. So, he shot for that highest level every day; I love the guy.

I had a good base. Now, what else did I have?

There was a good group of special teams players, and I added two defensive linemen to shore up specific roles. In my career, I had always liked to utilize defensive linemen in specific roles to create mismatches.

Next was an important personnel question: did we have a return specialist?

The Saints were using a free agent wide receiver out of Northern Illinois, Tommylee Lewis. Bill Parcells, a good friend of Sean Payton's, had somehow come in contact with Tommylee and had highly recommended him. Bill had a Hall of Fame career and knew what a good NFL player looked like. But the kick return game had not been a strength of any of his teams. Dave Meggett, who was his specialist with the Giants and Jets, was solid but not exceptional. Northern Illinois and the Mid-American Conference were not on our schedule. In this instance, Bill was not even close.

Tommylee was a great kid who worked his tail off, but his catching and accelerating instincts were a long way from NFL excellence. I'd had some outstanding NFL-leading punt returners such as O.J. McDuffie, Santana Moss, Chad Morton, Leon Washington, and Jeremy Kerley.

I also had learned a great deal about the mechanics of punt returning from the great Billy "White Shoes" Johnson and a number of his punt-catching drills. Running from one side of the field to the other. Catching with one hand. Turning one's back to the punter and reacting to the sound of the punt. Catching and running while coverage men are right on top of the returner. And catching the punt while holding another ball in practice.

I loved inventing and drawing punt return schemes and felt very comfortable with my punt return knowledge. I took all my weapons to New Orleans. We stayed after practice and worked as long as time would allow. Tommylee improved, but really he just wasn't quite good enough. Frankly, he was a participant in some of the most negative plays, both on offense and in the return game.

Brad Banta had told me that from his very first day in New Orleans he had lobbied for a punt returner, also not believing that this guy was going to get the job done.

My second game with the Saints was in Los Angeles versus the powerful Rams. In every area, they were impressive; we were not.

The kicking game was uneventful. Due to their great kickers, we had no return opportunities. I had never before been in a game when I had zero return opportunities. They had two somewhat solid returns. But in both cases our kicks were poorly timed and horribly placed.

We should have blocked one punt. The scheme was good, I just needed to adjust some personnel. But I did see a tiny bit of light in the tunnel.

After the game, I left the locker room and went back into the Coliseum and called my son John. He has always been very honest with me about my career, and I needed to hear his observations. John knows his football.

He said, "Dad, this doesn't look like one of your teams. When did you start kicking the ball in the middle of the field? When you did kick it correctly, you covered well.

"Your return guy looks like he can't catch, and your punt block looked good, but your guy can't run. The Rams looked like your old teams, and you guys looked like the teams you used to beat.

"Does your group understand what it takes? Dad, don't get discouraged. Make them play your way."

"Make them play your way!" I couldn't wait until Wednesday. Thanks, John.

The plane ride back to New Orleans from Los Angeles was the beginning of my *figuring it out* with the Saints.

The Saints do more of the "little things" for their players than maybe any other organization in the NFL. Only the President of the United States travels on a better plane. Everything is first class. Most of the players would sit up front in the largest international first-class section I have ever seen. We as coaches, administrators, and trainers would occupy the middle section and have two seats apiece. The very youngest players and anyone traveling with the team were seated in the rear of the plane in a somewhat normal configuration. The service and food were superb, seemingly with no end.

As always, the minute I got into the plane I went to work viewing the game film. Thank goodness for the luxury of the trip because the film was making me sick as hell.

Brad sat next to me and watched and graded the film with me. Preparing to watch the game for the third time, we began to get a feel for things. I kept hearing John say, "Dad, make them play your way."

What exactly did that mean, and how could we get this group to look like that? We watched every play over and over and studied each player. On a tablet, I drew each play and player, reconfiguring each time until we had constructed a lineup that had everyone in a position matching their skill level with what was being asked of each of them. We had a talented enough group. They just needed some adjusting.

I had been away from the field for nearly five years, so what was different that they weren't playing my way? I was operating on Sean Payton's practice schedule—it wasn't mine.

I told Brad to get a tablet, and we started breaking down every second of our schedule. And the light came on: I wasn't practicing them in the exact enough manner in which they were going to have to play. Everything we were doing in practice was adequate as preparation, but it was not nearly specialized or intense enough to attain the level of play I was expecting. That I always expected.

What we were doing looked good enough, but it really wasn't worth a damn. So, we were going to change our practice. Every play was to be at full speed. The contact level would be determined by the dress. If we were in shoulder pads and shorts—look out! If just helmets and shorts—a hell of a lot more physical than we had been doing.

On any play, I might stop some guys and make the others go full-out to the ball. Every play had an eight-yard rule: you better be going full speed for eight yards. Our eight-minute sessions would now be called the "Fastest Eight." We were going to run twelve plays in those eight minutes. Everything would be at a hundred miles an hour. Following our eight minutes, a water break would be absolutely necessary.

I instructed our film crew to use an extra camera and on a signal from me to a shoot a candid camera close-up. All of a sudden, during a film session, a player would be looking at himself on the screen, blown up to the size of the room, while everyone watched just that one player. And he better be looking at someone who looked like a highlight film to fucking suit me.

It gets your attention.

I decided to implement a kickoff coverage drill. I am not much of a "drill" coach, probably stemming from my time with Coach Shula, who was not fond of drills, calling them "mindless," preferring to practice techniques and skills within the framework of the team.

Coach Shula's film sessions were very demanding. He was not only commenting on what you were doing, he'd spend equal time discussing exactly how you should be doing something.

The kickoff coverage drill is used during training camp and has three defenders running the last 20 yards of the coverage going against three blockers with a ball carrier in the area from the hash to the sideline.

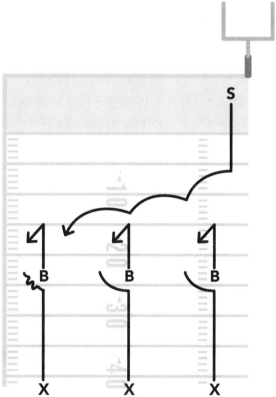

Rex Ryan once said to me that this was the best drill he had ever seen. It can be run at any tempo, from using bags for contact to full speed with tackling. Everyone can be included. The kicker and the safeties can run down behind the pursuit and properly execute their triangle on the ball. By watching the play on the end-zone tape, the contact part looks exactly like the end of a kickoff coverage versus a return, even though the players are only running 20 yards.

I very rarely had run the drill during the season. The games are all the full-speed contact needed, but I needed to get this group to learn how to play my way.

Thanks, John, because I could see a proper lineup and a method to improve. We just needed a catalyst.

Taysom Hill

On Monday, following our return to New Orleans, I was walking through the locker room when one of the players came out of the shower wrapped in a towel. Who the hell was this guy? He was about 6-2, 220 pounds and totally ripped. A powerful-looking guy.

I found out quickly it was Taysom Hill, a rookie quarterback from Brigham Young University. A QB? He sure didn't look like a QB.

I went right into Sean Payton's office. "Sean, tell me about Taysom Hill," I said.

He told me that, following high school, Hill went on a Mormon mission to Australia before entering BYU. He was a talented and athletic quarterback who dealt with several injuries during his college career, and there was some uncertainty concerning his play. He had been signed as an undrafted free agent by the Green Bay Packers, but then was released before start of the season. The Saints claimed him and kept him on the roster as an athletic-type quarterback with running ability, something different from their great passer Drew Brees.

Sean liked him as an athlete and wanted to one day look at him in a different style of offense. He told me that one of their scouts timed Taysom in the 40-yard dash in the low 4.4s. "Pretty darn good for a guy who looks like that," I thought.

I did some research and discovered that during his Pro Day, he ran a 4.4 and had a 38-inch vertical jump. Both

Taysom Hill

of those numbers would have led all the quarterbacks at the 2017 NFL combine in Indianapolis.

I told Sean that I had experienced some success with QBs of this type on my special teams units. Jim Jensen at Miami, and Brad Smith, Eric Smith, and Tim Tebow with the Jets. I said I would like to look at Taysom and see what he could do, and he said that was great—anything I wanted. Sean is a damn good coach and one who is always looking to improve, never sitting still.

My next stop was the weight room to talk to head strength coach Dan Dalrymple. Dan had been with Sean the entire time in New Orleans, and in my opinion was an old-school, hard-core, and excellent strength coach.

Of Hill, Dan said, "Coach, he can do it all. He normally works out with Drew Brees, who emphasizes stretching, flexibility, and cardio work."

Drew is the hardest-working player I have encountered in my thirty-two-year career. His weight room work is endless, but again mostly emphasizing stretching and flexibility. A little bit along the lines of Jane Fonda and her workouts, no disrespect meant to either.

Dan told me that sometimes following his work with Drew, Taysom would go over with the linemen and do 600-pound squats. He is a quarterback who can lift with the "Big Boys."

Now I had all the information I needed. I told one of my assistants to find Taysom and bring him to my office. He's a bright, engaging young man full of energy.

I said to him: "This conversation will last about two minutes. If you are interested, we will look at you at some very specific special teams roles. Easy to learn and that should fit your set of skills."

I wanted him to be a kick side Number Three on our kickoff coverage. Whenever we lined up, he would be free to run at the ball with no lane or area responsibility. On our punt return team, he would be rushing the punter from the edge.

As a kickoff return front-line blocker, he would always be in a double-team, and he would eventually learn the personal protector position on the punt team. Due to his running and throwing ability, that role would be a signature one and dynamic.

"Or," I told him, "you can continue to watch the game from the sideline dressed in sweats."

I was short and to the point.

He said that he would love the opportunity and was excited to try it out. He had never been on any special teams, but he was eager.

I met with him for a half-hour and taught him the Cliff Notes version of what he would need to know in his four roles. I had Brad Banta sit in with us, wanting him to be included in everything, and to know exactly how I was tackling these roles.

Brad already had *figured it out.*

"Sitting at my desk at the New Orleans Saints any morning during the regular season, I knew what was coming," Brad said. "My office was situated around the corner from the stairs entrance and the elevator. It was within earshot for me to hear if someone was coming or going via the stair door opening. Or the 'bing' made by the elevator arriving at the second floor alerted me.

"Either way, if you heard one of these noises, followed by a 'clickety-click' rhythm of a cane coming down the hallway, you knew that Mike Westhoff was on his way in. You then just prepared yourself. There came no 'good morning' or 'good to see you this morning.' Not even a hello.

"Instead, he might pick up an eraser and wipe away two days' work, saying, 'This shit won't work.'

"Or he might say, 'I couldn't sleep last night because thinking about this fucking guy kept me up.' Or maybe, 'I was driving in this morning and I got to thinking.'

"That's when the think tank—my office—started getting filled with nitrous oxide rather than the regular jet fuel. My office is where we would figure out a lot of problems. Give our group of special teams coaches—Kevin O'Dea, Deuce Schwartz, Mike—a wall-to-wall grease board, expo markers, film, internet, and time to think and talk things out, and solutions were abundant. Right, wrong, or indifferent, your opinion was expressed, discussed, and either shot down or put up on the board with good reason. He listened to everyone's opinion and gave consideration to each.

"We, as a group, were good at *figuring it out*.

"Whether it be personnel, blocking schemes, nicknames for positions on special teams, or reconfiguring a design structure of Mike's leg from the metal grafting, we solved many problems in my office. That is what we do as special teams coaches. That was part of the reason we were able to finish on top on special teams in the NFL during our tenure with the Saints.

"*Figure it out* is a mantra for special teams. We were good at it. We would sit around and discuss personnel morning, noon, and night. There was not one player that was discussed whose role we did not know on offense, defense, and special teams. How he fit on each depth chart. Who was up and down on the game-day activities. How much would he play on O and D. How he fit into the special teams units. What his strengths and weaknesses were. Where to put specific players to take advantage of mismatches.

"Who could be your 'jack of all trades' player to fill in if one of our starters was injured. Clock management scenarios. What play to run and when.

"We had to have answers for everything, and that is what my office was for: discussing the scenarios before they actually happened.

"Morning meetings just got the day started. Being on the same wavelength helped the process of figuring it out. From day one, we were speaking the same language and communicating our ideas openly and often. This open line of communication was key, and it spilled over to the players' confidence on the field. It showed up in their play, so much so that they were at a point where they were able to *figure it out* as well. They did not hesitate to approach us with ideas or problems that they saw taking place on the field. We—coaches and players—would come up with a solution and then watch it transpire at any time during a practice or game.

"Just think, all of this figuring it out started with a rhythmic noise coming down the hall and an abrupt statement in the morning. It is what working with Mike Westhoff is all about, and it set the tone for each and every day."

This day, it was all about Taysom Hill. It didn't take long to get going. The first period was our punt team. I lined up Taysom to rush against us. He exploded—and I mean exploded—off the ball, smacked my best wing under his chin, and rolled off toward the punter. It wasn't a perfect technique, but not only was this guy fast and athletic but—most importantly to me—he could hit and hit hard.

Everything he did that day, during and after practice, he did well. He had to smooth out some rough edges, but we had found a damn good player.

"Frankly, I didn't go to or stay at any of the special teams meetings when I was in college," Taysom said. "This was such a foreign thing for me, tackling. Growing up I never played defense. Maybe in high school there were a few extenuating circumstances when I played defense in the secondary because we were in a big game, a state championship game. Maybe the coach put me out there as a security blanket. But I never went through the drill work.

"It was definitely not in my head at all to be on special teams, but at this point I realized I had been through ten weeks of the NFL season, been released by Green Bay, and claimed by the Saints and moved my family to New Orleans. I was aware this is a really tough business to make it in. If they are going to create opportunities, I am not going to squander them.

"Sure, I was very surprised, but I was excited by the opportunity. It got me a jersey and got me on the field. I was shocked, but I wasn't upset in any way. I had conversations with Coach Payton, who said, 'This doesn't change how we feel about you as a quarterback. We feel you can add value to our team by doing this for this year.'

"I felt I had nothing to lose. I wasn't supposed to be able to do this and do it well. I was up for the challenge."

Sean asked me that night after the practice what I thought. I told him to make Taysom active for the game. He was going to be much better than expected. I was sure of that. I would bet on it. For thirty years, I had learned what it took, and this guy would be exceptional.

That night, after watching our practice film again with Brad, Kevin, and Deuce, and while standing in front of a board with our game plan on it, I told them: "Watch out now. Everyone is going to see what a real special teams unit fucking looks like. We look damn good, and Carolina is going to get smacked right in the face. Wait until Sunday."

I told my guys, "Thanks, you have worked hard and done an excellent job." And after my son John had told me to make them play my way, I was damn sure going to do it.

I couldn't wait until Sunday's game with Carolina: our newly configured special teams units and the debut of Taysom Hill. We won the coin toss, deferred, and kicked off. The Carolina special teams coach, Thomas McGaughey, an excellent coach and good friend of mine, told me a year or so later: "I looked out there and saw Number 7. Who the hell was he? A QB? What the hell is Mike doing?"

"You kick off and your QB runs right through my two best blockers and tackles us inside the minus-20. Oh shit! Who is this guy?"

Our entire sideline was watching Taysom and on that play they exploded. As he came off the field, he was mobbed. You would think that he had just scored the game-winning touchdown.

This was "playing my way."

Taysom continued to play brilliantly. He covered the next kickoff nearly exactly the same. I had moved him over one spot, but his assignment and technique remained the same, and he had the same result. Our special teams exploded, too; we were doing everything well. We ran a punt return for a TD, but it was brought back due to a penalty. Actually, it was a good call—you see, Mike Pereira, I can be fair.

Toward the end of a very close game, Taysom rushed their punter and was going to block the punt. Their guy punted the ball straight up in the air and we fielded it in great position, which gave a very short field to Drew, who drove us down to score and take the lead.

We won a very hard-fought game. In the locker room following the win, Sean Payton awarded the game ball to Taysom. From standing on the sideline in sweats to the game ball.

I couldn't have been prouder. We were a big part of the win and were beginning to "play my way."

Taysom moved on from having the easiest blocking assignment in our kickoff return to the most difficult one. He became our punt team's personal protector and was outstanding as a blocker, in coverage, and as a fake threat. Through the remainder of that season, he was one of the best special teams players in the NFC.

I am glad I cut through the locker room that day.

Turning It Around

The season was more than half complete. The Saints were back on the winning path, and I was again in a positive contributing role. Our special teams were good—damn good. Tom Morstead was doing everything well, blasting the ball and giving our opponents nothing. He was hitting the ball to the ceiling, and in the Superdome, that's almost unimaginable. He was punting the ball out of bounds, pinning them deep into a hole.

I had some great punters in my career, including Rohn Stark and Reggie Roby, and a No. 1 net punter in the NFL in John Kidd. But no one was as complete as Tom.

Wil Lutz was leading the league in points and kicking percentage. It seemed like he could drive to the stadium and make a field goal from the parking lot.

Our field goal and punt block teams looked as though they could block every kick. We made a change in our kickoff return positioning.

Following our Thursday night game in Atlanta, I was supposed to have the weekend off, and I was going to return to Florida, but the weather was awful and my flight was canceled. I returned to my office and spent a Saturday studying every kickoff return in the league. Our blocking, in my opinion, was the best in the NFL. Taysom Hill became our best blocker, but we desperately needed a return specialist.

We moved Alvin Kamara, our star running back, to the kickoff return role. Due to the change in rules and the ball being kicked from the 35-yard line, there were more balls kicked for touchbacks and far fewer returns. I lined up Alvin six yards deep in the end zone and told him to return anything in front of him. Any kick deeper than his alignment was not to be returned.

In my twelve years with the New York Jets, nine different players led the NFL in returns. No team or coach will ever top that. If Alvin Kamara had played for me under the old rules, I believe he would have topped Devin Hester, the great return specialist for the Chicago Bears.

"In the two and a half years we were together here, he was someone, you know, it was never I need more players or better players," Sean Payton said. "Mike had a great skill set of taking the talent that was available each week—and sometimes, based on injury, that would vary—and then putting a scheme that suited those guys."

Figuring it out.

Another Obstacle

I was now having a ball and loving everything with the Saints. All of a sudden, my whole world stopped once more.

It was a typical Thursday practice. We were indoors, and I had just finished one of my special teams periods. The team was taking a water break, and I walked over to the sideline when suddenly I felt a pop in my left thigh, followed by a clicking sound with each step. I froze, and my heart felt like it stopped.

In May 2012, five years earlier, a similar thing happened following a walk with my son John in Indianapolis. After a phone call to my doctor in New York, Dr. John Healey of Sloan Kettering, I was instructed to go to a hospital for an X-ray. While at the hospital and standing in a bathroom, my leg snapped in half, and I fell face-first into a toilet.

That was followed by a three-and-a-half week stay in the Indianapolis Medical Center, and a very complicated repair to my metal femur. The metal is two inches thick, how could it break?

Now, here I was on the practice field in New Orleans and seemed to be experiencing the same occurrence. I sat down and called for our trainer, Beau Lowery, the head of one of the NFL's very best medical staffs. He sure as hell didn't know what to make of this, and he got me immediately to a doctor's office for X-rays. As soon I saw the X-ray (after having seen a million of them), I could tell that the seam between the first and second piece was slightly askew, and something significant was wrong.

The X-rays were forwarded to Dr. Healey, who told me he believed he knew what happened but needed to view an MRI. I was given crutches to walk with and continued my normal coaching duties.

The following week, I was driven down to LSU in Baton Rouge to see Dr. Shaun Accardo, an excellent orthopedic oncologist and someone who had a knowledge of Dr. Healey and his work. Dr. Healey, in the very multiform field of orthopedic oncology, is first and no one is second.

After reading the MRI, Dr. Healey felt something was broken or cracked within one of the connections near the tip of my left femur. The leg was stable as long as I stayed on the crutches but would have to be seriously addressed.

Dr. Healey, who had become a good friend, told me he had to do some thorough examining and come up with a plan to solve a very complex problem. He said I should be very careful and that he would have a solution and be prepared to operate in New York sometime in February after the Super Bowl.

Well, now I had two really big events on my upcoming calendar, one that I was hoping for and one for which I was scared to death.

Dr. Healey and I put in a call to Troy Hershberger, the Purdue-educated engineer who was the department head for Biomet Inc. in the Patient Matched Products Department. Biomet is one of the world's largest joint replacement companies. They make knees, hips, and shoulders, but the complicated replacements are handled by Patient Matched Products.

They designed my original in 2008 and the repair adjustments in 2012. And now this new problem.

Troy was always trying to figure how my graft could have broken not once but twice. He told me that in their history they had three breaks, and I had two of them.

He also told me that on this new one, when his team looked at the X-rays, one of his guys said, "Oh fuck, what the hell are we going to do with this?"

I had told Troy about feeling some instability near the hip joint. He went right into action.

"When Mike walked, he reported that he could feel a wobbling and grinding sensation," Troy remembered. "That was not good, as we knew it was only a matter of time before it fatigued and broke through completely.

"I remember asking Mike what he was doing when it broke in an effort to understand what was going on here. He told me he had been working out with the team and standing on one of those 'wobble boards for thirty minutes or so a day to stay in shape and tighten up the glute area.' Clearly, we were not dealing with your typical patient who has about 80 percent of his femur replaced with metal.

"During this time, I recall that Mike was able to walk with a cane while keeping his motion to a minimum and thus not breaking the taper off completely. He would call me every few days to tell me how it seemed to be failing further and further as I would update him on how we were progressing with the implant. I recall that the Saints were making a playoff run at the time, and Mike telling me that this implant has to stay in one piece and make it until they either get eliminated or win the Super Bowl.

"I would turn on the Saints games and watch for Mike on the sideline and hope that he was sitting down—which he didn't appear to be doing. It was just a matter of time before it broke off completely, and I didn't want the implant to be the reason he was done coaching for the season. As if Mike would ever truly be done coaching.

"I was excited every time the Saints would win and advance, and then would break out into a sweat knowing the implant had to last another week. He was giving me those now-familiar half-time pep talks of encouragement.

"The new implant was completed and sent to Dr. Healey in New York, where it sat until Mike was ready to come off the field and get things fixed."

Troy's group and Dr. Healey are the best, and I appreciate how they went to work to come up with a solution to save my leg. Now, if I could just get to the Super Bowl.

Good, Bad, and Ugly

Every Monday following a Sunday game, the Saints would have a one-hour staff meeting before the noon team meeting to discuss that previous game. We referred to the meeting as the Good, Bad, and Ugly.

Sean was always pointed and direct. He wanted short, exact summations of what had taken place. I used to enjoy sitting there and looking at his face if someone was pontificating. I used to feel like he was thinking, *Would you shut the fuck up and just give me an answer?* I hoped he was thinking the same.

I had only been with the Saints for a few weeks, and I hardly knew any of the staff. I can only speculate about what they may have thought of some of my answers.

Sean asked me one time what I would do with a particular guy if he were activated for a game?

"We would Kumerow him."

The entire staff looked at me like, "What the hell is he talking about?"

Of course, I was referring to Eric Kumerow, the defensive end from Ohio State who was a first-round draft pick when I was with Miami. With Kumerow, we had needed to search to find a job he could handle without getting himself (and me) killed. To those of us who were special teams coaches, Kumerow had a very specific connotation.

Another time, Sean asked me about another activation. I said, "We want Elle McPherson, and you're giving me Hillary Clinton."

I had no fear of expressing my opinion.

At the staff meeting following the Carolina game, as part of my Good, Bad, and Ugly, the ugly was a penalty bringing back a punt return touchdown; everything else was good. I was complimenting our kick coverage and how much it had improved and how physical it had played.

Sean said, "It's the same people lined up a little differently, but it doesn't even look like the same team. Why?"

I told him, "We played exactly as we practiced. Exactly!" As my son John had instructed me, "Make them play your way."

Later in the day, Sean pulled me aside and complimented me on how the practice preparation and tempo had carried over to the game. He told me he was going to instruct the offense and defense to include something in their weekly schedule to gain that level of intensity.

"I think the world of him to begin with," Sean said. "He's a dynamic special teams coach and a difference maker on any staff he's been on. All of his statistical numbers, the teams that he has coached give evidence to that. He's someone that I think, first off, is an extremely talented teacher, and it starts with that. He can communicate his message well, he can demand the discipline during the week to create the opportunities that he's looking for, and you know he's never afraid to take risks, to take chances if it is well thought-out and calculated."

In the NFL, you can't beat the hell out of the players, but you can find ways to increase the intensity. In an NFL practice, due to the players' tremendous physical abilities, as a coach you have to learn how to control the level of intensity and be able to increase it by lessening the level of collision. Make them do something full speed but not from the same distance or for a particular length of time. Shrink the field. Take the 20-yard collision and add five yards. Demand 100 mph for short bursts.

Suddenly, our practices looked almost exactly like what I expected to see during a game.

I was always very appreciative of his saying that to me. I enjoyed my interactions with Sean, and it's one of the things I miss most, having retired from the Saints.

A Real Threat?

The 2017 season was closing rapidly, and the Saints continued to win. I had been on some good teams in my career, but this team was one of the best, and I believed we would be a real threat in the playoffs.

We had one stumbling block in our last game of the season versus Tampa Bay, and I am taking much of the blame.

Since my second game out in Los Angeles, our special teams had not lost a single play. As I have mentioned before, you don't win every play, of course, but we didn't lose one either.

We had an excellent group of blockers, so we just needed a chance to break one. Tampa scored early and had to kick off. I called a "Miami Right." We would double-team the kick-side Number Five and trap the back-side Number Five. We formed a pair of two-man wedges to block the 4-3-2-1 players on the kick side. When Alvin Kamara caught the ball, he actually was taking a step back that usually determines that the ball will not be returned. I always wanted our returner moving into the catch when returning the kick. Alvin later told me that when he caught the ball, he was going to take a touchback, but he looked up and saw a gigantic hole.

And a gigantic hole was exactly what it was.

Under the old kickoff return rules, I believe Alvin would have been one of the league's most outstanding returners, but on this particular play, any of twenty of my guys could have scored. Our blocking was great, we pretty much knocked down all the Bucs. So, 106 yards later, we had a touchdown and the longest kickoff return in franchise history.

What a great start to the game, and from there our kicking game was winning on most every play. We were hot and playing with great confidence.

Tampa fought hard, and the game went back and forth.

During my last five years in Miami, we were the No. 1 defense in the NFL. And with the Jets and Rex Ryan, we were one of the top defenses. This Saints' defense sure as hell wasn't in that class.

At times I thought they played well, but it was mostly Drew Brees and the offense that was providing the margin of victory.

Now that we had a special teams unit that was contributing, I just had to make sure we didn't do something stupid. But I got stupid.

Late in the game, our defense rallied and forced them to punt. My group had been doing everything well and I was cocky. The situation called for a "Giant Blue" punt return: a seven-man front doubling their kick-side flyer, and rushing the opposite side with three defenders, including Taysom Hill and Alex Okafor. We would be able to stop any fake, pressure the punter, force his punt to our left side, and ensure a solid catch and return to that side.

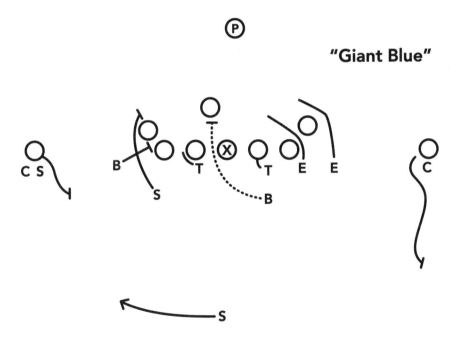

I was looking for a knockout punch, and I called a "Buccaneer," our term for an all-out eight-man punt block. We had practiced this block, and I really liked it. I wouldn't bet my boat on it, but I liked it.

We came off the ball quickly and came within an inch of blocking the punt. But they executed well and prevented that. Tampa's punter hurried his kick due to our pressure and hit a line drive. The punt returner must know how to play this type of kick. If you can catch it on the run forward, great. If not, get under control and fair catch the ball. If you can't make a clean catch, get away from the ball and let it hit the ground. Not my favorite thing, but sometimes the prudent play.

Tommylee got a late jump on the ball and tried to make a shoestring catch and fumbled the ball. Not a muff, which can't be advanced, but a fumble. Tampa picked it up and ran it in for a touchdown.

I was only a hundred miles from my home in Fort Myers, and I was ready to leave the fucking stadium and go home. My block call was dumb. I put our returner—I have made it clear how the Saints got him; he wasn't my favorite—in a bad situation. That was completely my fault.

These things are personal for me. Since the Carolina game, it was the only special teams play that we really lost, and it was a big one. I believe it cost us the game. Yes, as always, there were many contributing factors. We missed an easy chance to score, and we let them drive the entire field for the winning score. But the Tampa special teams' score negated our TD and gave them the chance to win.

I felt like shit; my call was to blame.

We finished the season 11-5 as NFC South champions. A bump at the end, but nonetheless a great season and a home playoff game. I needed for my leg to hold together for a couple more wins and a trip to the Super Bowl.

Almost There

The 2017 NFC playoffs were as dramatic and exciting as any in recent history.

After five years with the media, here I was back in the playoffs in what I believed would be a real dogfight. I felt the NFC was the stronger conference. New England, of course, is always a strong bet in the AFC, but I felt that the NFC was better balanced and would end up with the champion. I liked our chances. The schedule had been demanding, and we fought through it and were in a good position.

To me, the Rams were the favorite, followed closely by Minnesota, Philadelphia, and us, the Saints. Both the Rams and Vikings had beaten the Saints during the season, but we had improved since those games. We would be hard to beat. Our special teams were much improved, and I believed would give us a winning edge.

I couldn't wait—if my leg could just hold together, I could make a few more games and get to my first Super Bowl.

We played the first-round wild-card game against Carolina in New Orleans. We had beaten the Panthers twice and weren't going to lose at home. Not with the NFL's best home-field advantage.

It was a tight game and their quarterback, Cam Newton, played brilliantly. We persevered, 31-26. Now it was on to Minnesota for a tough matchup with the Vikings.

Personally, I felt great. I loved our game plan and believed we would win on every play. I loved our kickoff return chances, though I knew we would not get many chances. If we did, look out!

But we really only had one opportunity—and we came a step away from breaking it open for a touchdown. One thing I would have bet my boat on, though, was our punt block. We just needed the chance.

A few weeks earlier, we wanted to sign a free agent veteran defensive lineman to help with depth. George Johnson's name came up; I didn't know a thing about him. Kevin O'Dea had worked with him in Tampa and said he could help us on special teams.

Kevin was right. George started on four of six special teams and was excellent on two of them: kickoff coverage and, especially, on punt returns. For a defensive lineman to come in late and in the year and contribute, that is a smart personnel move. Our personnel director Terry Fontenot, now the GM of the Atlanta Falcons, was outstanding and made a brilliant move.

We designed a punt block in which we would line up George, who went 6-5, 265 pounds, in the A-gap next to the center. Right next to him would be David Onyemata, a 6-4, 300-pound defensive tackle. We then placed a fast running back on the inside shoulder of their tackle to neutralize him, and Taysom Hill against their wing on the outside edge. I knew their wing couldn't block Taysom.

Big Dave would crush the middle of their protection, creating a soft spot for George to penetrate. Taysom would beat their wing and either block the punt or force their punter into George.

The key to a successful punt block is having the correct person in the correct spot. Not fully understanding this results in never getting there or in roughing-the-kicker penalties. If you are roughing the punter, you didn't get the message.

This was a damn good block. We just needed a chance.

Down and distance and field position are critical components of a punt block. I made a mistake in Tampa. I wasn't going to make another.

With 5:15 remaining in the fourth quarter, we were trailing 20-14. Minnesota got a penalty, and our defense then forced the Vikings to punt. They had fourth-and-14 at their 40-yard line.

The 40-yard line is not the best spot for an all-out eight-man punt block. But fourth-and-14? I couldn't wait.

Some teams love to rush the punter from midfield. It looks cute, but they don't know shit. Due to the short punt, the punter easily quickens his get-off time and shortens his steps, and the rush team can't get there.

If you want to block a punt at midfield, show a base formation and set up one or two specifically designed rushers to attempt the block. Don't let the punter feel the eight-man pressure. Against Atlanta, we were in a similar situation and set up Alex Okafor, a pass-rush specialist, to rush the punt. He easily beat their wing and blocked the kick.

Dan Quinn, the Falcons' coach, told me later that play completely changed the game and won the game for the Saints.

This time, I called "Viking," our punt block. We had practiced it perfectly, and we were lined up correctly. We were going to get them. This was the play I had been waiting for.

And it worked just like we practiced. Taysom beat their man and was going to block the punt. Their punter hurried and drove the ball right into Big George's outstretched arm for a block. The result was great field position and the opportunity for Drew Brees, Sean Payton, and company to get a score and jump to a 21-20 lead.

"Mike spent time with me before and after and during practice, additional time, and also after all our meetings," Taysom said. "We would talk through every detail, what the expectation was for me on each individual play and unit, and my role on them.

"One thing I feel most grateful for with Mike is Mike had a vision for me, and there are people who didn't make it in the NFL who are much more talented than I am. I had the right coach and the right opportunity, and Mike was one of those coaches. Mike created the opportunity for me, and he believed in me. So, as I stepped out onto the field, I knew Mike—such a decorated coach; I knew his story—he would put me in a situation when I would be successful.

"As we stepped on the field, I knew it would work, and that is the best thing Mike did for us. As an athlete, to be put in the position to succeed is the greatest thing."

The teams later also traded field goals, and with just a short time remaining, Minnesota was trailing us 24-23. The Vikings had the ball at their 38-yard line with no timeouts remaining. Nine seconds on the clock. They had to try to get the ball to around midfield and get out of bounds. If the ball remained in play the clock would expire before they could get it stopped. Simply, our defense had to keep the ball in bounds.

Minnesota lined up with three receivers to the short side of the field, running a three-tiered route and hoping for a catch and to get out of bounds—or possibly a defensive foul to stop the clock and allow a very long field goal attempt.

During the five years I worked with the media, I spent hours preparing myself for situations. I had spent most of my career with special teams, but working with the media I was studying primarily offenses and defenses. I talked with coaches all over the league and with media members. Jon Gruden and Rex Ryan were a big help to me, and in this situation, I knew that you had to play a three-deep secondary. If you rush four guys, then you play a two-deep look, which unfortunately is exactly what we did. Not three deep, but two. That is, in my opinion, unsound defense.

Our safety, Marcus Williams, had to cover the deep sideline from being lined up between the yard number and the hash mark. Yes, he got to the spot of the pass in time, and he could have made the play on the ball or made the tackle. He did neither. And the Vikings pulled off the "Minneapolis Miracle" to win the game.

If we had been lined up in a three-deep scheme, we would have had a man standing right where the ball came down, with help coming over the top. The four-man rush was a mistake; I don't know who called it, and I don't care. But if three-deep had been called, we win the game. I will bet anything on that.

You can blame Marcus, but that is not where the blame should go.

Now, the season was over. The crowd stormed the field. I wasn't going to get on my crutches and fight through that mess. I went back to the bench and sat there for a half-hour.

No Super Bowl—again.

And now, a somewhat questionable surgery was ahead. I was sad and scared and just needed to go home to Florida.

Uncertainty and Certainty

Three days after the season ended so disappointingly, I said good-bye to New Orleans and drove back to Florida. The Saints had been a great experience for me. I went there not wanting to go and not knowing anything about the team. I was leaving three months later with some great friends, an appreciation of a terrific organization, and the pride of being a part of a really good NFL team.

I talked to Sean Payton before I left. He told me that he wanted me to return and that the Saints would do anything to help me with what was ahead for me. I thanked him for everything and said that I would like another year with the Saints, but I very much had to take one day at a time—yeah, I know that is sports' top cliche—and it was going to be a drawn-out process.

Back in Florida, every day was spent preparing for my trip to New York, to Memorial Sloan Kettering, Dr. Healey, and my tenth major surgery. Chemotherapy terrified me, and surgeries never upset me at all. But this one seemed different. It was very complex, and I was more than nervous.

Dr. Healey explained over the phone what the procedure entailed. My hip would have to be removed and replaced, along with a hip joint connecting to a metal femur that would attach to the remaining metal about halfway down my thigh. The problem was how to connect the tendons and ligaments that are needed to lift the leg to the metal.

He believed he could keep a three-inch piece of the femur bone, cut it in half, and lay the metal in the middle of the bone. Then he would fold the bone around the metal and secure it with a cable. The muscles, ligaments, and tendons were attached to this bone, so when it all healed, I would have a normal functioning leg.

Good luck, Mike.

I knew two things for certain: Memorial Sloan Kettering and Dr. Healey. He was maybe the only surgeon in the world who could pull this one off.

I also talked again with Troy Hershberger. He assured me that they had designed and engineered the very best piece needed. I trusted him and his team, and between them and Dr. Healey's team, I was in the very best possible hands.

Now, it was game time.

I shipped my car to New York. John Gamble, my good friend from our days together with the Dolphins and my fishing buddy, would fly to New York and drive me back to Florida. The surgery was set for the week after the Super Bowl, and I would stay in Garden City, New York, with my girlfriend Patti for a few days until the date. This one frightened me the most. I was getting older, and at seventy years old, I didn't want to be out for more than seven hours.

My son John drove up from Philadelphia and again accompanied me to the hospital. He has been with me for most of my surgeries and was an accomplished veteran of the process.

At Sloan Kettering, I talked with Dr. Healey before they wheeled me into the operating room that looked somewhat like the Starship Enterprise. Following a nearly eight-hour surgery, I could hear John saying, "Dad, Dad, wake up. Everything went great, you are going to be fine."

He had done that a number of times before. I can't imagine anything better to hear—or caring for, loving, and appreciating anyone more than I do my son John.

After hearing John's voice and waking up, I knew I had made it through fine. And now, the long road ahead.

Dr. Healey was next. This was his third major surgery with me, but this was different. He was excited. He said everything had gone exactly as planned. He couldn't wait to show me the pictures of the procedure. Seeing the raw, bloody inside of my leg was a little much for me, but I shared his enthusiasm. He is the best, and this was one of his best.

Trying to count the number of nights that I laid in bed and tossed and turned while searching for reasons why something had failed on the field would be an impossible task. I always believed that a key to being a successful coach or player was establishing a realm of ownership. In my mind, it was a complete and total ownership.

I know that the NFL is a "team sport," and there are many contributing factors to success and failure. That's why the head coach gets so much of the blame when things go poorly, but also—and very much so—accepts responsibility. And it's why he deserves so much of the credit for success. Realistically, I am aware of the multiple reasons for success or failure, but each week I put the entire onus on myself. I could easily feel that, to a certain degree, I had won the game, but I could completely believe that I had lost the game.

I accepted total ownership, and I wanted the players to feel the same. Many times, I presented them with metaphors for how I wanted them to view the game. I would tell them: "An interesting dynamic could happen this week in our game while we are on the road. The offensive players all eat the same breakfast and get sick and can't play. The defensive players, who can't tell time anyway, mis-set their alarms and miss the bus. So only the special teams make it to the game."

"And somehow, we *figure it out* and still find a way to win the game."

Ridiculous? I know. I know. But that's the attitude I want.

Each play is so important that the result of the game depends on the outcome of every play.

Final Game

The very last game of my thirty-two years in the NFL was while I was coaching for the Saints in the 2018 NFC championship game against the Los Angeles Rams. These were clearly the two best teams in the NFC, and a great game was in store. We had beaten the Rams earlier in the season in a high-scoring contest and had earned the right to play the game in New Orleans. The good old "home-field advantage."

It was my second season in New Orleans, and I knew it was going to be my final NFL year. I was going to be seventy-two years old. Having coached for thirty-two years and in more than 650 games, I knew it had been enough.

Winning that game, though, would bring for me the crowning achievement of getting to the Super Bowl. I had come close several times, but the game's ultimate showcase—and the Vince Lombardi Trophy, the sport's ultimate prize—had eluded me. I had some great years and arguably was the best specials teams coach in the league, but I had never been to a Super Bowl. I never felt that had defined my career, and I know a number of special teams coaches with Super Bowl rings who I could beat with my eyes closed. This was my last and probably best chance.

The Saints were an excellent team. Drew Brees was a Hall of Fame quarterback. Sean Payton was one of the NFL's very best coaches. We were a good enough team to win the whole thing.

We finished the season as the No. 1 special teams unit in the NFL. If you add up the various rankings, such as starting field position, turnovers, and scores of all thirty-two teams, you can get a good picture of special teams success. The picture can be varied and complex, and I had always done it in a particular fashion, but no matter how you compiled it, we were right at the top.

The Rams had a very good special teams unit, and over the previous five years, along with the Kansas City Chiefs, they probably had been the very best in the league. They had an excellent coach in John Fassel and a group of players that could make a game-changing play. Their real strength was in their specialists who, in 2017, all had been to the Pro Bowl—the first time in NFL history for that.

Greg Zuerlein was the kicker, Pharoh Cooper was the punt and kick returner, and in my opinion the star of the group was Johnny Hekker, the punter. Hekker was a four-time Pro Bowler and one of the NFL's elite punters. His directional and inside-the-20 punting were all spectacular, but what I was most concerned with was his ability to throw on fake punts. In his career he had attempted more fakes than any punter in history, twenty-two, and completed thirteen.

A big man at 6-5 and 240 pounds, he had an arm as strong as most NFL quarterbacks. The Rams did a good job of running their fakes and were not afraid to try them with Hekker at any time. I believed that at the time of the championship game, our units were playing better than the Rams, but this was the one thing I feared most.

After much planning and strategizing, we came up with a plan to combine our punt return, punt block, and "safe" units into one. I put four defensive linemen on the team. I have never seen four defensive linemen used on any basic punt return team in all my years. They were all very capable punt rushers, and with the size advantage—6-5, 290 against 6-2, 235—I knew that they could rush Hekker and pressure him and also be in position to defend any type of fake.

Also lined up with our linemen was Taysom Hill, our "jack-of-all-trades" quarterback who also was the best punt rusher in the league. He would always line up on our right side and pressure Hekker to his left, his favorite punting direction.

I felt it was a great plan, and we couldn't lose with it. I just had to perfect it.

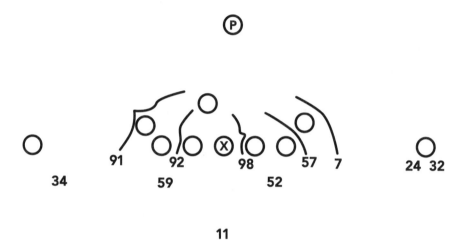

I loved this scheme and thought it was ingenious. One personnel group, no substitution, that could line up several ways and do everything. We could run our punt return, punt block (called Ram, coincidentally), and safe looks all from the same group and from a similar alignment.

Our punt return group was going to consist of those four defensive linemen: Alex Okafor (#57), David Onyemata (#98), Marcus Davenport (#92), and Trey Hendrickson (#91). They were all long, strong, and quick types who could reach the passer. Hence, on special teams, the punter.

Lined up with them was Hill (#7), in my opinion the top special teamer in the NFC. He was selected as the first alternate to the Pro Bowl team that year. The most efficient punt rusher in the league, Hill would be in Hekker's face all day long.

Our two special teams linebackers, Craig Robinson (#52) and Vince Biegel (#59), would make up the remainder of the front.

Hekker loved to punt to his left, and when hurried—which was going to happen all day—he nearly always punted to that side. We doubled the flyer to our right side with two of our defensive backs, Vonn Bell (#24) and Josh Robinson (#32). We singled the flyer to our left side with our remaining defensive back, Justin Hardee (#34). To help play for the fake, we moved him two yards inside of the flyer and four yards off the ball. On the snap, he was to backpedal while keeping an eye on the punter and the flyer. We wanted him to identify the play (pass or punt) before committing to a technique.

In the NFL, if the ball is in the air on a pass from punt formation and headed to the outside receiver, there can be no pass interference. There can be a personal foul, but no PI. The defender can grab and hold or collide with the receiver as the ball approaches and it's no foul.

By playing our cornerback off the line of scrimmage, we believed we were greatly aiding him in identifying the fake and enabling him to make the play. From this base formation, we had to make only one call, and the personnel, alignment, and assignments were all-encompassed.

"Splatter" was our return and could be run anywhere. We double-teamed their dominant kick side and singled the opposite flyer, trying to keep him away from the kick but at the least sustaining contact. Inside, we were always rushing five, with a rule of: rush until you are blocked, then block whoever is blocking you, preventing him from getting into coverage. One of our linebackers lined up on their best cover man and attacked him, driving him back first and then hanging on to block him. Our other linebacker played behind the line and was responsible for their personal protector for the punter, both for any run fake and as a blocking assignment.

The punt returner, not a strong position for us, was to favor his right side, catch the ball, and either explode straight up the field or stretch the field and "run to daylight."

"Ram" was our block call because I always used the opposing team's name as one punt block call. I never liked a lot of verbiage. Everything was short and sweet. "Safe" was our call to play for the fake. That had a specific alignment, and the front five would aggressively rush.

"Splatter" was the built-in return for "Safe" in case of a poor punt.

I loved the scheme. I believed it was one of my simplest but most creative ever.

Our practice preparation was excellent. Sean Payton knows how to get a team ready to play in a big game. Each day, we practiced against the fake punt, both the run and pass—especially the pass. I even had our backup quarterback, Teddy Bridgewater, stand in for their punter, Hekker, to make sure that I got the exact type of pass we would have to defend. There wasn't one time in practice, including the walk-through the day before the game, that I didn't like the way that we defended their fakes.

As an extra preparation for the game, I had our film guys put together clips of every fake punt that the Rams had run, even going back to their St. Louis days under then-head coach Jeff Fisher.

Fisher loved fake punts, but that didn't impress me because their teams were mostly terrible, and it is easy as hell to run a fake punt when your team is getting its ass kicked. But nonetheless, we studied and showed everything to our guys.

Through all of this, I—no one else, just me—made one colossal mistake. Hekker had a great arm and could throw anywhere, but he favored throwing to the outside receiver, the flyer, on his right side. Statistically, he punted to our right toward our double-team, but threw the fake to our left. It is why we lined up our left cornerback slightly inside and four yards off the ball. We believed that would greatly enable him to identify the fake and aid him in making the play.

Hardee, our left cornerback, had a great year in 2018. He ranked closely behind Hill as a special-teams player, and in some aspects he could have earned Pro Bowl consideration. Hardee was a proactive player. In my two years with the Saints, I had learned which exact roles he could excel at. We moved him all over the field but always put him in a position where he was exploding to the ball. We didn't ask him to react. Just GO!

On our kickoff coverage, we played him as a "Skim," a role designed to contain the back side of our coverage in an aggressive fashion. Skimming the return from the edge of the front to the edge of the rear. He was our right flyer on the punt team, and with Tom Morstead favoring punting for the right, he was always exploding into the face of the ball.

We adjusted his blocking assignments on our kickoff return but always in a specifically aggressive assignment.

So, in my biggest game ever, I made an error. I put a proactive player in a very reactive role. Even though I knew he could handle the assignment, and we had prepared and practiced it perfectly, it just wasn't something he did naturally. I should have flopped my guys on the corners, and put Josh Robinson, a more experienced defensive back, in the reactive position, and let Justin line up to the right, and in most situations, in the double-vise.

The game started out completely in our favor. We were leading 13-0 in the first quarter, and it probably should have been 21-0. Our defense was playing great; the Rams' offense couldn't do anything. Our punt return team was doing great; it looked as if we might block every punt.

In the second quarter, the momentum was clearly still with the Saints. Again, the defense stopped the Rams, and with a fourth-and-5 at the LA 30-yard line, the Rams had to punt again. Our punt return team was on the field in a "Splatter" call. The

Rams substituted a wide receiver (Sam Shields, normally a defensive back) on their right side.

Taysom changed our call to a "Safe" call. It was not much different from our return call but a little more cautious. Our left cornerback was lined up two yards inside of their flyer, four yards off the ball. He was to backpedal, keeping an eye on the punter and then reacting to the play.

The Rams, being the Rams, ran a fake. Hekker took one step as though he was going to punt, and then, just as he had done many times in the past, pulled up and threw to his favorite side, the right. Justin had back-peddled, but then in a reactive mistake, he turned his back to the intended receiver. They easily completed the pass. The Rams did exactly as we had practiced it all week, but a mistake was made.

They gained some momentum and finished the drive with a field goal. Had I made the personnel change, I believe that we would have properly reacted and stopped a fake, which in every other way we had properly prepared for.

To this day, I wake up and go back to that play and toss and turn over my indecision.

The game went back and forth from there, and the Saints could have won it in many ways. It will always be known for the infamous "No Call" near the end of regulation.

Our wide receiver Tommylee Lewis was interfered with by Nickell Robey-Coleman and also hit helmet-to-helmet. Neither was called. No flags. Everyone in the country, including the people in the NFL offices in New York, saw it. But there was no method for overturning the missed call.

It can easily be argued that it was the worst officiating mistake in sports history. No, not just the NFL—sports history. I believe that there needs to be a way to reverse such errors, maybe with an official in the press box who can stop play and demand a review. The ability to get the play correctly officiated is what everyone wants.

The proper call would have given us the ball with a chance to run down the clock to a handful of seconds and kick what should be the winning field goal from short range.

And earn a trip to the Super Bowl.

Instead, the game went into overtime. We lost on a 57-yard field goal by Zuerlein. The season was over, and my thirty-two-year career came to an end.

Following the game, as I walked out of the stadium with my six-year-old grandson Tom holding hands between me and my son John, Tom looked up at me and said: "I am sad, Grandpa Mike. We got cheated. That was a penalty, and we were going to the Super Bowl, and I was going to get to go."

I said to him, "My 'Best Buddy,' you are right, that was terrible. The Saints should be going to the Super Bowl. I finally was going to get a chance to go, and so were you."

I walked out of the stadium and never looked back. My thirty-two-year career came to an end—not the end that I wanted, but an end.

And I loved every minute of it.

CHAPTER 16

The Art and Science of Special Teams

Building a special teams unit is a complex and constantly evolving process. An active game-day roster consists of forty-eight players, and from that number, the offense, defense, and special teams units must be formed.

Rosters are broken down pretty much this way:

Special teams (3): Placekicker, punter, long snapper.

Offense (21-23): Two or three quarterbacks, eight offensive linemen, two or three tight ends, three or four running backs/fullbacks, between four and six wide receivers.

Defense (22-24): Five or six linemen, five to seven linebackers, seven to nine backs.

So do the math. The three specialists and the eight offensive linemen are firm numbers. Every other position is a variable and can be adjusted in a number of ways.

Many teams go with two quarterbacks nowadays because quarterbacks don't play special teams—except in the rare instance of being a holder on field goals and extra points, a job usually handled by the punter. Of course, if three QBs are not suited up, a team must have an "emergency" guy who could fill the void in some fashion, should injuries occur.

While the twenty-two starters, eleven on offense and eleven on defense, are firm numbers, most backup roles are determined by special teams positions or specific game plan needs. Assistant coaches are always protecting their turf. There is a tremendous amount of selfishness involved in a large team sport such as NFL football. The game has evolved from a time when a coaching staff consisted of eight to ten people to now, when there is around twenty-five.

For many recent years, the full NFL roster consisted of fifty-three players, plus twelve on the practice squad. Each week, the team would declare its forty-six active players. But in 2020, with the new labor agreement between the NFL and the players' union, the active roster was expanded by two players, with one of those designated as an offensive lineman to ensure there are at least eight available for a game.

For most of my career, I dealt with a forty-six-man active roster to compile my six special teams units. There has always been an argument that with fifty-three players being paid, shouldn't fifty-three be active for games? The thinking against that deals with advantages one team could gain through injuries.

Each week, usually by Tuesday night but sometimes as late as Thursday after practice for a Sunday/Monday night game, the head coach would decide who would be active. He was making his decisions based mainly on injuries but also by specific game plan needs, with most of the weight leaning to offense and defense—especially to the side of the ball with which the head coach is most active. So, if the head coach also is the offensive play caller, you can bet that the weight of his active game-day roster will lean heavily toward that side.

That active roster scenario has been dramatically affected by NFL rules changes. Many of those changes have been designed to protect the player and make the game safer. Head injuries are a major concern, and the NFL has taken dramatic measures to reduce the violence of collisions. Helmet-to-helmet contact is strictly forbidden and rigorously enforced. Players can be ejected for them.

Blindside blocks have been outlawed, and contact with "defenseless" players is heavily penalized.

These particular safety regulations dramatically impacted the kicking game. The ball was moved up to the 35-yard line for the kickoff. The shorter distance makes it much easier for the powerful kickers in the NFL to blast the ball into and out of the end zone. Touchback.

So, the number of "violent" collisions on kickoff returns is being greatly reduced.

In fact, the most dramatic rule changes in the NFL in the past fifteen years have occurred on the kickoff and kickoff returns. There are few returns due to the increased number of touchbacks. Wedges on kickoff returns—a long-standing blocking device—were reduced from four players blocking to three, with no more than two standing together. Now, there are no wedges of any type.

Then, double-team blocks could only take place between players on the front line.

Trap blocks were strictly regulated and had to initiate from a position that kick coverage players could identify readily. In order to slow down the coverage speed and violence of the collisions, the kickoff coverage players cannot have a running start and must line up in a balanced formation of five on each side of the kicker, in a static position one yard behind the 35-yard line.

There's also a great deal of money involved. Coordinators make in the range of $1 million to $4 million per year. Top assistants are paid from $500,000 to $1.5 million. At these numbers, self-preservation is a motivating factor. Making sure that one's particular area is productive is at the top of the food chain. It takes a strong head coach to navigate his way through specific and sometimes selfish needs to build the team and care for its general well-being.

How many defensive coordinators, if no one but they and the Almighty knew, would rather lose 7-6 than win 34-33? Knowing that their unit had been successful on that given day?

Special teams coaches have to be reactionary. We must adjust to situations during the game. Watching the NFL today, I believe that many offensive coordinators would rather throw the ball than go to Heaven. They enter the red zone and don't even consider running the ball. Yes, the pass is the most dramatic and sexiest play; running the ball is just too pedestrian, I guess.

The head coach must balance the roster, and the special teams coach must be prepared to adapt to assemble his units. Of the six special teams units, only the field goal and extra point squads (both kicking and defending) comprise mainly starting offensive and defensive players. The other four units—kickoff and kickoff return, punt and punt return—must be built to specific needs and with the remaining players on the team.

Kicking plays are unique because they cover the entire field and players must be able to perform in space. There is very little in-line (close contact) play, and special teams guys must have open-field skills. I knew exactly the type of players I wanted on my special teams units.

Size, a necessity at some positions, had no bearing in my decision-making. I wanted speed and quickness, with open-field balance and agility.

In my time in the NFL, if I had to pick one thing that I most excelled at, it would be involving the various aspects of the kickoff return.

During most of my career, nearly every kickoff was returned. I believed it was a game-changing weapon. I coached some great kickoff returners, and our ability to score and attain a dominating starting field position factored into the team's success.

O.J. McDuffie and Brock Marion at Miami. Chad Morton, Justin Miller, Leon Washington, Brad Smith, and Joe McKnight with the Jets. Alvin Kamara of the Saints. All these players at some point in their careers led the NFL in kickoff returns.

Practicing Special Teams

Being a successful coach in the NFL can be all-encompassing, and you take on so many roles. The head coach must be a very diverse administrator who must organize and direct his staff. He must know how to coordinate his personnel and scouting departments to build a team in his coaching image. He has to understand the draft and free agency in order to procure and sustain the type of personnel he wants on his team.

Some head coaches are Xs and Os guys. They can be very technical and can design, teach, and call plays. Some head coaches act as offensive or defensive coordinators. Don Shula could coach all the positions but stuck mainly with the offense and called our plays from the sideline.

Rex Ryan, with whom I worked four seasons with the New York Jets, was a defensive expert and called the defense much of the time.

Sean Payton called the offensive plays in New Orleans and was the best on-field teacher I ever saw in my career. He meticulously instructed each player on each play for a specific level of exactness that was sensational. I would watch our games and see a big play and remember watching the same play on Wednesday or Thursday in practice.

Some head coaches administrate the game for situations and clock management but don't call the plays. Jimmy Johnson did this well with the Dolphins. I don't know if he could call a play, but he could manage the game.

Coaches have to be teachers. I believe the first role of a teacher is to fully know your subject, and I feel that knowledge is always expanding—always. I had a sign in my office to remind me of that very idea: "It is what you learn after you know it all that really counts."

Teaching the specifics of a play is not sufficient. Everything must be taught in relation to your players' specific abilities. Your opponents' play design and their specific talents must be included. Precise rules of the game must be part of all teaching. The best-executed play for a touchdown will be brought back due to someone lining up illegally, or due to any other penalty that can prevent success. Plays must be taught in accordance with situations and clock management. The coaches' knowledge of the subject must be thorough and all-encompassing.

With my players, I wanted dialogue. They were free to question or suggest at any time, either in the classroom or on the field. I often quizzed them to challenge their knowledge.

Most times, the on-field discussion would take place during a post-practice film session. I demanded practice perfection and could be tough with my criticism, but I could also be extremely complimentary, offering praise. I wanted them to feel great about their performance. I wanted my players to be cocky. Not arrogant, but cocky. I wanted confidence, and I would try anything to instill it.

Dan Marino used to say, "You can't defend a perfect pass." He believed that if he threw the ball to the exact desired spot, no one could defend it. I wanted my players to look at everything we did. When it was done exactly, they would believe that no one could stop us. I used to stop the film of a specific play such as a kickoff return and, from the film, have a player go up to the board and draw the play. If the play was being executed properly, it could be drawn up correctly.

I then might show a clip of an opponent's play and ask the same thing. There wasn't the same exactness, and the play looked discombobulated, disorganized. The player could not draw it and would turn around and might say, "I don't know what the hell this is."

I would then look them in the face and ask, "How in the hell is this sorry outfit going to beat us? They shouldn't even be on the same fucking field."

Yes, I wanted cockiness and established a little bit of arrogance. But I most always showed the opponent a level of respect, though depending on their level of performance. The better they performed, the more I challenged us to match them—and beat them.

NFL practices are choreographed down to the minute. Every single thing is carefully scripted and planned. Before every practice, each unit will conduct a walk-through of the key ingredients of the practice. Everything is precise and explained so that there is a complete understanding of all aspects of the play. In my opinion, no other sport ever comes close to the level of precision of the NFL, particularly when the numerous variables are considered.

From stretching to warmups, individual drills, group work of all types, and into team work, everything is carefully planned and filmed. Each part of practice has a specific goal, and it is the coaches' responsibility to have those goals met.

During the beginning of practice, we worked with our kicker, punter, and long snapper on specific areas as they warmed up for their team work. Even during their warmups, I pressured them. I might move a field goal attempt outside of the hash area and make the kicker aim at a specific goal post. I would shrink the target and make him hit a certain number before we moved on.

Some days, I would secretly instruct the holder to alter every hold. No hold was to be perfect, and the laces were all over the place. Sometimes arguments took place, but I never relented. I'd just tell the kicker to "kick the fucking ball. I don't care if it is lying flat."

Occasionally, I would tell the long snapper to make every snap to the punter just a little bit off. Too high, just outside, maybe near the ground. I would tell the punter to move his body to the snap and concentrate on his technique. I wanted the punter to only concentrate on himself and not be concerned with the snap. I might tell the snapper after a poor snap, "Snap the fucking ball," never revealing the plan we had worked out.

We made our snappers work on exact spot snaps, followed by quickly working back and then out to blocking assignments. Every so often, we kept a bucket of water nearby and soaked the ball before each snap to prepare for a rainy game. Our long snappers snapped, then blocked sleds or lifted medicine balls—anything to improve their movement and balance following a snap.

Brad Banta, who snapped in the league for ten years, was the best at working those drills. He broke snapping down into minute details and drilled every single one to attain a level of excellence.

With me, there was never a "mindless" drill. Everything had a purpose.

"People always point to the twelve minutes at halftime for teams as the fastest in the NFL," said my former assistant Chris Mattura. "The fastest twelve minutes in football were Mike's Friday special teams period. Fridays are the shortest time-on-the-field, helmet-and-shoulder-pad practice of the week. We'd practice punts from the minus-1, fake punts, specific ball placement punts, punt returns, and our blocks, as well as kickoffs and kickoff returns.

"I ran the scout team. We'd get it all done in twelve minutes, fast, like machine gun fire. Mike was fired up the entire period, and the players responded. All twenty-two players, which included my scout team, needed a water break after the fastest twelve minutes in the NFL concluded."

The education process continues every day at the very highest level on the learning ladder, with the extremely intricate practice procedures of the NFL. Each play that is run, offensively, defensively, and on special teams, is drawn as a specific look to present an exact problem both in the scheme of the play and for the opponent's personnel.

My first experience with scripting plays in practice came in 1974 when I was a graduate assistant coach at Indiana University, working under Lee Corso. I was coaching defense, and every day in practice, I worked with the scout team defense—giving the picture of the opponent's defense to our offense. I worked as the defensive coordinator, and, after studying the opponent, I would call the defensive look against our offense during the team work portion of the practice. I loved doing this; I learned our opponents' defenses, and I could be creative in calling whatever I desired going against our offense.

All of that changed one day when Jim Gruden, Indiana's running backs coach and the father of Jon and Jay Gruden, came up to me with a stack of numbered cards containing drawings of defenses I was to call on their specific plays. It was the first time I had ever seen or heard of scripting. Now, even taking a shower may be scripted.

Jim Gruden: there are some pretty damn good coaching genes in that family.

Practices are exact; not a minute is wasted. Everything is walked through, then practiced at various tempos and speeds, building up to a full-speed scrimmage. Every part of the practice is filmed, watched, and studied. No error in practice is overlooked.

I demanded absolute excellence in practice. No detail was too small, and no mistake was tolerated.

The designing, drawing, teaching, and practicing of each play had a very specific goal, and I never settled for anything less than perfection, down to the smallest step or detail.

The Saints' Thomas Morstead *figured it out*.

"Mike was wonderful to me," he said. "Yes, he is a hard guy to play for. He knows exactly what it takes to be the best, and he constantly demands it. Mike is the poster boy for not giving a shit about what anyone says. He believes in his system, and he was beloved because everybody believed what he was saying—on any team he was with.

"Authenticity is all players are looking for. If you are a pretender, you will be found out very quickly. If you are insecure, it will be found out."

Thomas Morstead

James Dearth, who turned into a long snapper in the NFL with the Jets after playing tight end in college, *figured it out.*

"Mike's only goal was to 'lead the league,' and he was going to teach you very hard and detailed," James explained. "He would expect you to be able to coach your position right back to him. We would have to stand up and teach it. He never belittled anyone, but he would let you know if you didn't have it right.

"His game plans and drawings were the best I have ever seen. It's amazing the way he thinks, all the different things he would bring up. He wouldn't minimize any job. He used to say, 'Any job worth having is a job worth doing well.' He expected perfection from his players, and if they had no indecisiveness, they would be able to do their jobs really well.

"I don't know how he got this way. I know he learned a lot from Don Shula, but he is his own man. They definitely broke the mold after they made him."

O.J. McDuffie was the Miami Dolphins' top draft choice in 1993 as a wide receiver and punt and kickoff returner out of Penn State. O.J. had 415 career catches, and his ninety in 1998 led the NFL. He was the first player in NFL history to have ninety receptions and ten punt returns without a fumble. Only Antonio Brown of Pittsburgh in 2016 matched this record.

He also caught more passes thrown by Dan Marino than any other Dolphins receiver.

And yeah, he *figured it out* about my meetings and practices.

"I remember the first day I met Mike at his first meeting. I knew everything was going to be serious as hell when it came to special teams. I was there for a reason, and I know for a fact that I wouldn't have been drafted in the first round if it hadn't been for Mike Westhoff.

"Our practices were detailed and well thought-out. There was so much attention to the smallest detail, down to the inch on simple alignments. I learned quickly that my major role was going to be as a punt returner, and Mike made me catch a million balls from Reggie Roby. And if you could catch his missiles, everything was going to be easy. I practiced catching more punts with one hand than most people do with two. I learned proper foot techniques and gained great confidence.

"The first punt I returned in the regular season was against the Indianapolis Colts, and, even though I didn't catch it perfectly, I still returned it for a touchdown.

"The success that was enjoyed by special teams was the direct result of Mike's meetings and practices. Our schemes were unbelievable; we were very innovative. We showed something different every week, and we had to practice it perfectly or it would be repeated until we had it exact.

"Our scouting reports and game plans were so detailed. Everyone had to know exactly everything; there were no excuses accepted. He made us practice everything, and we were so detailed we knew everything about everyone. We never were caught off-guard. There's no way we'd have scored as many times on returns during my career if it weren't for the meetings and practices of Mike."

Then we have Taysom Hill, a Pro Bowl-caliber special teams player and, in my opinion, the best "hybrid offensive player" in the NFL. A quarterback from BYU, no less. He had plenty to figure out.

"Mike spent time with me before, during, and after every practice. He also met with me after our meetings and would explain and walk through every detail," Taysom said. "He showed me what was expected of me on each individual play and defined my exact role in each. He asked our defensive coaches to include me in their tackling drills. I had never done this before in my career, but with him no detail was overlooked.

"Because of the way Mike prepared me as I stepped on the field, I knew this would work. The best thing he did for me was to put me in a position where I knew I could succeed. He would present a picture in practice that was exactly the same that we would get on Sunday."

Leon Washington was a dynamic player at Florida State and then was a league-leading and Pro Bowl kick return specialist with the Jets. Opponents couldn't figure out how to stop Leon.

"Mike challenged me to be at my very best in each practice," Leon said. "He was the first coach I ever had who wanted me to practice exactly like it was during the game. He wanted me to finish—all the way to the end zone. That was unheard of in NFL practices. Players get too tired running that far over and over in practice. But he showed me the importance of always competing.

"Think about the different kick returners Mike had: O.J. Mc-Duffie, Santana Moss, Chad Morton, Justin Miller, Brad Smith, and Joe McKnight. And I am sure that I am forgetting someone. There is a reason they all led the league. Mike could identify players and how they would help the team. He had the total package: a smart, giving, and caring person, a leader. He could command a room the second he came in.

Leon Washington

"Practices? They were nothing like I had ever seen. On a kick return play, Mike would stand right in the middle of the field. From there he could see the entire play develop.

"His spirit and expertise showed up everywhere: in meetings, on the sideline, and on the field. Yes, even in the middle of the field.

"And Mike's meetings were the very best of any coach I ever met. You learned everything and had fun doing it."

Designing Plays

When a play is designed in the NFL, quite a number of factors are involved. In my designs, I always worked to gain an advantage and try to put my players in the very best position to use their skills. To be able to make the play and have an edge on our opponent. The chess match between the coaches, keeping in mind the skills of the players and the various situations, are key to any play design.

I had a base design for plays in each of my four main units of special teams: kickoff coverage, kickoff return, punt coverage, punt return. Each week, though, I drastically altered each of these areas to either enhance our personnel or attack the opponent's scheme or personnel. I was able to draw and show on the sideline every play change. Each week, I presented a vast number of different formations, plays, and personnel groupings.

One such example took place early in the 2011 season while I was with the Jets, playing in Baltimore against John Harbaugh. During the offseason, Harbaugh had brought in some key players to bolster their special teams.

As a special teams coach in Philadelphia, he had a solid level of success with very sound, fundamental units. He had Brian Westbrook as his return specialist, and David Akers, his kicker, had performed brilliantly. Those players had carried them.

As an opponent, I always felt that his units were well coached and very sound, but I never felt that he was innovative in any way. His team did very little to scare you as an opponent in any fashion. He took one of my kickoff return schemes and basically ran it his entire career.

In 2011 with Baltimore, he was doing everything to make his kicking game really special. While his previous units were nothing out of the ordinary, that year it looked as if he was going all out.

Going into the game, I felt that we had a very good kickoff return unit, and I wanted to shock the Ravens. I studied their personnel in their kickoff coverage team and wanted to attack their two best players. There is nothing worse than having gotten beaten on a play when your two best players come to the sideline, as good as they are, and they just got their asses kicked.

Their kicker, Billy Cundiff, was trying to kick touchbacks and was driving the ball into the end zone about five yards deep, but mostly in the middle of the end zone and with only about 3.5 seconds hang time. Four seconds is good; 3.5 and we are going to run it down your throat.

I lined up our kick returner, Joe McKnight, a young and talented running back out of USC, five yards deep and told him that unless he was driven backward, be prepared to run everything out.

KICKOFF RETURN

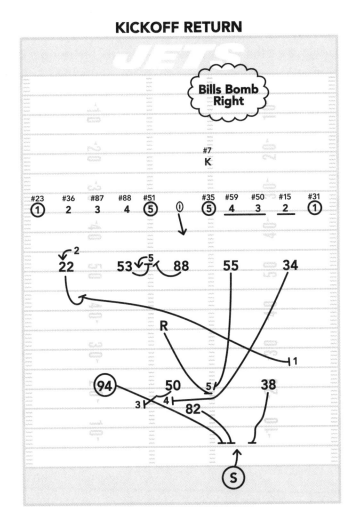

Brendon Ayanbadejo (#51), a 6-1, 225-pound linebacker out of UCLA, played ten years in the league and was a special teams standout. He had originally signed with Atlanta and spent time in Canada and NFL Europe. He played two seasons with Miami before joining the Bears and being selected to two Pro Bowls as a special teams player. He also made a Pro Bowl with Baltimore.

Ayanbadejo was fast, at 4.57 for the 40-yard dash, and exceptionally strong. With his speed and strength, he would penetrate the middle of the kickoff returns and create havoc. As I studied him, I was impressed with his kick coverage ability but noticed a weakness. When he took off running, he kept his head down and didn't look up until he was about five yards past the ball. He could really run, but he might be in store for a surprise.

I lined up my kickoff return with a five-man front. To attack Ayanbadejo, we used what I called a "Bomb" technique. Our center and guard were lined up at their normal 13 yards from the ball and were to take their normal two to three shuffle steps back as the ball was being kicked before turning and running to their blocking position and assignment. I taught the front line to shuffle back, watching the ball being kicked before turning and running. They were to keep their feet square and balanced before pushing off to run. Never "cross over." Crossing one foot over the other to turn and run puts your back to the ball and prevents you from reacting to an onside kick. If a team is looking to attempt an onside kick, it will look for a front-line player who is crossing over—and that is who it will attack.

They were to take their shuffle steps back and then to turn and attack ("Bomb") Ayanbadejo. We were hoping to catch him just as he looked up, and he would not see us "short-setting" him with a double-team. I had not shown a six-man front, so he had no reason to suspect anything different.

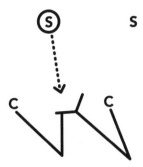

I always taught our double-teams with a "Post and Drive." We had the post man getting there first and setting up right in front of the defender at a ninety-degree angle, and then the drive player coming to his partner and setting up at a forty-five-degree angle.

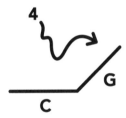

Defenders are taught to attack double-teams through the blocker on the side of the return. I wanted that blocker at a forty-five-degree angle to create more distance between the defender and the ball. Blockers want to drive the defender away from the ball or have him try to avoid them in that direction. If the defender tries to attack the forty-five-degree angle blocker, he will create a "bubble" in the line of the defense. Whichever one of the blockers the defender attacks, the other blocker will attack him, forming a tight double-team and blocking him away from the ball.

We were excellent double-team blockers, and we were going to dominate the defender. The technique of our right center wasn't perfect; he was late in his approach. We blocked Ayanbadejo but not nearly as physically as I would have liked. Later on that year, we used that same "Bomb" technique in San Diego, and they are still trying to find that guy. We blocked him out of the picture and pretty much off the field.

Kick returns have lots of moving parts. I tried to simplify mine with several basic premises.

Only two people had to know exactly where on the field to set up: the rover, who set the double-team, and the fullback, who set up the wedge. Wedging was legal back then but with only two players being together and forming the wedge.

This return was called "Miami Right, Bomb." The Miami Right designated that the opponent's right Number 5 would be double-teamed. The place on the field of that block would be determined by the depth of the kick and was game planned.

Normally, double-teams occur around the 30-yard line, but I wanted this a little deeper and closer to the spot of the kick. So, I chose the 25-yard line. I only assigned two people on our return team to know exactly where on the field to set up. Everyone else only had to look for them to know where to be aligned.

The rover set the double-team, and the fullback set up the wedge. Everyone else used them as their guide. The double-team was the focal point of the return. Everything else was based off that.

In this return, we were to double their right Number 5 on the 25-yard-line with our rover and right guard. Our right tackle was to shuffle back three steps and then turn and run to a point of two yards behind the double-team and run behind them to trap the coverage team's left Number 4. We were bombing the left Number 5, usually the man trapped, but now we were trapping the Number 4.

Our left guard ran back to his aiming point of the double-team and set up either three yards in front or behind the double (never on the same plane), depending on how his man was running. If it was fast, go beyond. If it was slow, set up in front of the double-team and block the left Number 3.

The fullback set the wedge 10 yards in front of the ball but never deeper than the 10-yard line if the ball was being run out of the end zone. If the returner ran the ball out, he had to catch up to the wedge. Spacing and distance are key ingredients of any running play, and I used these offensive concepts of the running game and applied them to my kickoff return system.

Leon Washington, a league-leading kick returner and a versatile running back, recognized that.

"Spacing and timing were critical words that Mike hammered on every return. How much space did I need from my lead blocker, and how much time did it take me to see the hole and make the proper cut? Mike knew that I needed to be seven yards from my lead blocker, a little closer than most. I was a running back and kind of hid behind my blockers and then exploded through the hole. Mike identified that right away."

Our fullback set a three-man wedge in front of the ball on the 10-yard line. The fullback and left end set together, and the right end set with them, but two yards outside the fullback. Wedges could consist of only two aligned blockers.

Our right end was assigned to block the kick coverage's right Number 2, who would be their kick-side contain man. And we would be kicking him out. That actually should be a very easy block.

The fullback and left end would, on the "GO" call from the fullback, start up and be responsible for blocking the right Number 3 and Number 4. Our returner, McKnight, was to read the block of our left end on their right Number 4. We always read the block of the man closest to the double-team on this side of the call "Miami Right"—first block on the right side of the doubled Number 5.

We added a wrinkle to this return and game planned a "Pop" call with our left tackle. "Pop" told our tackle away from the call side to run back normally, but only to around 10 yards, then stop abruptly and hit their back-side Number 2 player, forcing him to avoid to the side away from our calls, widen and slow his back-side approach. The tackle then would turn and run back at a forty-five-degree angle across the field to block the coverage team's play-side safety.

Baltimore's play-side Number 1 was Bernard Pollard, a five-year veteran and special teams demon. Pollard had been drafted by Kansas City in the second round out of Purdue and had a reputation as a big-time hitter. He was nicknamed "Bone Crusher." He put three New England Patriots out for the year, including the 2008 low hit on Tom Brady. He was big for a defensive back at 6-1, 225 pounds, and he was fast and tough.

While studying him, I noticed something different about the way he played the safety position. Most safeties run down with the coverage and, near the point of impact, they fall back to around five to eight yards behind the coverage, sliding in to be prepared to fill a hole in the coverage. I taught my safeties to keep outside leverage on the ball at about five yards behind, and with the kicker at 10 to 12 yards to form a triangle on the ball.

Pollard played the technique somewhat differently by staying deeper than normal. He would pull up at 11 yards, and then, if a hole opened, he would aggressively attack and fill the opening with a big hit. But with that distance, he left a critical weakness that I was going to attack.

Our left tackle using the "Pop" technique would have a great angle on which to attack Pollard, and he would never see us coming. It worked perfectly; just as he was getting ready to explode at the returner, we hit him right in the chest. The first thing that hit the ground was the back of his head, and his feet flipped over. He got blasted and probably still is wondering how he got hit so damn hard.

The return worked great. Every block wasn't perfect, but the timing was excellent, and their two best players were beaten—one of them destroyed.

McKnight went 107 yards for a touchdown and never had to break a tackle; we just blocked them all, especially Ayanbadejo and Pollard.

I liked playing Harbaugh. He was always a good challenge.

There are so many moving parts in a successful NFL play. Figuring it out is something I enjoyed and took great pride in. My favorite strategy was to defeat their best players. Teams' best players hated playing me and told me so many times. I was going to make their time playing us miserable.

I greatly respected them, but on game day, I hated them. Many times after games I would congratulate those players and would tell them if they were ever looking for another team, call me. I loved the way they played.

The Chess Game

One of the most underrated and underappreciated aspects of the NFL is the level of teaching and learning that takes place on a daily basis.

NFL football is an extremely complicated game. The variables and situations are endless. Every play is a combination of eleven different components moving against an equal number of eleven in countless varieties. The cognitive aspect of the NFL is on the highest plane.

There is no sport that comes close to football in the level of intellectual sophistication. It is by far the most academically complex sport. Coaches are much like scientists who sit in offices, watch hours of film, and design endless numbers of plays, trying to gain any sort of advantage.

Yes, it's a chess match beyond all such matches.

But unlike chess, when each piece has a specific move, every NFL position has a nearly endless selection of moves. And each one of those is further complicated by players' individual skills and athletic abilities.

Calling and then executing a play in the NFL requires a level of academic prowess that no other sport remotely approaches. Try this:

"Red right, 72 halfback short option."

That was one of our base plays when I was with the Miami Dolphins. Believe me, compared to much of today's sophistication, that play call is not even in the same universe.

The color designated the formation. Right determined the direction of the strength of the formation. 72 was the type of pass protection. Short option told every receiver what route to run. As you can see, so much had to be memorized—by everyone.

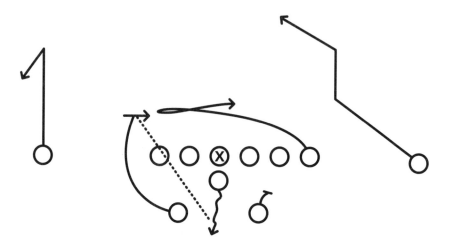

Each play, offensively and defensively, requires a great deal of mental preparation and execution. I used to tell my players that at their universities and colleges, the most revered professors might fail 30 percent of their class—and they are considered among the top professors on campus. If I as an instructor fail that many times, I will be fired at the end of the season, if not sooner.

Following my retirement from the NFL in 2012, I talked with the chairwoman of the education department at Florida Gulf Coast University near my home in Fort Myers about teaching a class to graduate-level students wanting to be high school teachers. Because I have a master's degree, I would be qualified to teach such a course. Many of today's educators are also coaches in any number of sports. The class would deal with many of the complexities of coaching. I have talked with several people who have taught such a class, and someday I may actually explore doing it. At this time, though, I was merely testing the water to look at the possibility.

During our conversation, the chairwoman seemed very interested, but she asked me what I felt was an unusual question. She wanted to know if I had ever taught a class. I immediately asked if she had ever taught a class. She said, "Of course, many times." I then asked if her results had been graded in the *New York Times*?

She looked at me like, well, "What are you talking about?"

I told her that every week my class got graded in at least three major publications. I couldn't afford to fail.

She probably never had experienced that level of pressure. Yes, I have taught class—hundreds of them.

Each day, a group of thirty or so young men from a variety of educational backgrounds would sit down in a classroom in front of me. My goal was simple: I was going to turn each of them into a student. An "A" student.

I didn't care what their educational background was—and believe me, it was varied—I was going to help them completely master everything I was presenting. I was going to turn them into experts of special teams play in the NFL. I wanted them to own their subject and take complete control. They were going to know the subject so well that they could get up front and teach it.

Many times, they had to do that very thing.

My favorite classroom was in New York with the Jets. Our team meeting room (my classroom) was a large amphitheater with very large, cushioned, and comfortable seats, with pull-up desk tops for taking notes. There were whiteboards in the front for posted notes or drawings, but most of the front was filled with a gigantic screen for film or drawings on an overhead projector.

Every player was equipped with a highly detailed notebook that can be four or five inches thick. The notebook is normally used as a reference. Everything for offense, defense, and special teams is drawn and defined.

I never taught from my notebook. At each meeting, I would distribute a handout with drawings and explanations of the plays we would be installing. This was all part of a player-centered learning environment. Each player had easy access to pens, pencils, and highlighters and could highlight specific assignments and techniques required on each play.

I would sit in the front of the class facing the players while drawing on a specific play that was being projected onto the large screen. Each player had the exact same drawing in front of him in his game plan. They were able to follow along and highlight or make notes on their individual copies.

I loved to look them in the face and ask questions and create a dialogue. There was no hand raising; this was cold calling.

"All right, Tom, describe everything you are doing here."

I expected tremendous detail from him in all aspects of his assignment.

During the season, each player on the opposition would be identified by his number, and we would then become specific as to that individual's abilities.

What does Steve Tasker, the great special teams player of the Buffalo Bills, like to do here? How will you attack him?

I tried to be as specific as possible. And when I was looking them straight in the face and having them instruct me on how to draw the specifics of the play—that was great.

At any time, I could project film of the play and dissect it to further enhance the learning process. The various levels of instruction, from visual to auditory and then to dialogue, were at the very top of the educational ladder, and this was only in the classroom. We hadn't even stepped on the field yet.

When my class started, everyone had to move into the front one-third of the room. No one was going to be sitting by himself in the back. I wanted dialogue and participation. Sometimes I would instruct one of my better students to sit next to someone who maybe was struggling some and work with him during the class.

The idea is to learn. The "how to" comes in a million different methods. I once heard that Dan Reeves—in my opinion the most underrated coach in the history of the NFL; I believe that he played and coached in more Super Bowls than anyone at one point—could do everything as a head coach. Building a team, he knew every situation and rule. He designed and called plays of every type. He had success with a variety of players, from John Elway to Michael Vick—you could hardly get any more opposite, and Dan made it work.

I know some really good head coaches who have had lots of success but couldn't draw a play to save their lives. Dan Reeves should be in the Hall of Fame.

In the winter of 1993, I received a phone call from Dan. He had just accepted the head coaching job with the New York Giants after spending the previous twelve years as the head coach of the Denver Broncos. He asked me a favor.

He told me that he was putting a film together to show to his new team, depicting how he wanted them to play. Through his research, he discovered that the successful Giants teams had been exceptionally tough and played very physically.

He was putting together clips of clean but physical play throughout the NFL. He told me that part of my special teams units were the most physical in the NFL, and he wanted my permission to show them. I was honored and extremely proud to be acknowledged by someone as renowned as Dan Reeves.

I said, "Of course and thank you."

One year, Dan went outside of football and brought someone into his organization who specialized in organizing and simplifying business. He somehow made his notebook and terminology more learnable and more student friendly. It clearly was outside-the-box thinking.

I'm not sure exactly what was done, but Dan was a brilliant coach and always looking for an edge.

And I made it very clear that we would stop at nothing to ensure the learning process worked. We'd have extra credit classes after practice and post-practice weightlifting on Wednesday and Thursday, sometimes even on Friday. Players would come into my office or into Ben Kotwica's. Ben would very carefully go over specific areas of the game plan with drawings, practice film, and game film. The learning process was NOT an option.

Ben did such an excellent job that, in my opinion, some games were won in those meetings.

I believe that copious notetaking is the most direct path to learning, and I tried to stay on top of it. At Wednesday morning's meeting, I passed out a new game plan and collected the previous week's. There was a cover page, and each player was instructed to put his name on the copy.

I thought my game plans and scouting reports were the best in the NFL. I had over the years seen several others, and I very much believed in mine. Back in the day, when we had so many special teams plays and were not restricted by the new rules, my game plan could be eighty pages. Eighty pages!

It was a depth chart, scouting report, and very specific game plan.

One year, when Eric Mangini had gotten the head coaching job with the Jets, he was talking with me about staying with the team. He pretty much said I could handle my area in any fashion that I desired. I was telling him about how I did my game plan and that I would absolutely not change it. He told me not to be concerned, that it was good.

"We have seen it several times," Eric said.

I froze. New England had "seen it? Several times?"

What did that mean?

He never explained further, and I never pursued it. But the Patriots were heavily fined for the "Spygate" episodes, so make of it what you will.

Occasionally, as I collected the previous week's plan, I would flip through them, checking the notes. Some were outstanding, neatly highlighted with very detailed notes. I sometimes would show them to the "class" on the overhead projector, and the entire group could clearly see the expertise. I never showed anyone's name, just the product.

Occasionally, someone's looked like shit, and I also would show it. I made it clear that I didn't give participation trophies. This was the NFL. If you were going to play, you damn sure had better be prepared.

Sometimes, out of anger, I would take the terrible report and throw it out the door, saying that I don't want this fucking piece of crap in my room.

"Mike brings with him a wealth of experience and knowledge—so much so I would argue he has forgotten more than any young coach even knows," said Deuce Schwartz, one of my assistants with the Saints. "Since the first day he entered the facility, his mere presence was infectious. I could write my own book on what I learned in a year and a half working with Mike. I admire his courage and fearlessness in his ability to constantly modify or tailor aspects of a game plan, meeting, or even attributes in his personal life in order to seek optimal results: in layman's terms, his knack for 'figuring it out.'

"One of my weekly responsibilities was drawing the plays for our game plan. This long and tedious ping-pong process involves actually drawing the plays; going to Mike and Bradford for editing; amending their changes; returning a new version for a few more modifications; then fixing those changes again until it was agreed the play was finalized for the players to see.

"To Mike's credit, even after we may have finalized the drawings, his mind was still churning. There were many mornings when I thought upon Mike's arrival into the office that we would start game planning a new special teams phase. I would be stunned to watch him walk in, not say a word to either of us—Bradford and I shared an office where we also conducted the crux of game-plan meetings—and begin erasing the entire grease board where our game plan was drawn while saying, 'This shit isn't going to work.'

"In a matter of seconds, I witnessed the hours of work I put into the drawings literally and metaphorically wiped away. We were back to square one.

"In these instances, I began understanding the importance of configuring and reconfiguring the plays in order to achieve the best results on game day—always figuring it out."

I am a movie fan, and the other night I was watching my favorite TV show, *Yellowstone*. Kevin Costner, the star, was talking about his beautiful ranch in Montana and said, "You can't buy this. You have to earn it. No matter who you are, you'll have to earn it."

That is how I feel about the NFL. There are no shortcuts. You have to earn it. Studying and learning are crucial, and you must pay great attention to detail.

As the players would leave the meeting room, no one ever bent down to pick up a scouting report that I had tossed in anger. They just walked right over it. The idea was that you damn sure didn't want that report to be yours.

Kevin Costner knows what it takes to have the best ranch in the country. I think I know what it takes to be the best special teams unit in the NFL.

I wanted to use my authority in a way that made the players feel that they shared in it. I wanted to take them above a bar they wouldn't reach by themselves.

Vernon Gholston

I took each of my four major units—kickoff coverage and return; punt coverage and return—and I broke down each of them into specific roles.

I never asked anyone to be able to do everything. I broke down the units into specific segments and varied them constantly. A bigger, slower player might have a specific role that matched his skills. I just had to maneuver that role to keep him in a position in which his abilities let him execute the requirements of the job. Make each role fit their specific skill levels.

This type of thinking brought about lots of extra work for me as a coach. My preparation work was endless. I had to design and draw everything. I might have ten alignments for kickoff coverage on any given week. Most teams would have one or maybe a slightly adjusted two. I believe that it was in this area that I excelled. By scheming and maneuvering, I could take less-talented personnel and win any given play by diminishing their number of roles, thus enhancing their ability to perform. As time progressed and my talent level expanded, I was only concerned about ranking at or near the very top of the league's statistics each and every week.

I categorized the players according to their various athletic skills: speed, size, strength, instincts, quickness, toughness, the ability to operate in space versus close quarters, and being a proactive or a reactive type of player. I took my various special teams units and separated the roles and fit the players into the specific roles. I was not afraid to reconfigure anything to get someone into a position in which he could excel.

One very specific example of this occurred while I was with the New York Jets. We had drafted Vernon Gholston, a defensive end out of Ohio State with the sixth pick in the first round in 2008. Vernon struggled; he never performed even close to the expectation level for a lofty pick of that magnitude.

A "high pick" outside linebacker can be a dominating player in the NFL. He can rush the passer and be disruptive on any given play.

Vernon did none of this. He worked hard and persevered, but nothing good was happening. I felt for him. A highly drafted and therefore highly paid player that seems to be failing at every turn soon finds himself all alone in the locker room. It's nothing overt; it is just a feeling.

Vernon was a good kid and had checked all the boxes of criteria for that level of a draft selection. I talked with Eric Mangini, the head coach of the Jets, who had prepared very thoroughly for the draft, and he assured me that Vernon had all the qualities that they were looking for with that pick.

I was absent from the Jets at the time of the draft while on a medical leave. When I returned and Vernon was in the midst of failure, much of the defensive staff voiced displeasure with the pick—blaming general manager Mike Tannenbaum and his being influenced by Bill Parcells and not wanting Vernon to drop to New

England on a later pick. Lots of fingers were pointed, but Mangini assured me that the hierarchy of the Jets was very much on board with selecting Vernon with the sixth selection of the draft.

Still, there was just no way he should have been taken No. 6 overall. Failure in professional sports may still pay well, but it can be cold and lonely.

One frigid day during the winter of Vernon's second year, with Rex Ryan being the new head coach, we had a massive snowstorm in New Jersey. Everyone was told to go home early to avoid the roads when they turned bad. I drove a Jeep and could drive anywhere, so I stayed late and finished some work then worked out in the weight room. As I drove home, I found a small diner about five miles from our office that was the only restaurant still open. I went in and sat at the counter; I was the only customer in the place.

The manager came over, having recognized me from the Jets, and we began to talk. He told me that I was sitting in Vernon Gholston's seat. He said that during the season Vernon came into his restaurant, sat at the counter by himself, and ate there nearly every night.

It upset me to picture him sitting there by himself, and I promised myself that I would find something for Vernon.

That next season, I designed a role for Vernon. Our kickoff coverage team was maybe the best in the NFL. We gave up nearly the fewest yards in the league and had one of the very best opponent's starting field position—a very important statistic. We moved people around, all over the place, and attacked the opponent's kickoff return squad. Remember, I treated kickoff coverage like a Bud Carson blitz on defense.

EXCHANGE RIGHT

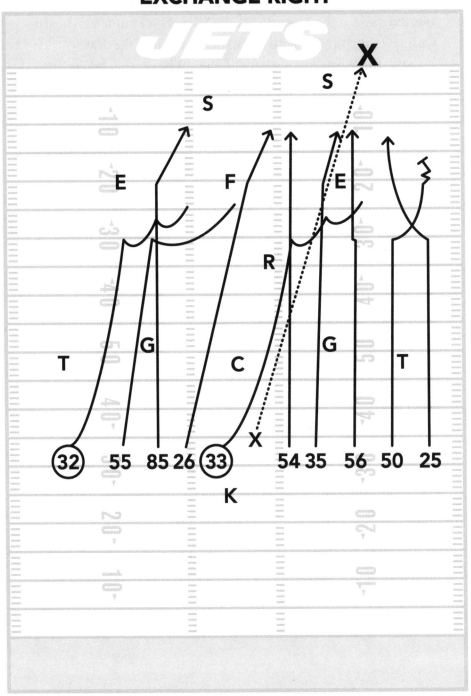

I always tried to construct my coverage and return units along the philosophical intricacies of offense and defense.

We were aiming for a spot and coming from everywhere. I always kicked to a side and flipped my coverage with a strong (kick) side and a fast side. We asked the kicker to place the ball from the yard number to the sideline and anywhere near the goal line. We were forcing the return team into a corner. We were using the sideline as an extra player in our coverage.

OVERLOAD AWAY (KICK LEFT)

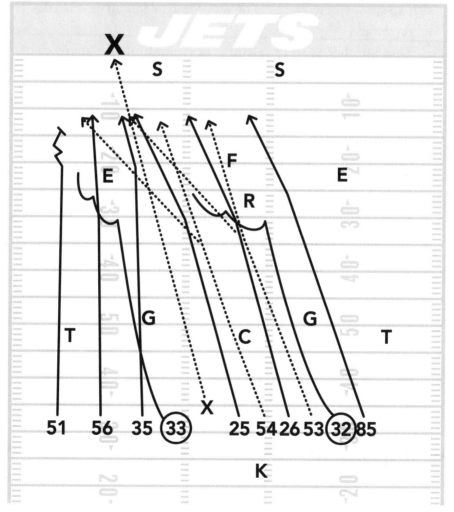

I aligned Vernon at the kick-side Number 2 spot. On my kick-off coverages, the numbers (R-1 to L-5) stood not only for the players' positions on the field but also a role and technique associated with that number. The R and L showed the direction of the kick and also designated the strong and fast sides of the kick. No matter where you were aligned, your roles and techniques were consistent. I had to match the personnel with their abilities that best fit the various assignments required.

In my drawings, I would show our player's number below the lineup positions and then draw a line, often coded by color or design, to show where and how he was going to end up on a particular coverage.

Our Number 1s were safeties; they could line up anywhere but had to end up five yards behind the coverage and three yards outside of the ball on their coverage side.

The kicker was to run down following the kick and end up five yards behind the safeties and directly in front of the ball. The safeties and kicker needed to form a triangle with the ball. I could stop the film on a particular play and with the laser point out how well we were forming the triangle. The kicker was the third safety and although maybe not the best tackler, if he were only required to fill a small area, it would enhance his chances of making a tackle if the ball carrier broke out.

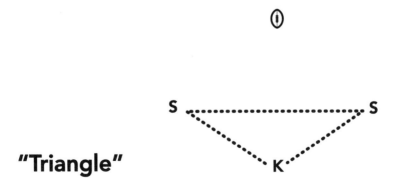

"Triangle"

How many times have we seen a ball carrier break free and only have to beat the kicker who is all by himself way behind the coverage team in the open field? Those plays usually end up in kickoff returns for touchdowns.

Our Number 2s were our edge players. The back-side Number 2 had a "skim" technique. He was always a fast and proactive type of player. His assignment was to "skim" the back side of the return team from the edge of the front wall of blockers to the edge of the back. Making sure that he got as deep as their deepest player, keeping leverage on the back edge of the return. He had the back-side contain, but it was very tight and very aggressive.

Our play-side Number 2 was our front-side contain player. He was a bigger, stronger type of player. He didn't have to be the fastest player, as he was only going to be asked to contain a very small area of the field. He attacked the play-side edge of the return, keeping outside leverage at all times and squeezing the ball carrier into the attacking part of our coverage.

Our Number 3s were our "ball" men. They were our fastest and many times our most aggressive players. Usually, defensive backs or wide receivers got this job—players who could run and tackle. They would line up anywhere. Sometimes they would even go in motion. They had "no lane and no contain" assignments and needed only to attack the ball. These were our disruptors, and you as an opponent had better know how to count because they were never going to end up in the position where they originated.

Often in a game plan, we would use three Number 3s, substituting for normally a Number 5. This would give us a smaller but faster and more aggressive coverage unit. Wedge kickoff returns were legal at this time, and we had to make sure our coverage unit was matching up correctly against the type of return that we were facing.

Our Number 4s were what we referred to as our linebackers. These were actually normal linebackers and would play in our coverage scheme as linebackers would in a normal defensive alignment. They would get right to the point of attack, then flow in behind our first level of defense. They would look for an opening and then fill and tackle as the opportunity presented. The players were quick, aggressive, and sure tacklers.

Size was not important here, as they were usually not the first wall of defense. Larry Izzo (a Pro Bowl special teamer), O.J. Brigance, James Ihedigbo, Kenyatta Wright, Bernie Parmalee, Jerald Sowell, Nick Bellore, and Craig Robertson were some of the standouts. These were all slightly undersized but extremely versatile and aggressive players and great tacklers.

Our 5s were our impact players. They were bigger and much more "point of attack" players. Often, they were placed at a spot to be double-teamed. That was somewhat sacrificial, but it enabled more versatile players to match up one-on-one in the open field and more easily defeat the blocker and make the tackle.

Throughout most of my career, we faced wedge kickoff returns. The most misused term in all of football was the "wedge breaker." It is a "never-picked-in-gym-class" media type of term. That description was never in my notebook or vocabulary. I never taught anyone to run into the front end of a truck.

Any one of my players facing a wedge looked to attack on the outside of the edge, creating a one-on-one situation. If attacking the center of a wedge, the player was to attack between two players, turning his body slightly at an angle to put more on one blocker than another and lessen his area of impact. No one ever said this was easy, but this is pro football and involves somewhat of a controlled violence.

Football is a physical sport. Hitting is a key aspect, but it must be controlled properly. I taught hitting from below the shoulder and above the knee. Helmet-to-helmet hits and blind shots were never taught by me, and I believed that my teams were among the most physical in the NFL—year in and year out.

Our kickoff coverage teams had very specific roles, and by showing the drawings on the sideline before the play, we could move individuals around and create the best matchups for our players. My kickoff coverage scheme was aggressive and somewhat risky; defensive teams who like to blitz take the same kind of risks. They can attack you and destroy you, but sometimes they get caught and can give up a big play. I took this same risk and occasionally got caught, but much more often we had some of the very best kickoff coverage numbers in the league.

Vernon was the play-side edge or contain player. I told him to see himself as a security guard. He didn't have to cover the entire lobby, just the elevator door. I assigned him a small area to work with. He wasn't good at it. He was great.

We had an excellent group, and he was a viable part. I am very proud of how it worked out for Vernon. He accepted the role and worked hard at it. I was proud and pleased that a small bit of creativity had such a positive effect on someone. He was finally sitting in a meeting, and with much of the team watching the film, he was seeing and having some very positive impact.

Did it make up for his other shortcomings? Probably not, but he was having some success, and on certain plays he could be a playmaker—and maybe bring a smile to his face, or a friend to have dinner with.

Sometimes the best parts of coaching take place in the smallest areas.

Why Did It Work?

Being successful in the NFL as a coach mostly is about becoming a head coach. But being a head coach is not for everyone. For some, it is just not in their makeup. And others just may lack the opportunity.

For me, I would have loved the chance, and I believe I would have made it work. But I had lots of obstacles in my path, and it just didn't happen for me. I don't believe my career is defined by my not having been a head coach.

I was chosen to receive that Lifetime Achievement Award by the Professional Football Writers of America for my accomplishments as an NFL assistant coach. This very prestigious award made me very appreciative of what I was able to accomplish as a coach.

But also, on the other end of the scale, I worked with several coaches who were completely lost in the NFL, and one head coach who was a complete joke, with zero NFL coaching qualifications of any kind.

Of course, I worked with Don Shula, the NFL's all-time winningest coach, a Hall of Famer, and, in my opinion, the best coach ever in the NFL. And I also worked with Sean Payton, to me another Hall of Fame coach (in the future), especially if he wins another Super Bowl.

Two things that these great coaches had in common were an incredible knowledge of the business and their attention to detail. I watched these great coaches teach the exactness and detail of NFL football, and, of course, if it was taught to the correct player, it would bring a particular level of success.

I believe that the level of success I had as a coach came from this exact premise. I never stopped or hesitated for even a moment on the constant learning process of exploring every minute detail of special teams in the NFL. I would sit for hours in my office and watch film of what everyone else was doing—some coaches in particular, and others maybe not so much. I would sit at my desk and draw plays all day and night. I didn't care where it came from. Finding a better way to do something was always at the top of my list.

Sometimes success is nurtured by being in the correct place at the correct time. For my development as a special teams coach, those two areas were perfect.

I became a special teams coach completely by accident. Every aspect of the job was new and completely foreign to me. For most of NFL history, special teams were a small part of the game. There were some notable coaching exceptions such as George Allen and Marv Levy—both Hall of Famers—but they primarily emphasized execution and being fundamentally sound. There was very little if any level of creativity.

One aspect that aided me in my way of thinking was having very little in the way of rules governing much. Now, almost all of what takes place in the kicking game is closely governed by rules emphasizing safety. In 1982, this basically did not exist. Wedges, traps, and double-teams on kickoff returns were all legal and could be designed a million different ways. Double-teams initiated inbounds could be extended out-of-bounds.

Hence, throwing an opponent's punt team gunner right through the Gatorade table seemed to be a good way to finish a block. Blind-side traps and peel-back blocks were taught and encouraged.

Movement and overloads on kickoff coverage were among my favorite aspects of creativity. If you were a long snapper on punts or kicks, someone was going to be lined up right over you, and your ability and courage were surely going to be tested. Most of the long snappers today would call home and ask for Mom if faced with what we presented them on every single snap.

That's the way the game was played. Much of the violence and physical level of play needed to be controlled and regulated. No one was trying to hurt anyone, but football is a very physical game. And the NFL, through its rules and equipment, has taken great strides to protect its players.

Franklin Delano Roosevelt, one of our great presidents, stated that he wanted his career to be judged by the enemies that he made. No, not by his personality, but by how he had done his job. I wanted to do things precisely and physically, and with as much creativity as possible. Everyone would hate to play me. I wanted my opponents to dislike me for a hundred different reasons. When everything was over and they got to know me, they might actually see a pretty nice guy—but only when it was all over.

I had two signs in my office that I tried to live by every day.

"You can't win with the players you don't have."

"If you always do what you have always done, you will always get what you have always gotten."

In relation to the first sign, I didn't have Deion Sanders or Devin Hester, but I will put up the number of league-leading kick returners that I had with anyone in NFL history. Sometimes I loved our personnel department, but most of the time? Not so much.

But I knew I could figure it out and find a way to make things not only work but be the very best or damn close to it.

The second sign meant to figure out a new and better way. Do the same thing, just make it look different. Add a wrinkle. Come up with something new. Do what they don't expect. Hit them harder than they have ever been hit.

I wanted to make my opponents absolute nervous wrecks. Did I achieve that? I don't know, but I think I might have come close.

One area I believe I excelled in was the philosophy of design. I wanted my coverage units, both kickoffs and punts, to be based on the exact premises of defense.

Kickoff coverage I saw as blitzing. I wanted to attack the return team with the same principles that a blitzing defense uses to attack an offense. I made sure that I sustained edges and always emphasized contain, but only slightly off the edge of the play and formation. Definitely not at a point of the field. I moved personnel around to create mismatches. I believed in attacking on various levels and stacking various players to confuse blocking assignments and mimic linebacker and safety positions of a defense.

One of the main principles of my coverage philosophy was to shrink the playing field and use the sideline as a coverage weapon. I flip-flopped my coverage and created a "strong side" and a "fast side." I overloaded the play (strong) side in a hundred different ways, with numbers and various personnel, and with the fast (weak) side squeezed the return into the overload and the sideline.

The rules have been greatly changed, and this type of coverage movement has been completely eliminated. In 2020, the kickoff coverage had to be lined up in a 5-by-5 balanced position. Playing on a kickoff return team and having to count my coverage movement was a full-time job. Today? My six-year-old grandson could count today's bullshit. Creativity was part of the job that I greatly relished and believed I excelled in. Coaching today? Not so much, frankly, compared to the opportunities that I experienced. Very little creativity, if any.

As a kickoff return team, I saw the play as an offensive off-tackle power running play. I broke down the kickoff return play that way.

The play started with a double-team. I have plays in which we could double-team five different players: three on the strong side and two on the back side of the kick. If you number the kickoff team from the outside in, we double players 3, 4, and 5 on the kick side and players 4 and 5 away from the kick.

I would call the return on the sideline and show a drawing of the play. Most of my teams kicked to a side. We were kicking off from the 30-yard line, not the 35 like today, and there were not as many touchbacks. My returns were designed to run mostly at the play side of the kick and counter away from the kick if called. I studied every kicker and believed that through his alignment or first two steps I knew exactly where he was going to kick the ball. From the sideline, standing directly opposite the kicker, I could see him perfectly, and I would signal to my guys the direction of the kick (as we saw it) and therefore which return we would run.

Every play had a counter designed with it. Everything looked like a kick-side return and then would break hard back away from the angle of the kick and the coverage.

Believe it or not, there is a lot of teaching that goes into a double-team. First of all, I wanted to be able to vary my position from which I would double. (I created a position player who I moved all over the field. From up near the front line to back deep in the return. I referred to this position as the "rover," and he could line up anywhere and had a million assignments.)

You never had to worry about memorizing these different looks because I would draw each one and show them before we went on the field. Each week, I would have ten to twelve different kickoff return schemes drawn.

The double-team is broken down into two parts: the "post" and the "drive." The post was one of the two players on the field who had to know exactly where to be aligned. He would drive back to a specifically designed spot on the field and set up slightly to the outside of the coverage man we were going to double and at an exact yard line.

Distance and spacing are two of the most important aspects of a running play and certainly of a kickoff return. The double-team must be in a proper relationship to where the kickoff lands. I wanted my double-team to be around 25 yards from where the ball normally lands. If the ball is usually landing around the goal line, I wanted to get my double-team usually around the 30- to 25-yard line. I took into account the hang time of the kick and the speed of the coverage team and set my double-team accordingly.

The post player set up at his spot, and the drive player only had to look for his partner to know where to go. The post player would align at a ninety-degree angle to his blocking assignment, and the drive man would get next to him at a forty-five-degree angle.

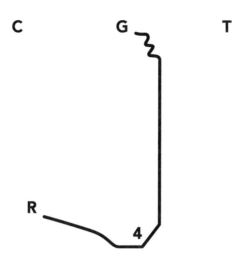

Kickoff coverage individuals are taught to attack a double-team block through the return-side man of the double-team. I wanted the double-team man to have to slow down slightly to bubble over the top of the angled blocker. This, to me, was going to increase the size of the "soft spot" in which we were aiming our return. The double-teamers would work together and drive their opponent preferably away from the called side, but basically anywhere he wanted to run.

We then trapped the next man in the coverage closest to the double-team. Our trapper only had to look for the double-team and run for a point one yard behind the double and look for his man either coming out from behind the double or flowing back over the top. Just sprint to the double-team spot and take whatever shows.

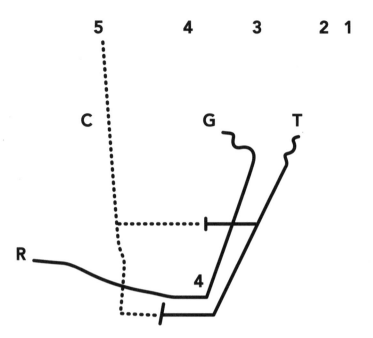

I believed that only a few people needed to be aware of exactly where to end up aligned on the field. Everyone else was there as an aiming point. This way, the learning process could be more exact.

The only other person who had to know exactly where to end up aligned was one of the wedge blockers. Most of my career, we were able to form a wedge with two or three players aligned together. I started in the days of the old "four-man wedge," but that was altered for safety. Two players could be lined up together on possibly 2 versus 2 or 2 versus 1. For me, only one player had to know when to set the wedge; to relate to a running play, they were lead blockers.

We set our wedge anywhere from 12 to 7 yards from the ball. Justin Miller, who led the league in kickoff-return yards, liked the wedge to be farther from him. He was exceptionally fast and wanted to feel as though he was chasing the lead blockers.

Leon Washington, also a league leader, wanted to feel as though he was hiding behind the blockers and could explode through anywhere. He felt better running five to seven yards behind a wedge.

Spacing and timing are crucial to any running play. They are equally crucial for a kickoff return.

One week before the 2020 college national championship game, I was talking with Jeff Banks, the special teams coach at Alabama. I had helped him at both Texas A&M and at Alabama, and I believe he is an excellent coach. I told him his kickoff return was out of whack. In my opinion, he wasn't having much success because his double-team was way too far in front of the ball. I said, "Your double-team is in Birmingham, and you are playing in Tuscaloosa."

I am sure he got the message.

Much of my career, I utilized a three-man wedge. They would be configured with two men side by side and one aligned two yards inside from his partners. The outside man was always aligned by himself. Occasionally, I used a four-man wedge in which they were aligned two by two.

These blockers were to retreat to a specific point in front of the returner, normally around 10 to 12 yards. Each individual had a specific blocking assignment or worked with his partner in a two-on-two blocking coordination. One specific member of the wedge would be responsible for setting the exact alignment and for giving a "GO" call just as the ball was being caught. I wanted everyone moving forward as the ball was caught.

The returner should be running or sliding forward as he caught the ball, and the wedge was also moving forward. The man on the outside edge of the wedge was usually responsible for the edge player in coverage: the Number 2 if counting from the outside in. This should not be a hard block, and if made while under control and not running wildly should easily be executed.

The next two edge players were responsible for the first two defenders outside of this double-team. Keep your feet and take the defender any way he wants to go. Believe me, these blocking assignments were mixed up a hundred different ways, but the principles were basically the same.

The return man's read was always the same, and it went from inside out. He read the block of his wedge man closest to the double-team. Between each blocker was a window. Read the return from the inside out and explode through the first open window. Then look for inside pursuit, an unblocked safety, and, lastly, the kicker. Make the unblocked defender move one way or another—and then you run to daylight.

Several times in my career, I aligned two return specialists. The blocking returner's rules were simple: come to a position two by four. That is, two yards outside of the ball and four yards in front of the ball carrier. The blocker's first rule was to pick up any defender who had broken free and was pursuing to the ball. His blocking rule was consistent: if the defender can tackle you, then block him. If not, head through the wedge and look for the most dangerous defender. I did not want the off returner turning back and blocking a pursuing defender who was too far back to tackle the ball carrier.

Hence, the "If he can tackle you" rule.

The backside blocking of any running play is designed to form a type of wall to cut off pursuit. The lead blocker is the "wall" man to a point four to six yards from the double-team and set up either slightly in front of the double or slightly deeper, but never on the same plane. Blocking on the same plane forces blockers to run into one another and keep them from moving freely to their blocking assignment.

His blocking assignment was going to be the second man down inside of the double-team. The first man down belonged to the trapper, and the four- to six-yard space created a small window to funnel the defender through. Many times, that man would see the opening and explode through, expecting an unobstructed path to the ball carrier. What he didn't see was the trapper coming from behind the double-team.

The next thing he knew, he might be waking up on the bench.

Now you know why they changed the rule. People have asked me to go back into coaching, but what the hell is someone like me going to teach?

The back-side wall would set up five yards apart and three yards either in front of or behind to his adjacent blocking partner. They would then run together, forming a moving wall to get to their specific blocking assignment and cut off the back-side pursuit. If executed correctly, this will resemble an offensive running play.

I used to love to be in a film study and stop the film and show a perfectly aligned play and ask if any coverage team could stop us when we're doing everything correctly.

When all of this was executed properly, any number of returners could have run for touchdowns and been a league leader.

One of my favorite things as a coach was to see if I could come up with something maybe different to gain an edge.

In 2018 with the Saints, we had a great punter in Tom Morstead, an excellent group of blockers and coverage personnel, and the NFL's all-time best personal protector, Taysom Hill. He could make every call, block like a fullback, and cover like a linebacker. We could also run fakes.

We were really good!

No, I didn't have a punter who could throw like a quarterback, as the Rams had. They had a great weapon and great success, but they went to the well too many times and failed way more than I could have accepted. John Fassel, the Rams' special teams coach who moved on to Dallas and kept trying all of his fakes, failed more in 2020 than probably anyone in history. Maybe two or three times more than anyone.

Of all the fakes I called in my career, I only failed once. Tim Tebow with the Jets ran one against the Rams. He should have checked out of it, and we failed.

In 2018, we were preparing to play Baltimore, and with their excellent defense, I believed we might be needed to help with some type of big play. As a special teams coach, if you can't make some type of big play, then in my opinion, you are not really special. Particularly if you have a level of talent.

I almost always only watched film from the end zone. From that angle, the picture developed more quickly for me. I was watching Baltimore's punt return team from the end zone, looking over the opponent's punt team and into the faces of the punt return team players.

I saw an opponent bring a flyer (or gunner) in motion back in toward the punter and then punt to the opposite side of the field. Many teams do this; it is very common. But I noticed something. When the punt team's personal protector wanted his man to come in motion, he lifted his arm out and to the side, and with his hand signaled for the motion. I noticed that as he did this, both of Baltimore's linebackers turned their heads in the direction of the motion man.

We then designed a punt fake to run Taysom Hill right over our left guard in a wedge type of running play. The play was called "Shark," and I would call it from the sideline. If the defense was in a look that we did not like, we would check out of the fake and punt the ball.

I called the fake. I did not consult with Sean Payton. He is calling offensive plays and is looking at his play call for an element of success. I am looking at the play for an element of failure. That will determine whether the situation is correct for a fake. I don't have time for questions. I was never reckless, and Sean trusted me.

Plus, I never failed. N-E-V-E-R.

We lined up in our normal punt formation with the "Shark" having been called. We then shifted our wing up to the ball and our flyer off. Taysom then reached out with his left arm and hand-signaled the flyer to motion in. Taysom was looking right in their linebacker's face. When the linebacker turned his head to look, we snapped the ball.

We blew them right off the line and easily got the first down. Our guard hit their linebacker right in the chest before he knew what was happening and knocked him right on his ass.

Our offense went back on the field with regained momentum and led us toward a victory. It was a great fake, well designed, called at the correct time, and extremely well executed. Sometimes when it works, it just doesn't get any better.

Being successful on Sundays in the NFL is built around several premises. Obviously, having great players helps. But in the NFL, everyone is nearly a great player.

Creativity and variance in design were my keys to any success, but practicing with precision and tempo were absolutely necessary to reach my highest level of performance.

Brilliant Minds

As I look back on my career and the abilities of the coaches with whom I worked, several jumped off the page.

Richard Mann, the receivers coach with the Colts, was the most fundamental and precise at his position of anyone I ever observed. Bill Muir and Doug Marrone were creative and disciplined offensive line coaches. But no one was more exact in his teaching than Bill Callahan.

Rex Ryan was the most creative defensive coach I ever worked with, but his staff—with the notable exception of Mike Pettine—

were not as demanding of exactness on the practice field as I believed they needed to be.

Rick Venturi as a secondary coach could turn very average players into very good ones due to his precise teaching.

Don Shula, of course, was the best. He knew and could teach every part of the game in the classroom, the film room, and on the field. His knowledge and instructing ability were at the very top of the NFL.

But the best on-field teacher that I ever watched was Sean Payton. He teaches every aspect of every play to his offense. His exactness is immeasurable. Every single step he taught in a precise manner. Everything has a specific reason and outcome if practiced correctly. If I were to be even a little bit critical of him, it would be in his occasional play calling. There are times when I wish he would run the ball more. It seems as though he would rather complete a pass than anything, but that is not unlike most really good offensive coaches.

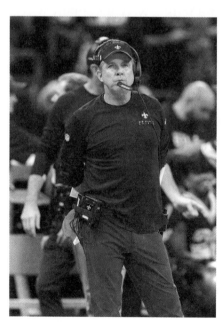

Sean Payton

In my practices, I wanted everything to be exact. I wanted to be able to freeze a film at a spot during a practice and the picture on the screen would exactly—and I mean exactly—mirror a drawing of the play being executed. If one person was out of position, the picture would be ruined.

There were several methods I used to try to achieve that specific level of excellence. I once read that Phil Jackson every so often while practicing his Chicago Bulls would have a "silent" section of his practice. No one was allowed to talk or make any calls. Everything had to be done through recognition, pointing, and feeling what your teammates and what the opposition were doing. I felt that if it was good enough for Michael Jordan, then it might be good enough for Michael Westhoff.

Occasionally, I would conduct a punt drill in which no one was allowed to speak. I would make the punt call, and everyone also had to nod or point as their only communication. Everyone worked through feel with the person on either side of them and communicated without speaking a word. I used the example of playing in very loud stadiums in which we had to be able to feel one another.

I also used to practice a "freeze" call with my punt team. In the middle of a punt protection play, I would blow a whistle signaling everyone to freeze. If you moved a step or two after the whistle, it was OK; just revert back to the position you were in and freeze. The exact stance and position were required. I wanted to be able to show the freeze position in the film session and see if it looked exactly like a drawing of a perfect punt protection cup. This has to be practiced a few times to get it executed properly, but we got it done.

One year when I was with the Jets, a number of coaches from the University of Michigan came to New York to watch our spring practices. We were an excellent special teams unit, and several coaches were observing my punt drill. Following the practice, one of their coaches came up to me and said, "Mike, I timed your period. You had twelve minutes and ran fifteen full-speed plays in which you protected against various defensive looks, punted, and covered five yards. Then, on the last one, everybody covered all the way to the ball."

He added, "You only substituted two players. When do you practice your second punt team?"

I told him that in the NFL only a few players are needed or substituted, and the "second punt team" will practice the next day versus my first-unit punt return team. The first team practices together every single minute and does everything full speed. That is how we get better and gain the most out of a practice.

I spent a great amount of time in film sessions and even occasionally during the practice coaching backup players and even practice squad players as they worked against my first team. I was very hard and demanding with my assistants if our scout team wasn't nearly perfect and showing everything with precision and at the correct tempo. If I had to wait one second for a scout team player to get lined up, someone was going to get his ass chewed out. But I also was very complimentary of scout team players and loved to compliment them in front of my entire team.

With me, everyone is accountable every single minute. I am not for everyone, but if you are really working at it, I love you and will show it in a hundred different ways. At the end of all of it? We will be at the top, and it will be one of the best times of your life. You will be nervous and hate me some of the time, but at the end you will look back and love how special it all really was.

CHAPTER 17

All-Star Special Teamers

L ooking back over my NFL coaching career, I have encountered the greatest special teams players ever. There were so many great names that I coached against. The superb return specialists Mel Farr, Devin Hester, and, in my opinion the very best of them all, Deion Sanders. Was anyone a better kicker than Adam Vinatieri?

Great cover guys? How about Hank Bauer, Elvis Patterson, Bill Bates, Mark Pike, and Joe Fishback? And tops among them all: Steve Tasker.

The Pro Football Hall of Fame has done an incredible job recognizing, remembering, and honoring its greatest stars, but I believe that it has made one major error in not including Steve Tasker. I went against him for many years, and he could affect a game more than any other special teams player in history. He made plays that changed games. He could block kicks and cause fumbles. He was selected to seven Pro Bowls and was the 1993 Pro Bowl MVP at a time when the game was actually played—not the pretentious joke the game is today.

For a decade, when you played the Buffalo Bills, who at that time were one of the NFL's most powerful teams, you had better account for Steve Tasker or you couldn't win the game.

In the NFL, from my first year in 1982 until my last with the Saints in 2018, I know those thirty-two seasons were the very best that there ever were and ever will be for the special teams part of the game. Today, due to the many rule changes, you just don't have the same number of plays. Kickoffs result in touchbacks, and punts are mostly from the 50-yard line area. Many of today's special teams plays are non-plays.

I am in my seventies, and I could cover a kickoff today.

I find compiling my Special Teams All-Star Team to be an exercise in euphoria. As I sit and go back through my rosters, one great memory after another comes streaming back to me.

So, as I look back, I believe in no uncertain terms that I witnessed the greatest players ever, and from that group I am going to pick an All-Star Team. But they are all going to be "my guys."

I believe that, over the years, guys who played for me can comprise the greatest team ever. It is hard to pick just one special teams unit, so I will present several names for each position and then try to narrow it down.

Kicker

The kicker is a good place to start, and I had some really good ones. Pete Stoyanovich at Miami; John Hall and Nick Folk of the Jets; and Wil Lutz in New Orleans. But the guy who in every way surpassed everyone was Olindo Mare at Miami.

He could do it all—an incredible athlete who could nail field goals and kick off as well as anybody. Only Hall of Famer Morten Andersen could challenge his onside kick. The rules were different then, but if the ball was kicked into the ground, all bets were off in going after it. While using his normal kicking approach, Olindo could at the last second drive the ball into the ground, sending it about twelve feet into the air and at one of the kickoff return team's frontline players. As that player was looking for the ball to come down, we would block him while another one of the Dolphins would recover the ball.

Olindo Mare

When we had the correct kick, we were 100 percent successful in recovering them. Believe it or not, we were even successful in a playoff game against New England at recovering the onside kick—three times. Three!

One was overturned because of a penalty, which I am still trying to find. But we recovered three.

Chad Cascadden when he was with the Jets recalled playing against an Olindo Mare onside kick.

"First off, Olindo's lineup was always the same," Chad said. "[It was] very difficult to read which direction he was going to kick the ball. Have you ever seen this kick? It's fucking impossible to know when it is coming. Because the ball hits the ground first, it is a live ball, and now I've got to recover it. Good luck. Me against four guys bearing down on me as I try to jump and catch a ball dropping from seemingly fifty feet. We all know how this is going to end for me.

"Honestly, that was the hardest, most well-designed play I have seen in my life."

Olindo Mare, at that time in my career, is my kicker.

Punter

Though Ray Guy is in the Pro Football Hall of Fame, I also believe I coached the three best punters in NFL history: Rohn Stark with the Colts and my good buddy Reggie Roby at Miami are the first two.

Reggie was an incredible punter who could hit the ball maybe higher than anyone ever. He was a big, powerful man at around 260 pounds, and he was a really good guy. My son John kind of grew up with Reggie and was a favorite of Reggie's. When I had to release Reggie due to contract problems, my son John would not speak to me for a week.

"Dad, you cut Reggie!" he said, and he stormed off to his room. I got the silent treatment.

But to pick just one, it has to be Tom Morstead of the Saints.

Tom works every day as hard as any NFL player I have encountered. No one prepares harder in every facet, mentally and physically, than Tom Morstead. He can hit every type of punt with great direction and hang time. He has an extremely quick get-off and is excellent at pooch punts.

But it wasn't all smooth sailing between us.

"I had been to a Pro Bowl and been the highest-paid punter in the league for a decade, yet Mike and I had a few tiffs," Tom said. "Mike would say, 'You are one of our A-plus players, whatever happens on the field, it doesn't matter if you do your job. Your bar is higher than most players can ever reach.' The way he communicated that to me was very powerful.

"Maybe some coaches don't want to mess up the mojo. He came in and didn't do that at first, but anything not acceptable was made very clear. I appreciated that. He didn't try to change how I punted, he just laid out the expectations, and they were very high."

I am a movie fan and am going to paraphrase a movie in my description of Tom Morstead. In the baseball film *The Natural*, Robert Redford plays an aging ballplayer named Roy Hobbs who has found his way back to the game and to greatness. Before the last game, in which a win would put his team into the World Series, Robert Redford is talking with his manager, Pop, played by Wilford Brimley.

Pop said: "My mother told me that I should be a farmer."

Roy Hobbs replied: "All I ever wanted to be was a ballplayer."

Pop then told him: "Well, you are the best player I ever had and the best hitter I ever saw."

I am going to say of Tom Morstead: "Well, you are one of the best players I ever had and the damn best punter I ever saw."

If I had Tom on two of my Jets teams, they could easily have been the best the NFL has ever seen.

"Mike was exceptionally knowledgeable but would own up to a mistake in a minute," Tom said. "When he first walked into our meeting room, even as arrogant as he was, you could tell that he was authentic. He saw things in certain players that maybe they themselves didn't realize they were capable of performing. He knew exactly what he was teaching, and he set the bar higher every day—maybe even higher than you ever thought you could reach. The way he taught and communicated was very powerful.

"Mike also acknowledged where he was not strong. He is genuine."

Long Snapper

The long snapper is not even a debate with me. There is only one, James Dearth of the Jets. He was really special.

A big, strong, powerful man at 6-3 and 270 pounds of muscle, he played during a time when teams were allowed to line up on the center and hit him. The center had to snap the ball and be able to hold his ground. That's totally different from today's specialists, who look mostly like high school gym teachers. James was a former college quarterback and NFL tight end who we developed into a long snapper. My first year at New York, I knew that James could be the snapper. I just had to train him. We worked endlessly.

And James *figured it out.*

"Coach Westhoff worked with me nearly every day," James said. "He would call me on the weekend and tell me to meet him in the (workout) bubble. The bad news: I got a call from him on a Sunday to meet him in the afternoon. It was Easter Sunday.

"The good news: because of him, I played eight years in the NFL and got set for the rest of my life.

"When I first came to know Mike, he really pushed me hard. He would say stuff like: 'I am not trying to kill you, but we will get pretty darn close.' Mike had the best special teams game plan book I ever saw. He expected you to take notes and see everything. He coached everything as hard as he could. He expected a lot of himself and demanded 100 percent from us. You didn't have to be perfect, but you had better be doing your best. Mental errors were never accepted.

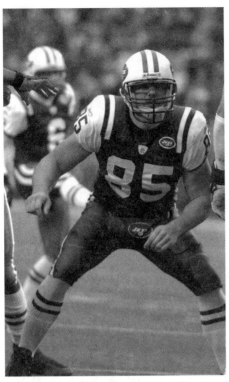

James Dearth

"He would say deep things in meetings that you might never dream of, but it showed that he was personable and really cared for his players. He would find ways to get to nearly every player. It made me feel like I was part of his family.

"I have seen him talk about players who he had to move on from, and he might get a little choked up over it. He cared about them so much. He is like family to me. He poured a lot into me and into my career. He believed in me. I would do anything for him. I don't know if he understands how grateful I am for that.

"With Mike, we had only one goal, and that was to lead the NFL. And we were damn good. We were always right near the top."

James Dearth could do everything as a long snapper and tight end. He could snap for punts and kicks, block and cover. I used him as our wedge on one of the NFL's greatest kickoff return teams, and if you looked hard enough, you might still see a Raider lying in the middle of the field in Oakland after James had sent him flying.

In a game against Kansas City in the Meadowlands, I over-shifted my punt team and left James the snapper at the end of the line, therefore making him an eligible receiver. After the snap to our punter, Tom Tupa, a former quarterback, rolled to his right. He threw back to James, who was running a wheel route down the left side, for a long gain. Coaches can be creative with good players.

I would take James Dearth over any snapper I ever saw.

Linebackers

Who are the linebackers on my Special Teams All-Star Team? Backup linebackers are usually the heart and soul of the special teams, and I had many. Craig Robinson was my best in New Orleans and one of the best in the NFC during 2017 and 2018. In Miami, I drafted Brant Boyer, who turned out to be outstanding but spent most of his career in Jacksonville and then became the special teams coordinator for the Jets. He will always be one of "my guys."

In Miami, I also had O.J. Brigance and Twan Russell. From the Jets, I had several: Jason Glenn, James Darling, Matt Chatham, Jason Trusnik, and Nick Bellore. Jonathan Vilma was a Pro Bowl linebacker who also was outstanding for me. He was one my hardest hitters. There is a St. Louis Rams player somewhere who still has headaches from Jonathan.

One year, believe it or not, Jonathan Vilma played every play on defense, and he was on our field goal block team and the punt return team. He covered every—yes, EVERY—kickoff that year and, at the end of the 2004 season as we were battling for a playoff spot, he covered every punt. I don't believe any NFL player has ever done anything like that: playing every defensive play and nearly every special teams play. Jonathan Vilma was very special.

So, picking even two linebackers was tough for me. Then again, it was actually easy to single out these two guys.

In 2003 with the Jets, Kenyatta Wright was the best special teams player in the AFC. He was not selected to the Pro Bowl, but that is the fault of the players and coaches who voted. When our defensive coordinator, Teddy Cottrell, brought him in from Buffalo, I was not the least bit happy and I told him so. I was not impressed by him in Buffalo and saw no place for Kenyatta on my units. Sitting in my office, he had the toughest first day of work ever. I could not have been harder on him.

"I was coming because of Ted Cottrell, and I was coming there to play linebacker and thought I would be a situational guy," Kenyatta said. "I didn't play a whole lot of special teams in Buffalo and none in college.

"So I come to the Jets and learn that linebackers play special teams. You look at the power of the head coach and offensive and defensive coordinators on teams, and it was totally different when I got to the Jets. You know how in New York they talk about the mob boss. Mike was the mob boss of the Jets. Everything ran through him. I think decisions were made through him.

Kenyatta Wright

"I didn't know that until after my first day there. Then I knew Mike was in control. He was very powerful, and I had never been on a team where the special teams controlled the day, the schedule, and everything.

"Mike let us know up front, 'You are here for special teams first.' I had in front of me (at linebacker) Marvin Jones, who had a chance to be in the Hall of Fame, drafted third overall. That tells you how good he was; I knew

I was his backup. Mike would reiterate it: special teams! He'd say, 'If I don't like you, you won't make it. You better give all you got every single day.'"

Kenyatta held his ground and assured me he was a damn good player, and I would soon find out. So, I told him I would start him with a clean slate—and he grew to be one of my favorite players and my best special teams guy at the time.

"You had to change your mindset as a player, and that's something I never really had to do until I got to the Jets," Kenyatta said. "Be a role player—that is something a lot of guys struggle with. But for me it was a new adventure. But to keep a job in the NFL, you've got to perform. You don't perform, you will be gone, no matter what (the job)."

A play that Kenyatta made covering a kickoff against the Giants and the great returner Brian Mitchell in 2003 was one of the best you will see. They were setting up to run a middle wedge, and Kenyatta exploded right into one of their blockers—an offensive lineman, by the way—and propelled him back and threw him into the ball carrier. He knocked them both on their asses.

His not making the Pro Bowl was a shame.

I know Kenyatta remembered another play he made that people still talk about.

"When we began two-a-days, and even in our early games, every play we wanted to dominate the other team, set a tone," Kenyatta said. "There was a time in San Diego, which had Tim Dwight, and we were ready. And I am thinking that I get to knock this guy out on *Monday Night Football*. Mike only set up those plays for certain guys.

"Seeing Tim Dwight flying in the air, and he didn't finish the game, that was what our special teams were all about."

Punt Returner

Picking the punt returner for my team was very easy—and very hard.

I really didn't have many choices. At New Orleans, we were very inexperienced and just not very good. Bill Parcells recommended Tommylee Smith in New Orleans. I was shocked when I worked with him after practice as to how nonfundamental he was. I worked with him every day and loved him as a person, but, hey, Bill, stick to something you are an expert at, not this.

As I look back on my career, an interesting punt return statistic stands out. At Miami, we had two relatively unknown guys in Nate Jacquet and Jeff Ogden, who both finished ranking second in the NFL in punt return average. Not exactly household names, but we had great blockers for them. We had great punt return teams that could rush the punter and also block for the returners. Jacquet and Ogden were average guys who benefited from a great supporting cast.

From a technical standpoint, one of the reasons for our success came somewhat from Jimmy Johnson. I never saw him much involved in Xs and Os. I am sure he could have been, though I never saw much of it. In this instance, however, he wanted me to play a two-deep punt return scheme. I had not previously done much of this and was not sure about it.

Yet the two-deep scheme, from Jimmy's encouragement, helped two average but solid players become league leaders. He didn't draw it up. I did. But it was a damn good idea, and it was his.

But I had two real all-stars: Santana Moss with the Jets and O.J. McDuffie with the Dolphins.

Santana was a first-round draft pick as a wide receiver from the University of Miami. He was the quickest, most explosive punt returner I have ever seen. Santana had the quickest start ever; he was sudden. He had great hands and led the league in punt returns. If it had not been for injuries and missed time, he would have been hard to unseat.

For me, though, the guy who was extra special was O.J.

Also a first-round draft pick, from Penn State, O.J. was a great athlete and could do everything. Superior hands and judgment. No one could catch the ball better than he could. I used to do a catching drill with the JUGS machine I learned from Billy "White Shoes" Johnson, the great returner, in which, after catching the ball, the returner would hang onto it by placing the ball under an arm or between his legs. The machine was set so that the returner would not have to run. Just see how many balls you could catch and hold onto.

Believe it or not, O.J. caught seven. Held onto seven, too. Try that some time.

"I know for a fact that I wouldn't have been drafted by the Dolphins in the first round if it wasn't for Mike Westhoff," O.J. said. "My ability to return kicks and play receiver was key. However, I knew my first responsibility was going to be on Teams!

"I caught a million punts and kickoffs during minicamps and training camp. I had the best punter in the world, Reggie Roby, punting to me in practice. If I could catch his punts, I could catch anyone's punt. The balls came down like missiles."

O.J. benefited from a good supporting cast and also from maybe some of my most creative schemes. But he was special and did it all. In my thirty-two-year career, he was maybe the best all-around athlete I had ever been associated with. O.J. was not the fastest player that I ever coached. But his vision, balance, and catching ability were second to none.

He also was a great starting wide receiver who led the NFL in catches—only to have his career cut short with a toe injury. That was a mess in how it was handled. Ask O.J. what ended his career, and you will get an answer that will knock you down.

I actually wish I had him later in my career when I was more advanced in my knowledge of return schemes. O.J. McDuffie with some of my more advanced special teams units would have been Deion Sanders and Devin Hester before Deion and Devin were Deion and Devin.

"There's no way I would've scored as many times on returns during my career if it weren't for Mike Westhoff," O.J. added. "The double-vise guys on the outside for punt returns were our starting cornerbacks. Nobody was getting to me. And we had the ten best blockers on kickoff returns. Some started on offense or defense.

"The first kickoff I touched in the preseason against the Atlanta Falcons went 90 yards for a touchdown. The first punt I returned in the regular season versus the Indianapolis Colts was fumbled by me and returned for a touchdown. So, I saw the good, the bad, and the ugly from Mike.

"Needless to say, the good times were the best. Mike is one of the best coaches I ever had."

I believe I am putting together the best special teams unit ever assembled, and O.J. McDuffie is my punt returner.

O.J. McDuffie

Kickoff Returner

Kickoff returns is the area where I believe I excelled the most. My experience as an offensive line coach helped me develop a recipe for success. I designed kickoff returns around the same principles as an offensive running play. Each was segmented into very specific areas, and each one was designed around a certain scheme and set of techniques.

"I coached with Westy for four years (2008-2011) with the New York Jets," says Bill Callahan, one of the NFL's experts at coaching offensive lines, "and what I admired most about him were his old-school coaching traits. He was compellingly principled in his philosophy of coaching.

"A lot of what he stood for as a coach was derived from his experiences being on Don Shula's staff with the Miami Dolphins in the '80s and '90s. I respected the fact that he didn't hold back his opinions about the personnel, team issues, or his unit in particular. He told it like it was, good and bad. Some people—players, coaches, and front office personnel—didn't particularly care for that because it hurt their feelings, but he couldn't give two shits, and I respected him for that."

Each return was based on seven specific areas:

- play-side double-team
- setup
- trap
- backside wall
- wedge
- lead or seal
- read

Each of these was particular in detail and scheme, though there were numerous variations to each area. Also, with each play-side return, there was an accompanying counter that started out the same and then would break and run away from the play-side look.

From this philosophy, just like our offensive play design, a million different plays could be run and a new scheme could be added each week.

The first time I saw a double-team blocking scheme work was by Pete Rodriguez of Washington. He showed a double-team with a lead block. It was a simple but very effective scheme, and he had some great success.

Pete was not one of my favorite coaches—maybe because he didn't like me. We were competitors, not friends. He told me once after we had gotten to know each other a little better that he thought I was cocky and unfriendly. He was probably right, but I respected him and thought he did a very good job—including having bested me in some of our matchups. Not everyone can say that.

I took his double-team and completely altered it. I moved the double-team to coverage men at any position and at various yard lines. I incorporated the wedge with the double-team and a trapping scheme. I altered the techniques in blocking the back side of the play, the lead blocker, and the read technique of the ball carrier. Having a counter off the double-team was a major change.

It is very common for coaches through film study to copy, borrow, or steal something from our peers. I coached against some of the very best in NFL history. No, I did not say specifically special teams coaches; I mean coaches. Period.

Pete Rodriquez, Brad Seely, Joe Avezzano, Wayne Sevier, Mike Sweatman, Bruce DeHaven, Joe Marciano, Russ Purnell, Tom McGaughey, Scott O'Brien, Dave Toub, Darren Simmons, and, of course, my good friend and one of the NFL's all-time best, Joe DeCamillis.

John Harbaugh was a good special teams coach and has done exceptionally well as a head coach in Baltimore. But he always has had a great kicker and return specialist, and his numbers are good but not exceptional. I never felt that he was creative or very innovative. He stole one of my kickoff returns and ran it his entire career. I also helped him on some very specific individual matters and was not reciprocated in a fashion that would have meant a great deal to me personally. So he is not making this list. I doubt he cares, but he is not on it.

As I've mentioned, Alvin Kamara—our star running back in New Orleans—was great in 2017. He could have been, at another time, one of the NFL's all-time best return specialists.

In 2018, we used him occasionally, and he was always productive. At Carolina, he ran one for about 60 yards. I was happy, but also disappointed; he should have scored.

We had a good blocking unit in New Orleans, but with today's rules, you just don't get enough chances. Player safety is the emphasis and touchbacks—non-plays—guarantee that.

In Miami, I had O.J. McDuffie and Brock Marion as my kickoff returners. O.J. was productive but, as I have mentioned, more of a punt returner. Brock was a great athlete and outstanding punt blocker. He was good but didn't quite have the speed to be special.

In New York, now there we were really special.

Jonathan Carter, Jerricho Cotchery, Chad Morton, Justin Miller, Leon Washington, Brad Smith, and Joe McKnight all were NFL leaders in kickoff returns. I know that Devin Hester and the Bears were great, but it was one guy: Hester. Not seven different players. I firmly believe the New York Jets were the best kickoff return franchise the NFL has ever witnessed. EVER!

We put up some great numbers. We were always near the top in average starting field position, always giving our offense a strong starting place. In 2002, Jets Coach Herman Edwards made a bold move to replace quarterback Vinny Testaverde with Chad Pennington. It worked brilliantly and propelled us to the playoffs, but there was some praise that I never heard. Our kickoff returners gave the Jets the best starting field position in the league. Chad played on the shortest field, and he never mentioned it. He is not one of my favorites and never will be. I believe he was part of a very good overall team, nothing else, and certainly nothing really special.

Also, in 2002, we had another very eye-opening number. We were playing Oakland in the twelfth game of the season, and I was preparing my game plan. I noticed that Chad Morton was leading the league in kickoff return, and Santana Moss was leading in punt return average. Even more special was that Chad was second in the NFL in punt return average. We had the top three spots. Try to beat that!

Jonathan Carter didn't quite have enough attempts but what he did was the best: Jonathan could outrun anyone and could've led the league easily with more attempts.

Jerricho was one rep short of qualifying but was among the league leaders. He was a terrific athlete, a great returner, and an outstanding special teams player.

Justin had it all. An explosive defensive back from Clemson, he could run around or through anyone. I have a film clip of him running a middle trap return for a TD against the Colts. What was amazing on that play was he had four players escorting him into the end zone: Leon Washington, Brad Smith, Eric Smith, and B.J. Askew.

Both Leon and Brad led the NFL in kickoff returns, and Eric and B.J. were outstanding players. It is not hard to be a good coach if you have those kinds of players. I would bet a lot of money that you could never show me a film clip of three league-leading returners all running into the end zone on the same play.

Joe McKnight was with me at the end of my time in New York and probably ran my all-time favorite play: a 107-yard touchdown in Baltimore. He was a good player and a great guy. I loved him. His life ended tragically in a road rage incident in New Orleans.

Joe was not a confrontational individual. I was terribly saddened and will always miss him.

So, of all my returners, it is very difficult to pick just one. Chad Morton, with his two TDs in one game against Buffalo, is hard to beat. Still, if I have to pick one—and this is *my* All-Star Team, after all— it is going to be Leon Washington. He was the best of the group and one of my favorite people.

Leon had no trouble figuring it out.

"What separated Mike from a lot of other coaches I played for is Mike had a unique ability to make the game fun," Leon said. "You never felt like that going into someone else's meetings. It might be, 'Here we go again.' You looked forward to being with Mike, and it was great from that aspect.

"He is charismatic, has a sense of humor, but at the same time can command respect for his coaching and his ability to lead special teams—and to lead a team.

"Mike being the coach he is and having coached so many great athletes, he knew my running style was a little different than a Miller or a Chad Morton. I was a running back. My spacing and timing—critical words he hammered in—were important. How much space I have from the lead blockers and how much time I have to get through the hole or make the right cut were key.

"Justin needed to be 12 yards away, and Mike knew with me I could be seven yards. I needed to be a little closer so I could hit (the hole) like a running back. Mike identified that right away.

"On top of that, there was the mental aspect of the game. He is one of the very best coaches I have ever been around for the mental part. I knew all the rules of the game, what to do in situations. He prepared us for every situation. We were ready.

"For example, on kickoff return rules, if the kicker kicks the ball near the sideline, a player from the return team could put one foot out of bounds and touch the ball and the kick is considered out of bounds. And the return team gets the ball at the 40. I don't know how many guys would know that. It's one of those moves that rarely happen, but Mike coached that every week.

"We played the Bills in 2008, and I was able to execute that play, and it helped us win that game in Buffalo.

"What made him really great is the fact he had a sophisticated scheme for the way he coached, and yet he made it seem simple. Terms like 'Check with me,' which would mean Mike would look at the kicker and his walk-off and see where and how he would kick it. And then we would look over right before the ball was kicked off, and Mike would give us a play. Mike would have called the play in the huddle and then signaled right or left. He was never wrong.

"That type of coaching is unheard of, pretty much.

"Coming up with things on the sideline and making adjustments during a game and knowing personnel—you're talking about one of the best people in identifying players on special teams. Then knowing where to put players to help them succeed.

"Just something about his personality. If we were playing a team he felt we were better than, which was most teams that we played, he would say: 'Are you kidding me? We're going to let this outfit come in and beat us?'

"Another was 'PLEASE' when he disagreed.

"His meetings were among the best of any coach I'd ever met. You learned, and you had fun, and you better be aware.

"It was an open door for Mike, and that was the way he coached his players. Yeah, he's a free spirit who loves to go fishing in the ocean, who loves the game and his players. He wanted you to be free and play hard and smart, and you just went off his words and did it.

"His ability to teach the game and take a complicated scheme and make it seem easy is what made him special. When you meet Mike, you will know in the next thirty seconds this is a guy I will fight for on the football field. That, combined with a scheme like that, it's a combination that works well.

"Mike is unique. Not to knock another coach. Mike's personality and charisma and everything about him is unique. You don't see that type of coach come around too often.

"I was able to take some of Mike's philosophies he coached and took them to other teams. That first year I was in Seattle, I made some first-team All-Pros and had three return TDs. Coming straight from New York, you knew that was a carryover from Mike. In the style I ran, the way he taught me with spacing and timing, I would hit the hole on returns the way he drew them up.

"I don't know the percentages, but I am sure the number of plays he won is way in his favor. In the time I was there, we had the top two or three returners in the game, and our cover teams would finish in the top five. He was winning a bunch of plays.

"I can't count how many games special teams played poorly and would be the reason we lost a game under Mike Westhoff because that was never the case. With Mike, we knew with our special teams we always had a chance to win the game."

Offensive Players

A very much overlooked aspect of putting together a special teams unit is being able to find offensive players to fit into roles that include being able to tackle.

I always found that it was easier to teach defensive players how to block than to be sure that an offensive player was able to tackle when put in that position. Many times, the player can revert back to his high school days when he probably played both ways, but being able to tackle the great return specialists of the NFL is not for everyone.

Try and stop Deion Sanders in the open field when you haven't made a tackle in four years.

Good luck.

Some of my best players over the years were running backs or fullbacks who had great athletic skills and could also really tackle. In Miami, Tony Paige was a terrific blocking and receiving fullback for Dan Marino, but he also did everything for me. On our punt team, he was an excellent blocker who could also run and tackle.

An interesting play occurred with Tony in Chicago in 1991 against one of Mike Ditka's great Bears teams in a cold late-afternoon game. The Bears needed a win to ensure home-field advantage in the playoffs, and Mike later wrote in one of his books that this loss was the beginning of the Bears' downfall. Toward the end of the game, we blocked a punt and recovered the ball on the two-yard line. For me, that block was a very rewarding coaching maneuver.

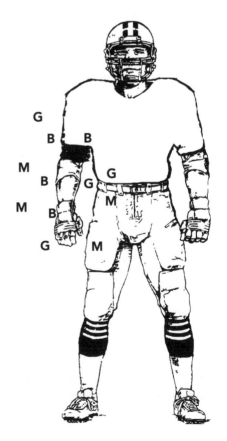

I used to chart opponents' punt snaps. I had a drawing of a player, and I would mark a letter for the opponent in the spot of the snap (L=Lions, G=Giants).

The drawing was configured as if looking at their punter from the vantage point of our punt return team. I noticed that Chicago's center, when having to block to his right, snapped the ball every time outside of the punter's body by about one foot to his right. I designed a block in which, at the last moment, we would overload the center's right side, and he would be forced to block in that direction.

Sure as hell, he snapped the ball over there, and Bryan Cox blocked the kick. The ball rolled toward the Chicago goal line, stopping at the 2. We scored, and the game went into overtime.

I don't know how many coaches charted punt snaps back then.

In the overtime period, we won the coin toss and took the ball. I knew from film study that their kicker, Kevin Butler, liked to hit a hooking line drive kickoff to his left side that would hit around the 25-yard line and roll hard toward the goal line—especially if he had the Chicago wind behind him.

They took the wind, and now I had what I wanted.

We lined our front-line center right in front of Kevin. As he lined up to kick, we walked our center to our left side, setting up a seemingly large hole through which to drive his kick. I believe that he saw that opening, and it must have looked like Interstate 95.

But we had lined up Tony Paige, who had one of the best sets of hands on the team, on the 25-yard line in the middle of the field. As Kevin approached the ball, Tony slid over to his right to be directly in the kick's path. Kevin hit his line-drive kick, and Tony was standing right there. He caught it and returned it to around the 40-yard line.

I don't imagine that, kicking off with the wind, Mike Ditka was too happy about giving Dan Marino the ball near midfield. A couple of passes later, Pete Stoyanovich came on and hit a field goal, and we went home with a great upset victory. Tony, in a small but strategic manner, played a big part in that win.

James Saxon was another fullback I used on special teams in Miami who contributed greatly. At the Jets, Jerald Sowell was one of my most productive players. Aside from being one of the best people I have ever met, he was one hell of a player. He covered kicks and made tackles as well as any defensive player I ever coached. Jerald belongs on the best special teams unit ever.

Although I had him at the end of his career and only for a short time, Michael Bates could be discussed as one of the greatest. He went to the Pro Bowl as a return specialist and "cover man." Mike could really do it all.

John Conner is another offensive player I need to mention. He was a fullback at Kentucky who came into the NFL as unprepared as anyone I have seen. My assistant, Ben Kotwica, kept him after practice to help John with his assignments. When Ben asked him to get his notes out, he was shocked at what he saw. John's backpack looked like a fourth-grader's. It basically contained nothing useful.

So, Ben started from scratch and, over time and with great effort from John, Ben helped him grasp his assignments and learn all he had to know.

John ended up being one of our really good players, certainly one of the most physical. His nickname, "The Terminator," was given to him by Rex Ryan and fit him like a glove. John worked his tail off and with some big-time help from Ben became an excellent player.

I can't discuss offensive players on special teams without bringing up Brad Smith. Brad was a quarterback from Missouri. My first-ever assistant, Sam Gash, and I went out to the University of Missouri to work him out. I coached for twenty-four of my thirty-two years in the NFL without an assistant; I just never felt I needed one. Or wanted one. I was going to do things my way, and they were more trouble than they were worth.

But Sam—he was my first, and I loved working with him and respected him. He went to the 1999 Pro Bowl as a fullback without ever having a rushing attempt. Sam could block and knock your head off. He was as tough a player as the NFL has ever had.

Brad Smith

Sam was with us for the 2005 season, was a great help, and fit right in with my way of thinking.

"I was just getting into coaching when I met Mike," Sam said. "I knew of him for years. I was in New England and Buffalo, and he was down in Miami and then in New York. So, I knew his reputation. Any time as a player having to go against one of Mike's teams, you knew the return game was going to be awesome.

"Just watching Mike, it inspired me coaching special teams. Watching him use Justin Miller, a high draft pick who couldn't get on the field on defense, and basically I was told by Mike, 'Let's figure it out.' And that was Mike's deal. He could take players on offense and defense and were not adept at doing it at that level, and he'd take them on special teams and make them stars.

"It also didn't matter what color you were or anything. You might see coaches putting people in certain classes. Mike never saw that. What can this guy do for me on the field? That's all Mike cared about.

"He saw things in guys maybe other coaches didn't. Mike's special teams were top five or so every year, no matter how bad the team was otherwise. Mike made a success out of whatever he did.

"Mike would have made a great head coach. In terms of knowing a team and having the pulse of the team, I think no one in the history of the game was better than Mike."

As Sam and I visited Missouri's football department, it became clear how much everybody admired, respected, and loved Brad Smith. In all my scouting trips, I never experienced such praise. The coaches and administration were sick he was soon leaving school for the pros, and the secretaries were sad and even crying. Yep, everyone loved Brad.

For me, he did everything right. I could use him anywhere on our kickoff team. He could play any role. He was perfect for personal protector on the punt team. He could block, cover, change formation, and run fakes. He was a real weapon.

He started off as a blocker on the kickoff return team and greatly aided Pro Bowlers Justin Miller and Leon Washington. When it was his turn to be the return specialist, he promptly led the league. His 97-yard kickoff return touchdown against Pittsburgh helped push us toward the playoffs and could be argued as one of the Jets' top returns in their history.

Brad Smith was the ultimate teammate and one of the unsung heroes in the National Football League.

I took great pride in finding special teams roles for every type of player. I just had to *figure it out*. And that's what I did.

Guys Who Could Do Everything

A part of my All-Star Team will focus on the diversely talented players who could do everything. Two of the greatest, Zach Thomas and Larry Izzo, I have discussed earlier in detail.

The guys came from every position: safeties, running back, tight ends, linebackers, and, believe it or not, quarterbacks. One thing, though, that they each had in common was that they played an extremely physical game.

I wasn't a coach who ever talked about hurting a player. I never prescribed a "bounty." I taught that all contact be made below the shoulders and above the knee. I honestly believe that my teams were the most physical specials teams units to ever play in the NFL. I know that this will irritate many people, but I will go up against anyone. I coached a lot of very aggressive players, and our schemes were designed to create collisions.

Our kickoff coverage moved and ran people all over the field, and the various levels that were presented were designed along the lines of defensive blitzing. We could create overloads to attack a blocking scheme and gain unblocked players.

Our kickoff return schemes were designed around very physical offensive running plays. We could double-team and run that with our "post and drive" concept, which was very aggressive. Behind our double-team was a trap. It could come out of seemingly nowhere, and someone would get blasted.

Our wedge assignments were so specific that they also became very physical. We peeled back across the field and knocked safeties into the bleachers. Football is a hitting sport, and the NFL is a big-man's game. I believed that the contact should be violent but controlled.

Most of what I designed is illegal today, and some of the changes I agree with. But, as I stated earlier, I never sought to injure anyone. I believe I taught the game the way it is meant to be played. Showing a clean, hard hit on the big screen in a meeting room is the most exciting play in the game. If it is not about hitting, play soccer.

Today, it is all about "throw and catch" and how much money the quarterbacks make. No wonder TV ratings have dropped. I am right where I belong: appreciating the great way that the world's best sport was played and should be played.

Our punt return teams could "double-vise" an opponent off the field and over the Gatorade table or into the kicking net. We blocked as many punts as anyone ever, and that was achieved with good teams for which punt blocks must be called strategically. If you are coaching a bad team, it is easy to call a punt block—you have nothing to lose.

You know, the easiest coaching job in the NFL is the special teams coordinator with a poor team. No one cares what he is doing, and he can get away with risky calls that with a good team fighting for a playoff spot might not be pertinent. Some coaches have built a reputation for being aggressive, and they wouldn't know a playoff game from touch football in the backyard.

If you want to watch physical punt return team play, watch Taysom Hill, David Onyemata, and Alex Okafor of the Saints. It will be hard to find a more physical group.

My punt teams used multiple formations and kept defenders off-balance and therefore less aggressive against us. We would "Slam" protect, in which the wing on the snap of the ball would fire off the ball and smack the outside rusher. He would then bounce out and release when the ball was punted. This technique was something that anyone playing that position loved because it was so proactive and let them play very aggressively.

I had some great players who were extremely skilled but also aggressive. One of my very first such players was Jim Jensen with the Dolphins. His nickname was "Crash." Does that tell you anything?

Jim was maybe the first great hybrid player. He was a tight end/halfback/fullback/wide receiver/quarterback. As a special teamer, Jim was on every unit. He could block, tackle like a linebacker, block a punt, and throw a fake. Jim could snap for kicks or hold for them. He could punt, and he could placekick. Anywhere I played Jim, he would excel. Jim Jensen was a player who won games. Coach Shula knew a little something about personnel.

Brock Marion with Miami also could do everything. He returned kickoffs and blocked punts. He was a great weapon we could play anywhere.

Rashad Washington was a safety with the Jets and one of my most physical players. His trap block on a "Miami Right" kickoff return versus Tampa is one of legend. Physical legend.

Chris Baker, a Jets tight end out of Michigan State, was one of the NFL's top special teams blockers. I never saw a better open-field blocker on kickoff returns. Against Buffalo, he drove a defender out of bounds and ran him through our bench, knocking everyone down—including Herman Edwards, our head coach.

Also from the Jets was B.J. Askew, a fullback from Michigan. Very few people ever tackled any harder than B.J. did. Watch his kickoff coverage against San Diego, or when the Falcons tried to block him one game against Atlanta.

Another one of my guys was James Ihedigbo, a free agent safety from UMass. He was smart and tough. I played him everywhere and always got the same result. He had a complete knowledge of his role and a physical level of play that made every opponent nervous to go against him. When "Diggs" was the trapper on our kickoff return teams, someone was going to get knocked down.

He played hard, he played physical, and he played according to the rules. I can remember him receiving only one penalty, a mysterious holding call in San Francisco that brought back Leon Washington's return that would have been the winning touchdown. During the next week, the NFL's officiating office said the call was improper after reviewing it. A little late, Mike Pereira, head of officials.

Another outstanding player I had with the Jets was Eric Smith. A safety from Michigan State, he was without question one of the most versatile and absolutely the brightest player I ever coached.

I gave Eric the toughest job every week, and he handled it every time. He was the best punt blocker I ever had. He executed the schemes perfectly with only one exception against Houston when he was a half-step late and did not make the play. When anyone was punting against us, they had better know where Eric was located.

Eric Smith

I am not sure how to prove this except through incredibly heavy statistical analysis, but I believe that Eric Smith was on the field for more special teams touchdowns than anyone in NFL history. Kickoff returns, punt returns, and punt blocks, and if you throw fake punts into that equation, I believe he would easily be the leader. When you walked into an NFL meeting room and saw Eric Smith, it made your whole day. You knew that someone was absolutely appreciating and understanding every part of the message.

"I think Mike was probably the reason I played as long as I did in the league," Eric said. "The special teams things he did kept me in the league longer than I would have played anywhere else. He knew how to look at guys and see what they did best and figure out how to put them in position to make them successful.

"I feel like with me, I was going to know what to do even when things go crazy. This was when teams could run guys everywhere on kick teams. I would be able to take what he was teaching us and sort it out, learn it all, still get my blocks. Mike put a lot of decision-making on me; a lot of my roles had the most changes in them, but he knew I could handle it mentally."

More Taysom

My final All-Star Team member—and by no means the least important—is Taysom Hill in New Orleans.

The whole process of discovering him and getting him started is a story for the ages. Coaching in the NFL for someone like me was all about giving someone an opportunity, a fair and equal opportunity. I wish more of our country could do that very thing.

Taysom is a special athlete, as we all know now, having watched him play so many roles so successfully in the New Orleans offense. At 6-2 and 230 pounds and able to run the 40-yard dash under 4.5 seconds, Taysom has all the physical skills. What truly stands out about him, though, is his toughness and his ability to throw.

I had Tim Tebow in a similar role with the Jets, but they were not even from the same football planet. Tim could run with the ball, but he could not throw and wouldn't hit anyone. If I had put him on the kickoff coverage team, he would have been playing baseball years before he headed to the diamond.

Tim won the Heisman Trophy, and I believe he deserved it, but in the special teams football role, he was not in the same league as Taysom Hill.

Taysom is one of my all-time favorites. Joe Lombardi, the former Saints quarterbacks coach, used to tease me about "my guys." And Taysom made him a better coach and helped him earn an opportunity to be a coordinator.

From starting from nowhere to climbing up the ladder to a nice new contract, I could not be prouder of anyone more than I am of Taysom Hill. Of the eleven positions. I would line up on my special teams All-Star Team, Taysom could start at each one of them.

"Mike is a storyteller. He loves to tell stories to have everyone sharing experiences he has had," Taysom noted. "My favorite thing about Mike as a coach—the first thing you think about with Mike—he has this confidence about him. And if something went well on game day, it was his idea and he knew it was going to work, which we kind of laughed about.

"But what we knew and talked about, I knew Mike wouldn't put me in a situation I couldn't be successful at. So, when I stepped on the field, I had so much confidence because when he put me on the field, I knew he wouldn't put me in those (negative) situations. That gave me added confidence. Maybe that is the reason he did it."

Bernie

One more player remains to talk about—and he goes in a special category.

Bernie Parmalee

I don't know of any player who started more in obscurity and moved to such a prominent role as a special teams player as Bernie Parmalee. The current running backs coach of the Jaguars, he was cut for the second time from Miami's training camp and was headed home. I sneaked him out on the field anyway for one last practice.

After that was discovered, I thought Coach Shula was going to fire me.

But the boss knew that it didn't really hurt anything, and he was a tough guy who liked tough guys. Bernie got a second chance—and played nine years.

Oh yeah, Coach Shula kept me, and I lasted for thirty-two years. And I am the only one of his assistants to be awarded the Lifetime Achievement Award by the NFL writers.

One thing Bernie could do better than anyone was hit. He was my all-time most physical player, and I had a ton of them. His ferocious hit during the punt drill of a morning practice after he had been cut is what got him started.

"Let me tell you something about that defining moment," Bernie said. "I was in my first NFL training camp, and I had gotten released. I went back to my hotel room to pack and prepare for my trip back home the next day. I suddenly got a knock on my door. It was Mike. He told me that I could play in the NFL and that I just needed to keep trying.

"He told me to still come to practice the next morning, keep my helmet on, and hide in the back during stretching, and then make sure that I was really ready to show something.

"Now I really didn't know what to do because I was just released. I'm a young guy trying to make the team, and I have just been cut and he wants me to come to practice. Well, he was the coach, so what the heck? What do I have to lose?

"So, I did what Mike said to do. The next day I got dressed at the facility, and I went to practice and hid in the back with my helmet on. I was a rookie, so not too many people knew me anyway, so I didn't get noticed.

"The first period of the practice was a punt drill, so Mike knew I wouldn't have to hide for too long. He told me to go in on the punt team at my regular left tackle position. And to go like hell.

"On the last play, Mike cleared the field and told everyone that the play was live. When that ball was punted and we were covering down the field, all I thought of was making the play. I made the play with a vicious hit.

"All I know is that things changed from that point and somehow I ended up sticking around. I know that Coach Shula said something to Mike. I don't know what the extent of that conversation was and I don't really want to know.

"It did work out in my favor. Thank God!"

Bernie was clean and tough. Never a cheap shot. Everything face-to-face, man-to-man. A kickoff tackle of Rocket Ismail of Oakland in a game in Miami, I would argue, was the hardest special teams tackle ever in the NFL.

There was no better person in this business. I respected Bernie, and I loved him like a son.

And Some More of My Guys

So many players have excelled for me in special teams roles. At Miami, some of our team's stars shined equally for me: Jarvis Williams, Louis Oliver, Tony Paige, Bryan Cox, Troy Vincent, James Saxon, Zach Thomas, Jason Taylor, Trace Armstrong, Sam Madison, Brock Marion, Brian Walker, and Patrick Surtain. Those were some great players who helped Don Shula and Dan Marino win a lot of games.

Jason Taylor is in the Pro Football Hall of Fame, and Zach Thomas should be headed there. Troy Vincent, Sam Madison, and Patrick Surtain are three of the best cornerbacks to ever play. All those guys while I was at Miami had one thing in common: no matter what special teams role I asked of them, they each completely excelled.

Jason Taylor could rush the punter and scare him to death. Zach Thomas could line up on the kick return team and knock the hell out of anyone. Running back Tony Paige and linebacker

Bryan Cox were exceptional starters but maybe even better special teams players.

Louis Oliver and Kerry Glenn were, in my view, the best punt return team double-vise the league has seen. They made the NFL change the rules.

Great special teams units always have a few starters who contribute mightily. I believe I had a formula that worked for these individuals, and only on very few occasions was I disappointed

Key special teams positions are the flyers or gunners on the punt team. I had some great punters through the years—none, unfortunately in my twelve seasons with the Jets—but with those outstanding punters I did have some great cover flyers. Reyna Thompson in Miami was my first, but Bill Parcells brilliantly stole him when we had to expose several players in the somewhat beginnings of free agency. Reyna was a track star from Baylor and helped Bill to his success with the Giants.

Fred Banks, Mike Williams, Kirby Dar Dar, Jerricho Cotchery, Wallace Wright, and Justin Hardee were all outstanding. If I have to pick two, though, they will be Isaiah Trufant of the Jets and Trent Gamble in Miami.

Those two guys could do everything. They were extremely fast, could really tackle, and were great athletes, especially skilled at downing the ball inside the 10-yard line. You noticed that I said the 10, not the 20. I believe that is the most significant stat in football. With today's kickoffs resulting in touchbacks, so many offenses are starting at the 25. It doesn't take too much to reach the 50. Punting the ball inside the 10, not the 20, is the only realistic goal.

The best thing about this All-Star Special Team is these are all MY GUYS!

"I think the friendship he has had from players is deep," Tom Morstead said. "He sees a deeper level of capability in players than most players see in themselves. I think that is powerful if you can handle the style of coaching he gives you. He saw things in certain players that maybe players didn't even realize they were capable of performing."

I know that playing for me is not the easiest. I can be gruff and somewhat harsh, but I know something about living with and functioning with pain. I deeply respect what it takes to play in the NFL.

I sincerely cared about them as individuals and would go to great lengths to support them. Very few loved them any more than I did.

CHAPTER 18

Special Moments

During the preseason in 1988, two very special incidents occurred. At the beginning of July, I finished my last chemotherapy session and started the process of returning to a normal, healthy life. I was coaching for the Dolphins and resumed my duties and began training camp.

We played our first preseason game against the 49ers in London, where I had my encounter with Coach Bill Walsh. He congratulated me on a job well done during practices and talked with me about someday joining his staff. It started a small relationship that we shared over the years.

After I left Jackson Memorial Hospital in Miami following my last chemotherapy session, a flood of emotions swarmed me. I was going home with a chance to rest and rebuild, but most importantly, no more drugs. In my opinion, only chemotherapy patients truly understand the process. Friends and family love, empathize, and want to share, but unless you are wearing the wrist band, you really don't know. They want to know, but they don't and can't know.

In 1988, I went through the treatment without the help of today's antidotes such as Zofran and others. Try that on for size! I didn't have a hair on my body, and I was a shade of green. I wore a full leg brace, and it didn't take much to bring a level of nausea. The good news? I had one month to get ready for training camp.

Camp started normally—and I was ready. I was walking with a cane, and I counted five hairs on my head. We'd have two weeks of camp in Miami, then a trip to London and a chance to meet Bill Walsh.

The NFL was playing some preseason games in various international locations. Games were played in London, Barcelona, Berlin, Mexico City, and Tokyo, for example. The two teams would meet in the various cities and practice against each other for the week. Families were included on the trips, and the NFL set a specific schedule that protected the players and made for a productive and enjoyable week.

I was feeling strong and was getting back to normal. My wife, Marilyn, accompanied me, but our son, John, was too young and stayed at home with his grandmother. I couldn't wait for the chance to spend a week on the field with the game's two greatest coaches: Don Shula and Bill Walsh.

Working with Don Shula every day for twelve years was the greatest opportunity of my life, but now I had the chance to closely observe another icon. The two coaching staffs came together to discuss the schedule. Coach Shula was very adamant about the schedule, and Bill Walsh seemed agreeable and willing to compromise.

These two brilliant coaches competed on every play during the practices. Those practices were disciplined and intense. Bill Walsh's West Coast Offense has many times been referred to as a "finesse offense." Finesse? You have never been on the 49ers' practice field if you believe that. The 49ers could knock the hell out of you. They practiced extremely physically. Our two teams got into fights in every practice. San Francisco's "finesse" would smack you right in the mouth.

I took every opportunity to get as close as possible to Bill Walsh and observe his teaching. His exactness stunned me. His detail was incredible, broken down into what seemed like the most minute points. Nothing was overlooked. It had to be perfect, or it wasn't good enough. Over and over, he perfected his team.

Coach Shula was a great teacher and perfectionist, and now I was observing another version of the same exactness. I was very proud of my level of teaching. I designed, practiced, and demanded a precise level of expertise. I believed that I could out-scheme and out-practice any of my opponents. I believe that I learned these skills from the best, and I worked every day to implement them and constantly improve on them. While working with Coach Shula and now observing Bill Walsh, it didn't take much to fall into their competitiveness.

I felt that during the week the 49ers had the edge during practices. They seemed to win most of the drills and sessions—except one area. I believe I was ahead in our competitive kicking sessions. Coach Shula always believed in the kicking game, and I carried that spirit to these matchups with the 49ers. We edged them in every kicking session. Our offense with Dan Marino won its share, but I felt that I won each and every one.

It was a great week, followed by a much better-than-average preseason game. We won a hard-fought and well-played game. And then, I experienced one of my favorite NFL moments.

As I was walking off the field, Bill Walsh came up to me and congratulated me. He said that I had done a great job all week and that I should be proud of my coaching abilities. He told me that I had won all week and should keep my head up: I was going to get better and was already a damn good coach.

Years later, after Coach Walsh had retired from the 49ers and was working with Stanford, he had gotten sick and was fighting cancer. We had exchanged several notes and had talked about dealing with chemotherapy.

On June 6, I received a note from him:

Mike:

Thank you for your kind words. They mean very much to me. I consider you one of my family. Thank you for sending General MacArthur's creed.

Bill

His kind and encouraging words to me following our preseason game in London gave me a level of confidence that I carried with me for my entire career. His successor, George Seifert, talked with me about joining the 49ers, but it got tangled up and never happened. I admired the 49ers, and it would have been interesting working for them. But Bill Walsh's words and note to me hold a very special place.

Mike Ditka

Another such incident occurred following our second preseason game versus the Bears in Chicago. We lost to the Bears that evening, and I was sitting by myself in the end zone waiting to board the bus for the trip to the airport. My guys had played well, and I was gaining some positive perspective and confidence.

I was just beginning to regain my health and starting to feel normal. I still didn't have much hair, and I was self-conscious about how I looked. Hence, my staying by myself and shying away from others.

As I sat there waiting, Mike Ditka came out of the dressing room and was heading to his car. He looked bigger than life: tall, well-dressed, forceful, confident—and with a big cigar. He was the boss in Chicago.

He came over to me and said, "What the hell are you doing out here by yourself, Michael?" I told him some bullshit, and he looked at me and smiled.

"I know why you are sitting here," he said. "You are going to be fine. You are doing great. Each day will get better. Keep your head up, you are a damn good coach. You kicked our ass today."

He handed me a business card and said, "There is a number here that you can call me anytime you need to talk. Two Pittsburgh guys. If you need something, feel free to call."

He put his hand around my head for a second, then walked away.

I will never forget his words or his gesture of kindness. I never did call him, but I did talk with him many times over the years. Mike Ditka is a big man in so many ways. Greatness comes in many forms. Sometimes the smallest of gestures are all part of what makes someone so special.

Mike Ditka was a great coach, but he also is a great man. What he did for me following that game in the end zone helped build me back into the person I hoped I could be again.

Thanks, Mike.

Al Davis

Another Hall of Famer and iconic football figure I had a special relationship with was Oakland Raiders owner Al Davis.

Everyone knew of Al Davis the assistant coach, head coach, general manager, scout, and owner. No one in NFL history had more roles or performed them at the level of Al Davis. Hell, he was even AFL commissioner for a short time.

In my opinion, he was a football genius. He knew every part of the business and could work on every level. He could manage and coach everything.

My first contact with Al Davis came immediately following the retirement news conference of Don Shula. I was in the team's meeting room at the Dolphins' complex, the site of his retirement announcement. I was the only assistant coach who personally attended. Everyone else watched on TV from their offices. I wouldn't have missed it for anything. I worked with Coach Shula for a long time, and I was going to be there for the end.

When I got back up to my office, Al Davis was on the phone. He was with George Karras, his assistant, and they told me there would be a first-class plane ticket at the airport and to come out to California to discuss my coming to work for the Raiders. I told "Coach Davis" that I was honored, but I needed some time to sort out things and would call him back in a few days with my answer.

I had always admired the work of Al Davis, and he was not an easy person to say no to.

My son, John, was in the ninth grade at St. Thomas Aquinas High School, maybe the best high school in America. Certainly the best football program and a brilliant academic school. He did not want to leave. Actually, neither did I!

But working for Oakland intrigued me. I loved the physical style of football the Raiders always played, and I knew that I would fit in and could contribute at a very high level. I believe if I had gone there, Oakland would be the team synonymous with special teams excellence and physicality.

There were two other occasions when Al Davis talked with me about joining him, and one of those times he actually offered me another job.

I would always see him in Indianapolis at the NFL's Scouting Combine and got to spend time talking with him. The old Colts football stadium was attached to the Indianapolis Convention

Center, and, for years, we all walked through it to get to our hotels. The Convention Center was large, with plenty of empty rooms and hallways. I wore a full leg brace and walked with a cane, so this was a perfect place for me to walk for exercise. Every day I was at the combine I walked through every inch of the Convention Center.

One such day I was walking back toward the hotel with Al Davis and talking football—and my maybe joining him in Oakland. As we were leaving the Convention Center, I said goodbye and turned to start my exercise walk. He asked me where I was going. I told him that I liked to walk through the Convention Center because it was mostly empty and I could get in a solid workout. He asked me if he could come along.

Of course, I said yes, and he told his entourage to meet him shortly in the hotel. Then Al Davis and I took a quiet walk together.

We only did this a few times. As we walked, we talked special teams. He wanted to know everything and questioned me why I was doing things a certain way. He was incredibly bright and asked brilliant questions. He only walked a short way with me and then turned and headed for the hotel.

We repeated these short walks together on several occasions. Each time, Al Davis would ask if he could walk with me!

These trips were not very long, but I was deeply honored to have had that brief but meaningful relationship. I never regretted not going to Oakland, but I can't help but wonder what working for Al Davis and the Raiders would have been like.

Joe D

One other coach with whom I have had many special moments is Joe DeCamillis.

Back in 1993, Dan Reeves told me he was promoting one of his assistants who happened to be his son-in-law, Joe DeCamillis. I told him that I would be happy to talk with him and would contact Joe to get the ball started.

Back in the '80s and most of the 1990s, a man named Ray Pelfrey conducted a kicking clinic in Reno, Nevada, around April 1 each year. Ray was a former high school teacher and coach who made quite a name for himself as a kicking instructor. He moved to Reno for tax purposes and established a thriving business. Ray was very good; he knew more about kicking than anyone I ever encountered.

His expertise was taking ex-college players who had been released from NFL training camps for maybe just not being quite good enough. Ray would work with them and bring out their very best.

At this April clinic, his pupils would work out for NFL special teams coaches and display their wares. It was a worthwhile and enjoyable trip. Every year we'd travel to Reno, take a look at some very good players, and enjoy the camaraderie of the casino and atmosphere. I am not much of a gambler, but each year I looked forward to the trip. The workouts were excellent, I became good friends with Ray, learned a lot about kicking from him, and enjoyed some trips over to Lake Tahoe. A number of very good players were signed by NFL teams out of these workouts: punter Matt Turk and kicker Jay Feely to name a pair.

I talked with Joe DeCamillis and told him to meet me in Reno a few days before the start of the workouts. I met him at our hotel in Reno, handed him the keys to my SUV, and told him to drive to Lake Tahoe. We visited all my hangouts, restaurants, and bars, and for four days covered everything. I drew up and talked about every part of the special teams game. We discussed everything— and a great friendship was born.

Joe had a very solid background, and he was a quick learner and exceptionally bright. For years, we would share our thoughts and challenge each other constantly. During the season, it was common for us to talk early on a Tuesday night about our respective upcoming games plans. We helped each other immensely, and, in my opinion, we won a lot of games on Tuesday night.

No, I didn't say "helped win." I said "won" a lot of games, and I firmly believe it.

After spending several years in New York, Joe traveled with Coach Reeves to Atlanta and took that team to the Super Bowl. Joe then had stops in Jacksonville, Dallas, Chicago, and Denver, this time winning the Super Bowl with the Broncos. Joe has that much-sought prize, the Super Bowl ring. I am envious, but I couldn't be happier that my good friend has one and did so much to help his team attain that very special prize.

Following the stop in Denver, Joe returned to Jacksonville as the special teams coordinator. Earlier, while at Dallas, a life-altering incident occurred. During one of their spring practices, a severe storm hit Dallas and collapsed part of the building in which they were practicing. Joe was struck by some of the wreckage and severely injured his neck.

The damage was dramatic and required a very complex surgery. Joe's healing process was extremely difficult, but Joe is as tough as they come. He fought through the hard times, continued to work, and persevered to maintain as normal a life as possible.

I found out about the accident on TV, and I couldn't reach Joe. I talked to Dan Reeves, and Dan told me everything that occurred and kept me involved at the beginning.

When I first saw Joe after the accident, even though it was months afterward, I was shocked. His head and neck were so rigid in order to promote the healing that he had to turn his whole body. That first time I really got to see him was after the season. They were coaching the Pro Bowl, which was in Miami that year, and I went over to it and met with him. I would always tell him "little by little." I knew because I had to deal with that kind of stuff with my leg.

As I knew he would, Joe pushed through all of it, healed well, and looks just great today.

Several years later, while at Denver, Joe helped the Broncos win a Super Bowl. Peyton Manning was the quarterback and, as always, one of the NFL's brightest stars. But he was nearing the end of his career, and Denver's offense wasn't quite the weapon it once had been. The momentum for success came from the brilliant defense and Joe's special teams.

But the year after their Super Bowl victory, Denver experienced some difficult times. Manning had retired. Head Coach Gary Kubiak had some health issues and was forced to miss some time. One such game took place in San Diego, and Joe was appointed interim head coach. Wade Phillips was the defensive coordinator, with several head coaching stints on his resume, but nevertheless it was Joe who took the reins.

Joe handled the head coaching role exceptionally well. His decision-making and clock management were far better than several of the head coaches with whom I had worked. He made an excellent challenge of an officiating call and won; that's an area in which many NFL head coaches are clueless.

At the end of the game and down two scores, Joe used his timeouts properly and quickly ran his field goal team on the field to get three points and save a timeout.

Everyone prepares for kicking a field goal without taking a timeout. Words such as "Mayday" or "Geronimo" or "Hurricane" are used to dictate this situation. Joe used this, and then the Broncos recovered an onside kick. He now had the ball, saved some time, and had a chance to win the game.

Joe later told me he wished he'd instructed the offense to put in another quarterback with a stronger arm to throw the needed

Hail Mary pass at the end of the game. He was very much thinking like a head coach.

After Kubiak had to step down, I can't understand why Joe wasn't asked to interview for the head coaching position. Dave Toub, the special teams coach from Kansas City, was asked to interview. Dave is a good coach and had done very well at both Chicago and Kansas City, but certainly not any better than Joe had done. I have gone against both. Please: bringing in another special teams coach—who didn't get the job by the way, and lost out to an average candidate—was extremely shortsighted in my opinion. Joe's particular area of the team had excelled, and when he took a turn as the head coach, he performed exceptionally well.

Sometimes the absolutely very best thing is what is right in front of you, and you never see it. I believe I was in that situation twice in my career, once at Miami and once with the Jets. And since I have left those two teams, they pretty much have been terrible.

You know, I loved to make points and dramatize situations with stories or anecdotes. In my player meetings, I often used such stories. I remember making a point to my players of acknowledging and appreciating where they were and not being enamored of other areas that may look more appealing. "What is right in front of your face might be what you can't see, and it may be your very best option."

One story to reinforce my point:

Believe it or not, Sherlock Holmes and Dr. Watson were camping out on Sanibel Island. In the middle of the night, Holmes woke up Watson by saying, "Watson, wake up and look around. Look to the heavens. Tell me what you can observe and what deductions you can make from your observations."

Watson looked up and said, "It is a beautiful night, and I have a clear, unobstructed view of the heavens. I see thousands of stars and can recognize several constellations and galaxies, and within those, solar systems. Possibly much like our own. It may be possible that in those solar systems, if there is a source of light, like our sun, there could possibly be some form of life."

Holmes replied, "Watson, those thoughts are excellent. Your observations are right on, and your deductions are brilliant. But Watson, sometimes what is right in front of you and you cannot see is what is of the most importance. The fact that you have such a clear and unobstructed view of the heavens, is it possible that you have missed the fact that someone has obviously stolen our fucking tent?"

To me, what is obvious is that the Denver Broncos have not found their fucking tent. In my opinion, in the past several years, due to their looking past their best option, they have been terrible and have dropped from the very top to near the bottom. So, know what the hell you have and figure it out. Joe DeCamillis is an excellent coach, would have been a great head coach for Denver, and I am proud to say that he is also my very good friend.

Beat His Ass

When this particular incident occurred during my career, I had reached a level of success and was very well known and respected in my profession. I don't want to use any names here; I don't want anyone to be offended or hurt.

It was a cold Sunday game day. I always rode the second bus to the stadium; I never wanted to arrive there too early. I had gotten off the bus and was walking to our locker room when I ran into an opposing team's coach who was a former colleague with whom I worked for several years. We were friends, but not great friends. We stood and talked for a while.

He asked what I thought was a very unusual question: "Mike, do you know our special teams coach?"

I said, "Sure, but not real well. I know him as a colleague, not as a friend. He is doing a good job. You guys are having a damn good special teams year."

Then he said, "Yes, that's the problem. He makes sure we all know it, and he never lets us forget it. He is so damn cocky and arrogant. He walks around here like he owns the place."

He then told me, "Mike, you know me, I would rather win today than anything, but if you could bring him down to Earth a little, I would be eternally grateful."

He never said another word, just turned and walked to their dressing room.

I went to our locker room and began the pregame routine that I followed throughout my thirty-two years of coaching. I put my briefcase down and got my field pass. Normally, I didn't need it because many of the stadium guards had been there for years and recognized me. I walked out in the stadium in my topcoat and Irish cap.

As I entered the stadium and walked toward our bench, there was music playing. This particular stadium was famous for its classic rock. My favorite.

They were playing "Eye of the Tiger." I couldn't have been in a better pregame mood.

There were some Jets fans in the stadium early, and they were yelling at me. It was very gratifying and enhanced my pregame mood.

The game was a hard-fought battle, and we won at the very end. For me, it couldn't have been more positive. We had a great special teams day. Excellent kick coverage, not giving them an inch. We made all of our kicks and punted them in the hole all game. We had a solid punt return and pressured their punter into an error. We had zero turnovers and only one penalty, but it was our kickoff return that broke the bank. We had two very positive returns past the 30-yard line.

The icing on the cake was a 100-yard return for a touchdown. Scoring a TD on special teams is a rarity in the NFL; many teams go seasons without scoring a TD. I had come up with a new, very complicated scheme. It was designed to go up the middle following an intricate double-team and trap-blocking design. We also came all the way across the field and picked off their safety. I had never run this before, nor had I seen anyone else try it.

Our returner started somewhat to his left to set up the blocks, and then cut slightly to the right before exploding up the middle. My heart jumped. I am sure my opposing counterpart had a similar but opposite reaction.

Yes, a special teams touchdown is a major accomplishment in the NFL—and this one pretty much put the game out of reach.

As I was crossing the field after the game to shake hands with the opposing coach, I saw the coach with whom I had talked before the game. He never stopped or said anything to me, but just looked me right in the eye and tipped his hat. You know, as if he was saying: "Thanks Mike, you brought that guy back to Earth. He needed some humble pie and you fed it to him."

Oh yeah, "Eye of the Tiger" is one of my favorites. Any time I hear it, I go back to that very special moment.

Mass

There is another part of my NFL journey that I would feel terribly remiss if I didn't spend at least a short time talking about: the night before a game's religious services.

NFL players and coaches spend much of the year away from their homes, families, and normal routines. From the beginning of training camp in late July through the four (or sometimes five) preseason games of August. Then the seventeen-week season of sixteen games and one open date that now has become eighteen weeks and seventeen games.

And, hopefully, the month or so of the playoffs, finally ending in January or February.

When you hear about jobs that are 24/7 and 365, the NFL is all about that.

One of the many great considerations that the NFL has for its players and coaches has been to provide for us to participate in a weekly church service. On the night before every game, the team is together in a hotel, either at home or in the opponent's city. Meals, snacks, and a variety of meetings and film sessions comprise the bulk of the schedule. On each one of those nights, time also is set aside for a religious service. Ours consisted of two opportunities: a Catholic Mass and a nondenominational service, bible study, or spiritual guest speaker.

One thing you can be sure of: everyone in that building is nervous, and I mean NERVOUS. For the players, the anxiety varies from the physical concerns to the mental stress of performing in front of such an audience on Sundays, at such a demandingly high level. The NFL is a violent collision sport. Every effort is made to be as safe as possible, but people get hurt. So, there is always a level of anxiety every week.

As coaches, we are performing right on the front line. Each week, we are in front of 80,000 people and millions more watching on TV. Everything we do is being evaluated, discussed, and criticized by the media. Following the game, everything is second-guessed. Many of us, especially coordinators, are graded each week in the media.

How many people have their job performance graded each week in the media? The level of anxiety is way beyond what most people ever experience.

Don't get me wrong. It is all part of the deal. The job pays great and is one of the most prestigious in the world. For me, coming out of the tunnel each week in front of that tremendous crowd was the thrill of 100 lifetimes. I got to do it 657 times.

My anxiety on the night before the game centered on: was I properly prepared? What might our opponent try that is a little different? Did I have my guys thoroughly prepared? I had to make sure I stayed on top of every situation. How could I make this night before the game's meeting the best ever? If I were them, how would I try to beat Mike Westhoff?

One thing I could always count on was the half-hour Mass that I attended in hundreds of hotel rooms all across the country and, even in several instances, overseas. I loved the serenity of the Mass and how it brought me closer to seeing a bigger picture of life and my small role in God's Kingdom.

Each week, I got to spend some valuable time with some of the very best people that I have ever encountered. Our Catholic priests were each different and very special.

With the Miami Dolphins, we had two excellent but very different personalities. Father Ray Geiser had entered the priesthood after having served in the military—not as a chaplain but as a normal soldier. His life experiences were more thorough than many priests, and he was able to take the most complex religious point and simplify it, breaking it down to a point of extreme common sense. To this day, more than three decades later, I can remember some of his homilies nearly word-for-word.

How many people can recall what their priest or preacher said last week?

Frank Chambers was a young priest who spent a number of games with the Dolphins. He was a brilliant theologian with about ten degrees. From Father Frank, we learned the history of the Catholic religion and how it fit into our lives today. Father Frank's brilliance helped us see through the history and philosophy of the church and how our lives could be affected and enhanced by the teachings of the church.

Father Frank lives on the campus of Villanova University, where he was an undergraduate and currently is one of their directors of admissions. Villanova can be sure that Father Frank will find the brightest of students anywhere in the world.

During my twelve years with the Jets, I had the honor of becoming good friends with two great priests. Father Tom Hartman was a "superstar" in the American Catholic church, if there is such a thing. He was connected to the Vatican in Rome and traveled to various locations in the world to solve problems and promote the church. He personally knew Pope John Paul and was friends with Mother Teresa. Each week, he participated in a TV and radio show and shared a newspaper column with Rabbi Mark Gellman. They shared and sometimes debated principles of Catholicism and Judaism.

Father Tom was brilliant, and each week he helped all of us personalize and better understand and appreciate our faith. He suffered from Parkinson's Disease and, along with Michael J. Fox, helped raise millions of dollars to find a cure. I spent hours talking with him, and we had dinner together every few months. My time and friendship with Father Tom was one of the greatest experiences of my life.

Monsignor Jim Vlaun was the other incredible New York Jets priest. Msgr. Jim may have been the most genuinely caring man I have met. He was also brilliant and, in his own special way, could make each of us feel the value and warmth of our faith. He might be the kindest man on the planet. He saw life and religion through such a positive yet realistic vision that you couldn't help but be inspired.

Each week, many of us in the NFL who attended these services experienced a level of comfort that was both rewarding and fulfilling.

Motivations

In each meeting the night before a game, I had a specific message I was trying to convey. My stories, quotes, or even films were methods to inspire and entertain my players to dramatize a point.

One time in New York, I was trying to make a point to our kickoff coverage team. At that time, unlike now, every kickoff was returned and therefore must be covered. I had a fast, aggressive group, and we were leading the league at the time. I had T-shirts made with a cheetah on them. I wanted to play like attacking cheetahs.

On a Friday night—my only night off, by the way—I went to a library and found a film on cheetahs. I edited it and showed it in my Saturday night meeting. I didn't show much of the kill; it wasn't necessary, and I'm not really much into that sort of thing.

The players loved the film and wore the T-shirts proudly. We all did, including myself. We were the best in the league and attacked like cheetahs!

I also showed a film clip of a Robin Williams movie, *Patch Adams*, which was based on the true story of a troubled young man who checked himself into an asylum. While a patient, in a specific meeting with an older patient who was a professor, he discovered an aspect about himself that unlocked his problem and got him started on a career as a famous physician. The short clip dramatized the ability to look at one's self and figure out strengths and weaknesses.

Did it help anyone become a better football player? I don't know, but if I could generate any level of self-examination, then maybe I was succeeding.

Toward the end of my career, at the beginning of training camp, I showed a clip from a Charles Bronson film, *Hard Times*. Bronson played a bare-knuckle fighter during the Great Depression in the New Orleans area. He would fight for money in vacant lots or warehouses. In one scene, he and his opponent faced each other in the ring, surrounded by a cheering, betting mob. Bronson's opponent looked at him and said, "You look a little old for this, Pops."

POW.

With one punch, Bronson sent him flying—completely knocked out.

I would then tell the players that I want our opponents to see me as Pops. I was nearly seventy, but maybe I still had something left in me.

I would also tell them: "No one knows anything about you, and that is exactly how I want you to hit them." I wanted us to strike hard and fast—the most physical opponent they had ever faced.

It was entertaining, fun, and exciting. I would not be afraid to try anything to gain an edge.

While coaching in New York, I read a story about a very successful CEO of a major company. During an interview, he was asked about the foundation of his company. He said it came from his grandfather, who founded the business. His grandfather immigrated to America from Eastern Europe. While he was entering the U.S. at Ellis Island, he went into what he thought was a restaurant. He sat down at a table and looked for a waiter.

After a few minutes, a gentleman came over and told him this was a cafeteria. He spoke a little English and was somewhat able to understand. The man said: "In a cafeteria, you go up and get a tray and walk through the line and take whatever you want, and at the cashier you pay for whatever you selected."

The CEO said that over the years his grandfather remembered that America was much like a cafeteria, and he molded his business on that principle. You can have whatever you want if you are able to pay for it. But more importantly, are you willing to pay the price?

I would tell the players, "You wouldn't be in this room if you didn't have the ability to make this team or do the job successfully.

But are you willing to pay the price? Are you willing to study, work hard enough, and do what it takes to get the job done?

"The NFL is a big cafeteria. Are you willing to pay the price?"

I had no problem graphically pointing out what I thought that was and how to pay for it. I believed that success in the NFL was a constantly evolving process. I wanted my players to always be aware of where they were in the process and how to improve every day.

As Bill Parcells pointed out with an empty gas tank in a locker, "How much gas is left in your tank?"

I never stopped—every meeting had a specific message—and I loved it.

CHAPTER 19

Thoughts for the Future

As I have watched the current NFL game, I have been flooded with emotions.

First, there was somewhat a sense of relief that I was not coaching the bullshit I was watching. Don't get me wrong: I love and respect the NFL. However, the complete diluting of the kicking game saddens and sickens me. Part of me feels a great sense of pride in how I and a very select group of NFL coaches molded the kicking game from a point of implausibility to one of creativity, excitement, extreme physical play, and the opportunity for each play to have a substantial influence.

In 1982, my first year in the NFL, the kicking game plans could have been drawn and handed out on the back of a napkin. Fifteen years later, each week I was preparing an eighty-page game plan, depth chart, and scouting report to be distributed to my guys each Wednesday morning. We took the kicking game and changed it into one of the most creative and exciting parts of the game.

As a special teams coach, I came along at precisely the right place and time. There was virtually no originality and very little regulation. We could pretty much do anything—and I tried everything. It was a great time to be a special teams coach. I am very proud of how I helped turn the job into a coordinator's position—with the responsibility, authority, and compensation that the role deserved and requires.

Much of the change that has taken place in the kicking game has been the result of rule changes due to safety, and in my opinion in some instances, the guise thereof. Eliminating wedges, traps, double-teams, blind-side, and peel-back blocks, along with outlawing sustaining blocks out of bounds, while trying to lessen the speed and therefore collision of kickoffs and kickoff returns, has all been the result of "safety" rule changes or adjustments.

The wedge attack was strategically taught and designed to hit between players on an edge. Quarterbacks lead receivers right into the teeth of defenders, and concussions occur each week. Do we tell quarterbacks not to throw into a defended middle of the field? No—we just eliminate a kicking play and make sure everyone knows it is all about "safety."

I never taught dirty, cheap football, but I always taught extremely physical play, and I am very proud of it. You see, I have spent nearly all my adult life being very physically uncomfortable, so I have the deepest concern and respect for what the NFL players endure. I care about safety, but I also care very much about the integrity of the game. I loved the NFL kicking game and everything associated with it, and I am very disturbed at the level to which it has descended.

I want to use a numerical example to dramatize my point. In my first thirty years with the NFL, not counting field goals or extra points (either kicking them or defending them), I averaged twenty-two plays a game. In my last two years, (seasons 31 and

32, with the Saints), it was seven. Yes, the number dropped from twenty-two to seven.

I know the Saints play many of their games indoors and their great offense didn't punt much, but still, each week the special teams were getting only between five and ten plays. That was all. I am not counting kickoffs resulting in touchbacks; I am in my eighth decade of life, and I could cover those kicks.

Also, when teams now start at the 25-yard line after touchbacks, it doesn't take much for them to move to the 50, typically eliminating two punts and two punt returns per game. Before you know it, you have dropped from twenty-two to seven plays or so.

I have been asked to come back and coach. For me, no way. Seven plays, and most all of what I previously did is now outlawed? What the hell am I going to do?

In 2018 before a Saints game, I was approached by Troy Vincent, an NFL top executive who had a great playing career with the Dolphins and Eagles. While I was at Miami, I went to Wisconsin to work him out and helped in drafting him in the first round. Troy is a good football man, exceptionally bright, and I believe that he will someday follow Roger Goodell as the next NFL commissioner.

Troy told me that there was somewhat of a movement to eliminate the punt, and he wanted my thoughts. No, I was not shocked or even surprised. I knew that there are a number of people who would nearly eliminate the kicking game if it was possible. I don't know who is the leader of this movement, but from what I have been told, Rich McKay, president of the Atlanta Falcons, is the "man behind the curtain" for this line of thinking. I guess maybe he will be asked to express his opinion and reasons.

I am sure everything will hinge on "safety." I am for finding solutions, not destroying a great part of the game.

I asked Troy why eliminating the punt was being discussed. He told me it was the most injury-riddled play and the most penalized. I delved into each aspect. I explained to him that, first of all, the punt was the longest play in football and therefore vulnerable to various problems.

I wanted to know what type of injuries had occurred. He told me they were mostly soft tissue injuries. I asked when during the year did those happen. He said, "All year, but mostly early in the season."

OK, two things with the new schedule: much of the offseason and training camp has been drastically shortened, and I believe that many of the players are not in top football condition. Also, in today's game, nearly all the veteran starters play almost none of the preseason, leaving mainly all the regular plays to the backups for what now is a three-game preseason schedule.

Now, it is opening day, and they have to sprint 60 yards to cover a punt. They have done very little of this, and someone pulls a hamstring. No one should be surprised. What did you think was going to happen?

The punt is in no way a violent play. It is nearly three times longer than a play from scrimmage and covers much of the field, therefore certain types of injuries can occur. As the season progresses and players become more accustomed to the play, the injuries are much less frequent.

"The most penalized play in football" is what Troy told me. And I believe him. OK, what can we do to solve this problem? I believe several things can make a difference.

First of all, the play must be coached in a particular manner. For the return team, holding and the block in the back are the most frequent penalties. As a coach, if you teach your players "how to hold," and you practice the technique, you will rarely be called. Players need to know that holding penalties are called on your feet, not your hands and arms. Teach your players to grab and lock on anywhere inside and on the torso. Don't wrap your arms around your opponent or anywhere near his head. Run with your opponent and stay locked on.

Grabbing and holding requires exceptional hand strength. I used to buy "squeeze balls" for my players and required them to have the ball with them all of the time and to be constantly squeezing the ball to attain a level of hand strength. I personally did this for years and was instructed by my doctor that, due to all the metal in my leg, he wanted me to squeeze the ball as I stood on the field to help with my circulation.

I wanted the players to have exceptionally strong hands, so that when they grabbed an opponent it felt like they were glued on. Find a way. *Figure it out.*

Also, do not separate. Hence, the holding penalty comes from the feet, not the hands. And if you begin to separate, be prepared to push your opponent away and then try to regain the blocking position. Remember, if the official sees you holding, he is thinking, "Hold, hold, let him go." You can do the same and not twist or yank your opponent down but remain locked on.

This stuff is what training camp is for. Teach them technique and film them. Coaches need to teach how to properly execute techniques without being penalized.

The block in the back is simple; as a coach, you must drill into your players never to attempt blocking anyone if you cannot get your head completely in front. I took a "soft" approach to this. I let my guys know that if they couldn't get their head in front, it was OK. I was never going to criticize them. Just hold your position or move on to another defender.

Good punt returners are hard to tackle in the open field. If you can't get your head in front, let your man go and we will see what happens. I let them know I would much rather that we lost our block than block in the back.

By coaching and practicing these two blocking techniques properly, coaches can make a dramatic reduction in the number of penalties called.

Next, I would instruct the officials not throw the flag if a foul was not egregious and not in the vicinity of the ball carrier. Use some common sense; let them play. What was the foul? Did it affect the play? If not, do not throw the flag.

Thirdly—and this is a major change—I would require the flyers (gunners, end man in the formation) who may release on the snap must be lined up within one yard of the numbers. Not out next to the sideline where we see so many today. They use the sideline to protect themselves. As they release and they are contacted, they let themselves be pushed out of bounds. The blockers cannot come after them, and they can run free for a short while, angling back in toward the field of play without being blocked. Therefore, they are protected.

Take this away and the number of sideline fouls will greatly decrease. Also, this will help aid the exciting punt return play. This change in alignment will help the block on the punt team's best weapon, the flyer.

Also, this alignment by the flyer brings his blockers in closer to the punter. With the ball on the hash mark, and if the punter is kicking in that short side direction, then the defense is lined up much closer to him and can be a factor in the rush. Most punters offset their alignment slightly away from the side of the punt, thus keeping them in the middle of the protection cup. But this alignment shortens the distance to the "block spot."

S

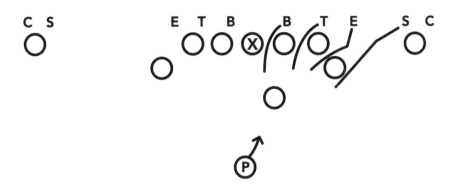

This makes directional punting more difficult and will help the return team to block the flyer and force the punt more into the middle of the field. This will help bring back the exciting punt return play.

Penalties will be reduced, and we will see more punt returns and punt blocks. I am trying to bring the kicking game back into the NFL. I wish I had more help.

I helped create the special teams coordinator coaching position, and I can see the day when an owner will walk in to see the general manager and head coach and ask: "Why am I paying this guy one million dollars a year when he is coaching only seven plays a game?"

If they are not careful, the special teams coaches of today would be able to write a book about their jobs on the back of their driver's licenses. They just don't coach many plays during the game. The special teams job has become pedestrian.

But, thankfully, not to Sean Payton.

"It's a shame there's not more assistant coaches having an opportunity to be in the Pro Football Hall of Fame," Sean said.

"Mike would be one of those candidates as a special teams coordinator in an elite level relative to his skill set and his production over the years. Not only a close friend but a well-respected coach and someone that I am sure . . . you've come across the people he has impacted. So, he's got that magic about teaching and coaching, and he can create that edge, and the players believe in him I would say wholeheartedly.

"I think the world of him as a teacher, as a coach, and a communicator, and we greatly benefited from his experience and him coming here."

My favorite part of special teams coaching was the kickoff return. I believe it is where I was the most creative and successful. O.J. McDuffie, Brock Marion, Chad Morton, Justin Miller, Leon Washington, Brad Smith, Joe McKnight, and Alvin Kamara were all among the NFL's best-ever kickoff returners. I am sure they all greatly benefited from the design and execution of the scheme.

Now, the kickoff return has become a non-play. The rule changes have basically eliminated the most exciting play in football. Nearly every kickoff results in a touchback, and we just don't see many returns.

Those rule changes have taken away almost all of what I believe were some of the most creative play designs in NFL history. I certainly was not alone in this, but I believe that I had a great deal to do with the entire process leading to those plays.

The new rules also have changed when and how the kickoff coverage team aligns and starts. Everything possible has been done to lessen the collision impact of the play.

But I believe that with these rule changes I propose, the collision aspect of the play has been dramatically lessened and the play could again be exciting—if not for so many balls kicked deep into or out of the end zone.

I want to put the play back into the game and would do so by adding a third ball. Currently, each team provides balls picked by their quarterback to be used when they are on offense. Those balls can be pretty much anything as long as they have the thirteen-pound air pressure checked by the referee before the game. This is pretty simple, unless maybe Tom Brady's guy releases a little pressure after being inspected. That is very easy to do, and I believe exactly what occurred in that deflated balls "scandal."

Also, for each game the referee takes six balls right out of the box and lets each team's equipment manager brush and mold the balls to make them a little bit more pliable and more friendly to kick. I would now add a kickoff ball taken right out of the box and used only for kickoffs.

This ball would be harder and much less pliable. Therefore, it could not compress as well when kicked and would not explode off the kicking foot. It would be more like kicking a rock, and now, instead of landing six yards deep in the end zone, it might come down on the two-yard line, forcing a return.

The collisions would be reduced, and the play would be similar to a punt return. Stay as safe as possible and put the play back into the game. *Figure it out*, and make it work.

After all, if Grandma has a leaky pipe, you don't have to move her out of the house.

Figure it out and make it work.

I coached thirty-two years in the National Football League. I was part of some of the most exciting plays the game has ever seen. I believe I greatly helped change the game and, in my opinion, very much for the better. NFL football is the world's greatest team sport. It combines mental and physical attributes that no other sport even approaches.

We need to work to keep it together, not pick it apart and allow uncaring individuals to dilute the greatest game ever.

PHOTO CREDITS

ACKNOWLEDGMENTS

I would like to thank the following people for their help with this book:

Bradford Banta, Judy Battista, Hank Bauer, Bill Callahan, Chad Cascadden, Jess Cohn, Brandon Coward, James Dearth, Joe DeCamillis, Kristen Farrell, Dan Galbraith, Sam Gash, Bob Glauber, Kerry Glenn, Chris Hayes, Troy Hershberger, Taysom Hill, Larry Izzo, Ben Kotwica, Anita Marks, Chris Mattura, O.J. McDuffie, Tom Morstead, Louis Oliver, Bernie Parmalee, Sean Payton, Deuce Schwartz, Eric Smith, Patti Tenaglia, Zach Thomas, Leon Washington, Stu Weinstein, John Westhoff, and Kenyatta Wright.

And, of course, Barry Wilner. Without his help and direction, I could never have written this book.

And the National Football League for providing me with the opportunity and environment to work for thirty-two years in the very best job in the world.